CONCURRENT PROGRAMMING

WILEY SERIES IN PARALLEL COMPUTING

SERIES EDITORS:

J.W. de Bakker, *Centrum voor Wiskunde en Informatica, The Netherlands*

M. Hennessy, *University of Sussex, UK*

D. Simpson, *Brighton Polytechnic, UK*

CONCURRENT PROGRAMMING
Fundamental Techniques for Real-Time and Parallel Software Design

Tom Axford

University of Birmingham, UK

JOHN WILEY & SONS

Chichester · New York · Brisbane · Toronto · Singapore

Copyright © 1989 by John Wiley & Sons Ltd.
Baffins Lane, Chichester
West Sussex PO19 1UD, England

Other Wiley Editorial Offices

John Wiley & Sons, Inc., 605 Third Avenue,
New York, NY 10158-0012, USA

Jacaranda Wiley Ltd, G.P.O. Box 859, Brisbane,
Queensland 4001, Australia

John Wiley & Sons (Canada) Ltd, 22 Worcester Road,
Rexdale, Ontario M9W 1L1, Canada

John Wiley & Sons (SEA) Pte Ltd, 37 Jalan Pemimpin   05-04,
Block B, Union Industrial Building, Singapore 2057

British Library Cataloguing in Publication Data available

Library of Congress Cataloging-in-Publication Data:

Axford, Tom.
    Concurrent programming : fundamental techniques for real-time
and parallel software design / Tom Axford.
        p. cm.—(Wiley series in parallel computing)
    Includes bibliographical references.
    ISBN 0 471 92303 6
    1. Parallel programming (Computer science)   I. Title.
II. Series.
QA76.6.A98   1989
005'.35—dc20   89–16637
                                                                         CIP

Printed and bound in Great Britain by Courier International, Tiptree, Essex

Trademarks

Contents

Preface

Concurrent programming is not an easy subject in which to achieve mastery. It contains many subtleties and traps for the unwary over and above all the usual complexities of 'ordinary' sequential programming. This book aims to introduce the techniques and algorithms of concurrent programming through a practical, down-to-earth approach. (It is assumed that the reader is already well versed in programming in high-level languages such as Pascal, and also knows the basic principles of computer architecture and machine code, including interrupts.) The material covered starts with the low-level methods commonly used in much existing real-time software, and then moves on to the more sophisticated high-level techniques that have been developed in recent years and which are being applied increasingly to real-time and parallel systems. I have attempted to strike a balance between including lots of algorithms on the one hand, and covering a wide variety of concurrency mechanisms and languages on the other. The intention throughout is to introduce important basic techniques which will be of practical value to those who intend to write real-time or parallel software for modern computer systems.

One of my main aims has been to emphasise simplicity and elegance. I would justify this emphasis on three grounds; educational, philosophical and practical. Firstly, on educational grounds, a simple approach encourages the more diffident or reluctant reader to make the effort necessary to understand the subject. It also helps to increase confidence. On the other hand, there is a very real risk of becoming over-confident. Most beginners in computer science have little difficulty in understanding basic concepts such as that of a stack, yet, when asked to write a set of routines to implement a stack, are surprised to find that they make logical errors and take much longer than they expected to correctly implement this 'simple' software. It is equally easy to become over-confident in concurrent programming.

The remedy that I would suggest is to acquire sufficient *practical* experience of using these techniques in realistic applications. This book is not intended for purely theoretical study. A selection of the techniques described should be put into practice by the reader at the earliest opportunity. The only other effective remedy to over-confidence that I am aware of is to follow a very formal approach and show how to rigorously prove every algorithm as it is introduced. This book does not adopt such extreme formality.

Secondly, on philosophical grounds, simplicity is attractive and worth putting effort into trying to achieve. The beauty and aesthetic pleasure in the study of any branch of science comes largely from discovering new and often quite unexpected simplicity and regularity in what previously appeared chaotic, even unintelligible. Major advances in science usually arise from finding simple ways to describe that which previously appeared complex. Computer science is no exception, yet many programmers automatically tend to prefer the complicated because 'complex algorithms and data structures are usually necessary to achieve optimum efficiency'. While such arguments in favour of complexity are sometimes justified, all too often the complexity comes first and the justification is sought later. (Of course, another pervasive reason why complexity itself is popular is its close association with status in a competitive world. All too often, the ignorant have more respect for the author of a complicated solution than of a simple one.)

Thirdly, on purely practical grounds, simplicity pays. The traditional programmer's concentration on efficiency above all else is now an anachronism. Software reliability is a higher priority than maximum efficiency in many applications, and simple software is overwhelmingly more reliable than complicated software. Of course, what we would really like is *both* simplicity *and* efficiency. Very occasionally just such algorithms are discovered and this is one way in which the state of the art is advanced.

My emphasis on practicality does not imply any lack of sympathy with more theoretical and formal approaches. Indeed, I am a firm believer in the value of analytical methods in software development, and am convinced that formal methods for program verification and other types of analysis will eventually come into widespread use in all branches of software engineering. Nevertheless, formal methods as they exist today are still in their infancy and are difficult both to understand and to apply in realistic practical situations. Observation suggests that the great majority of software developers do not possess the mathematical experience needed to be able to take formality in their stride. They often avoid highly mathematical literature and may even be somewhat afraid of mathematical terminology and exaggerate their own lack of experience in its use.

The approach adopted in this book is first and foremost a practical and utilitarian one, quite deliberately. Formality and rigour have been pushed into a back seat, but they have not been forgotten. The aim has been to avoid frightening off too many of those readers who lack a strong mathematical background, yet to introduce a little formality wherever it can be done fairly painlessly. By emphasising the need for greater software reliability and the importance of systematic and detailed analysis in achieving this, I hope to convince at least some of my readers of the value of the more formal approaches and to whet their appetites (and their confidence) to learn more about these emerging and very important methods.

The core of the book is based on a course of twenty lectures on 'Real-Time Systems Programming' that has been given to second year undergraduates at the University of Birmingham since 1981. The original emphasis of this course on real-time programming has been broadened to include the applications of concurrency techniques to parallel processing on both multiprocessor and distributed architectures. At the end of most chapters I have included a short set of exercises, the solutions to which have been gathered together in an appendix. Although designed primarily as a textbook, the practical content and approach may also appeal to professional software developers wishing to learn the basic techniques of concurrent programming.

I have much pleasure in expressing my sincere thanks to many colleagues and students, both past and present, at the University of Birmingham, who have provided the stimulating and enjoyable environment in which I have worked for many years now, and which made this book possible. I would also like to thank all those who provided helpful comments on draft versions of this book, in particular Rachid Anane, Antoni Diller and Peter Greenfield. Special thanks are due to Peter Edwards, Tim Dean and Jo Whitfield of the Royal Radar and Signals Establishment, Malvern, who made many valuable suggestions concerning the material of Chapter 10 and helped to clarify my understanding of the Mascot design method.

Finally, I would like to make clear my intentions in using masculine forms of the pronouns 'he', 'his', etc. when referring to general categories of people, such as programmers, which include both sexes. I find constructs such as 'he or she' and 'he/she' stylistically clumsy, as are attempts to word everything in the plural or express everything in impersonal terms. Hence I have retained the use of 'he' and 'his', but *all such masculine forms should be understood to include the corresponding feminine forms.*

Chapter 1

Introduction

1.1 Basic Concepts

What is concurrent programming and why is it important? We begin by attempting to give a simple answer to this question and a justification for studying this topic.

In a nutshell, concurrent programming is the technique of writing programs that do more than one thing at a time. A very common example is a multi-user system that can be used by several people simultaneously. Further examples are computer systems used to control other equipment, whether it be the control of a factory, an aircraft or a domestic washing machine. In virtually all such cases, the computer will have to do several things at once.

Typically, the system requirements will demand that several tasks be carried out simultaneously. We will see later that it is quite possible to implement such systems on uniprocessor computers even though such machines are capable of executing only one instruction at a time.

Parallel computers are also becoming quite common. These contain more than one processor and hence are inherently capable of doing several things at once. To be used effectively, such parallel computers must employ concurrent programming techniques, even in situations where the user requirements do not demand it.

Hence concurrent programming is of central importance to two major areas of computing: *real-time* and *parallel* programming. These terms are defined as follows (although neither term is used with very great precision by computer professionals generally):

1

1.1.1   Real-Time Systems

Definition   A *real-time* system is one in which timing requirements are an essential part of its specification.

'Timing requirements' includes things such as the maximum allowable time delay between a specified input and the responding output action. By far the most common type of timing requirement is such an upper limit on a response time; for example, a computer controlling a chemical plant may have to respond to the detection of overheating by shutting down the chemical plant within a very short time to avert the danger of an explosion.

In many cases, the response time is not specified very accurately; for example, the chemical plant may have to be shut down within approximately one or two seconds to avoid danger of explosion. Clearly, in such a case we would tend to play safe and make sure that the response occurred in much less than one second. The point is that the timing requirements of a typical real-time system are very imprecise (although there are some exceptions, in which actions may be required at precisely defined times).

A non-real-time system has a specification in which timing requirements are much less important, the specification concentrating on other matters such as the system functionality (i.e. specifying the outputs as mathematical functions of the inputs), cost, performance, reliability, etc.

Examples of Real-Time Systems

Operating Systems – One of the main functions of a computer operating system is to handle input and output to peripheral devices (e.g. to access files on disc). Now, peripheral devices operate at speeds that are tightly constrained by their mechanical construction or by standardised interface protocols. If the operating system is to perform efficiently (or sometimes even to work at all), it must service each peripheral device more-or-less at the speed of that device. For example, it must be prepared to read a block from disc when the read head is positioned over the required block. If the operating system is too slow, the block will pass by and it will not be available again until the disc has done a complete revolution and the block is back under the read head once more. The time for the disc to do a complete revolution is quite long in computing terms!

Furthermore, operating systems are usually required to operate many different devices at once. This imposes quite severe and complex real-time requirements upon the system.

Transaction Processing Systems – These include point-of-sale (POS) systems such as those used in supermarkets with laser bar-code readers at the checkouts; automatic tellers in banks; ticket booking systems for airlines, theatres, etc. Such systems must have response times of a few seconds at most, or customers can become impatient and business may be lost as a result.

Industrial Process Control – Included here is the computer control of all sorts of industrial processes: whether it be a car production line, an oil refinery, a chemical plant or simply a specialised piece of machinery. Such computer systems are used not only to determine the sequencing and timing of complicated series of operations, but also to gather and process performance data, for quality monitoring and control, for detecting and rectifying exceptional conditions (such as a machine jamming), and many other purposes. Real-time requirements are common in these systems.

Embedded Systems – The term *embedded system* refers to any computer system which is built into a larger piece of equipment and functions as a component of it. Embedded systems are becoming extremely common: in the home, from burglar alarms to compact disc players and central heating systems; elsewhere, from military weapons systems to photocopiers, and from fly-by-wire aircraft to printing presses. Again, all these systems have real-time aspects to them.

Communications – E.g. System X telephone exchanges, data communications networks, cellular car telephone systems, satellite communications, military communications, local area computer networks, local area networks for distributed computer control of factories, ships, aircraft, etc. The great majority of modern communication systems rely heavily on computers and the software is typically required to meet stringent real-time requirements.

1.1.2 Parallel Systems

Definition A *parallel* system is one which is implemented on a computer with two or more processors which run concurrently.

This definition is understood to exclude systems which have several processors, but only one of them is running the program we are interested in. For example, there are many common multi-processor systems which to the normal user look just like single processor systems because any single user program will be run on only one of the processors. The only program that knows of the existence of the other processors is the operating system, which simply shares the work between the various processors, but never splits individual jobs. Thus, such a system is parallel from the point of view of the operating system, but it is not parallel from the point of view of ordinary user programs.

Similarly, most modern computers contain several extra processors for controlling peripheral devices. These generally run fixed programs which are permanently stored in read-only memory and so are not available to the programmer (even to the operating system programmer). Such systems are not normally described as parallel (except from the viewpoint of the hardware engineer).

If we describe a system as 'parallel', we are saying something about its implementation; whereas if we describe a system as 'real-time', we are saying something about its specification. Parallel implementations are constructed almost exclusively because they can give greater performance than sequential implementations. With the continuing advances in integrated circuit fabrication techniques, an increasing number of parallel computers are available commercially, most of which require specially designed parallel software to take full advantage of their very high performance capabilities. For example, several popular parallel architectures are based on the Transputer chip (Inmos Ltd., 1988b).

Although modern parallel processors offer super-computer performance at remarkably low cost, they are still not very widely used. The main obstacle is the high cost of redesigning existing software. This is further aggravated by the need to design the software with a specific parallel architecture in mind. The present state of the art does not allow us to write one parallel program in a high-level language which can then be run efficiently on all parallel computers. Unfortunately, different parallel architectures require different types of parallel languages.

1.1.3 The Need for Reliability

In many of the examples mentioned above, the reliability of the computer system is of crucial importance. For example, in the latest generation of aircraft, both military and civil, 'fly-by-wire' technology is used. This simply means that computers control the flying surfaces, and the controls operated by the pilot, such as the joystick, are simply input devices attached to the computers (effectively just high-quality versions of the joysticks used by many computer games). The pilot's controls give no direct mechanical linkage to the ailerons and rudder, as is the case on more traditional aircraft. In such fly-by-wire aircraft, failure of the computer systems is likely to result in total loss of control of the aircraft which will often mean considerable loss of life.

A *very* high degree of reliability is therefore essential. Techniques are known for achieving very high reliability in the hardware (in fact, most computer hardware can be made much more reliable than traditional mechanical systems, which are more subject to wear and tear). Software reliability is, unfortunately, much harder to handle; both to measure and to control. Bugs in software are essentially errors in *design*; software does not 'wear out' or suffer damage through ill treatment in the way that hardware does (excluding deliberate alteration of the software as in those malicious and deceptive techniques which are often referred to by the colourful names of 'software viruses', 'trojan horses', etc.). Hardware is often so much simpler in its design than software, that bugs in the design are relatively rare once the hardware is in full production. As the technology of integrated circuits advances, however, more and more complex hardware designs are being built, and the design reliability of the latest computer hardware is becoming a major problem also, just as it is with software. Traditional methods for improving hardware reliability (error detecting and correcting codes, replication of hardware, etc.) do not cope with design faults, either in the hardware itself, or in the software running on it.

Because of the increasing importance of reliability to the many new safety-critical applications of computers, Chapter 12 is devoted entirely to this topic, and discusses both the traditional ways of improving reliability and new approaches which are currently the subject of much research activity.

1.1.4   Concurrent Program Design

A conventional computer executes a sequence of instructions and hence we think of programs as essentially sequential (i.e. they do one thing at a time, in a specified order). Most of the well-known programming languages, such as Pascal, support only this type of programming.

Concurrent programs contain several parts which are run concurrently. Each of these parts is itself strictly sequential and is called a *process*. Some programming languages, such as Ada, Modula-2 and Occam, support concurrent programming. The special facilities provided by such languages are described in detail in Chapters 8 and 9.

Definition   A *process* is part of a program which is itself executed strictly sequentially, but which may run concurrently or pseudo-concurrently with other processes in the same program.

On a uniprocessor computer, it is not possible for more than one instruction to be executed at any one time. Thus, in the time scale of a single instruction, concurrent processes are not possible. On a longer time scale, however, several processes may be interleaved so that each runs for a short time, then another is run, and so on (this is called *timesharing*). The time at which one process is suspended and another reactivated is generally not under the control of any of the processes themselves, but, instead, it is controlled by the operating system. Over a long enough time scale, the processes appear to run truly concurrently, although it is always true that at any given point in time only one of the processes will be executing. Other terms which may sometimes be used synonymously with *process* are *task, activity* or *thread of execution*.

In such concurrent systems, the processes themselves have no control over the times at which one process is suspended and another started. This is both an advantage and a disadvantage. It means that the programmer can ignore the problems of timesharing the processes; this is all done for him by the operating system. On the other hand, we do not know when each process will be run or for how long, and, furthermore, it may vary from time to time. We must regard the processes as effectively running asynchronously, i.e. we cannot rely on being able to predict the relative speed with which they run, which runs first, at what point each is suspended for another to have a turn, or any other aspect of the timing of the processes; nor can we rely on any of these characteristics even being reproducible. This indeterminism with respect to the relative timing of the processes makes conventional debugging very much more difficult than is the case for ordinary sequential programs. From the programmer's point of view, this is probably *the* major difference between concurrent programming and sequential programming.

Concurrent programs can also be implemented on parallel systems. We distinguish three types of implementation of concurrency, as specified by the following three definitions:

Definition *Multiprogramming* is the execution of concurrent processes by timesharing them on a single processor.

Definition *Multiprocessing* is the execution of concurrent processes by running them on separate processors which can all access a shared memory (possibly in addition to some local memory on each processor).

Definition *Distributed processing* is the execution of concurrent processes by running them on separate processors which can communicate by a message passing mechanism. Each processor has its own local memory, but there is no shared memory.

We will use the term *multiprocessor* for a computer on which multiprocessing can be implemented, and *distributed processor* for a computer on which distributed processing can be implemented. Both multiprocessing and distributed processing are sub-categories of parallel processing.

All three types of implementation of concurrency will be discussed in more detail in later chapters.

1.1.5 Cooperating Processes

Independent programs in a time-sharing system are seen as independent concurrent processes by the operating system. If the processes are all completely independent, they will not interact with each other or need to communicate in any way.

If a single program consists of more than one process, however, those processes will normally cooperate with each other (there would be little point in putting them together in one program otherwise). There are two main categories of cooperation between concurrent processes:

> **Communication** – Data is passed from one process to another, either in the form of a message sent by one process and received by another process; or in the form of a shared memory area which is accessible by more than one process.

> **Synchronisation** – A partial sequencing of points in the various processes is specified. For example, one process may have to wait for another process to do something before it should proceed.

Although we have said that functionally independent processes have no need to cooperate with each other, they may have to in a situation where they are competing for a limited quantity of resources. For example, if two processes both want to use the same tape unit, one process must wait for the other to finish before it can start. We will see later that this type of synchronisation between processes can use the same basic mechanisms as are used by processes which need to cooperate because they are performing different parts of the same overall function.

1.2   Some Basic Concurrency Problems

Several important problems are now described in abstract terms. Each is really a class of related problems out of which we attempt to abstract a common structure. For the moment we only state the problems, in later chapters we will look at various types of solutions. These problems are all fundamental to concurrent programming and crop up over a very wide range of application areas.

In the design of concurrent programs, just as in the design of other types of programs, a good approach is to try to relate the problem to familiar 'standard' problems for which solutions are well known. This approach is particularly important for concurrent programs because the special difficulties in debugging concurrent programs make radically new program designs very suspect until they have been very thoroughly analysed and used. When reliability is important, it is a good idea to stick to known techniques using known algorithms which have been thoroughly tried and tested.

Most of this book is devoted to the study of solutions to these basic problems in a wide variety of different circumstances.

1.2.1 Concurrent Processes on a Uniprocessor

A fundamental problem on any ordinary uniprocessor computer system is to devise a means of implementing the concurrent execution of a number of processes. This must be done by interleaving the execution of the processes, so that one runs for a short time, then another runs for a short time, and so on. The problem then splits into two parts:

> **Process switching** – the mechanism by which the currently running process is suspended and another process started.

> **Scheduling** – the algorithms which decide *when* to switch processes and *which* process to run next.

Solutions to the problem of process switching are described in Chapter 2. Scheduling strategies are quite a specialised topic in their own right and generally beyond the scope of this book. The interested reader is referred to texts on operating systems, which often include a discussion of scheduling (e.g. Peterson and Silberschatz, 1983; Deitel, 1984).

1.2.2 Mutual Exclusion

Mutual exclusion is one of the most important and fundamental synchronisation problems encountered in concurrent programming. In certain circumstances, it may be necessary to ensure that parts of two concurrent processes do *not* run concurrently. These are called *critical sections*.

Definition   A *critical section* is part of a process which must not be executed concurrently with a critical section of another process. More precisely, once one process has entered its critical section, another process may not enter its critical section until the first process exits its critical section. We say that *mutual exclusion* applies between critical sections.

Often, in more complex situations, there are a large number of critical sections but not all need be mutually exclusive with each other. Instead, they can be partitioned into distinct *classes*.

Definition   A *class of critical sections* is a set of critical sections, all of which must be mutually exclusive with all the others in the same class. Critical sections from different classes need not be mutually exclusive.

The Need for Mutual Exclusion

Mutual exclusion is often needed when concurrent processes communicate with each other by using a shared memory. If two or more processes share a common data structure, it is typically necessary to enforce mutual exclusion on the sections of these processes which access the shared data, otherwise it may become corrupted when two processes try to access it simultaneously. To illustrate how this corruption can occur, we examine in detail the following example of a shared queue.

Consider two processes, both of which may put items onto a shared queue (for the moment we do not worry about the processes which take items off the queue). Suppose the queue is implemented as an array, *queue*, and an index, *tail*, to the last item put into the queue. The relevant code in the two processes will look something like the following (written in a Pascal-like pseudocode).

Process 1   **Process 2**

```
. . . .

. . . .
tail := tail + 1;
queue[tail] := data1;

. . . .

. . . .
```

```
. . . .

. . . .
tail := tail + 1;
queue[tail] := data2;

. . . .

. . . .
```

Shared: *queue : ARRAY [0..queuesize] OF anytype;*
         tail : integer

Local: *data1, data2 : anytype*

> *Whenever writing algorithms which involve two or more processes, it is important to make it quite clear which variables are local (used by only one process) and which variables are shared (used by more that one process). In the examples given in this book, we will generally give Pascal-like declarations for the variables, and write these after the pseudo-code for the processes. These declarations will be labelled as either shared or local. Programming languages which provide facilities for writing concurrent processes have their own rules for indicating which variables are shared and which are local.*

An Execution Scenario — Suppose the execution of these processes is interleaved so that Process 1 executes *tail := tail + 1*, then, before it has a chance to continue with the next statement, the operating system interrupts and switches to Process 2, which executes *tail := tail + 1*, followed immediately by *queue[tail] := data2*. A short time later the operating system interrupts again and switches back to Process 1 which proceeds to execute *queue[tail] := data1*.

Let us put some numbers in and see what this does. Suppose the initial value of *tail* is 6, so *queue[6]* is the last item that was put into the queue. The next item should be put into *queue[7]*. In the scenario described above, however, *data2* is put into *queue[8]*, then *data1* is also put into *queue[8]* (overwriting *data2*, which is therefore lost), while nothing is put into *queue[7]*. The queue has clearly been seriously corrupted!

The solution to this problem is to require the two statements concerned with putting data into the queue to be a critical section, so that once Process 1 has started executing *tail := tail + 1*, Process 2 may not start executing *tail := tail + 1* until Process 1 completes execution of *queue[tail] := data1*. In subsequent chapters, various methods for ensuring mutual exclusion of these critical sections are described.

Accessing Shared Data — Generally, the only safe way to write processes which access shared data areas is to make the section of code in each process which accesses the shared data area into a critical section. The basic rule is: whenever any process does anything to a shared data area to temporarily put it into an inconsistent state, that code must be made into a critical section so that when the critical section ends, the shared data area has been made consistent again.

In our example of a queue, an inconsistent state occurs after incrementing *tail*, before putting the data into *queue[tail]*, because at that point in time *tail* does **not** point to the last item of data put into the queue. The specification of the particular representation of a queue that we chose to use requires that *tail* always points to the last item of the queue, and any process that accesses the queue expects this to be the case when it begins its access.

Exceptions — It is not always necessary to enforce mutual exclusion when accessing shared data. If, for example, two processes access two quite separate parts of the shared data, then mutual exclusion will probably not be necessary. If it is possible to treat the shared data as being made up of several smaller data objects which are accessed separately, then mutual exclusion need not be applied between accesses to different objects. In effect, each data object defines a class of critical sections accessing it.

If in any doubt about whether or not mutual exclusion is really necessary, the only safe approach is to apply mutual exclusion. The only disadvantage in making sections mutually exclusive when mutual exclusion is actually not needed is a possible reduction in execution speed. If both processes try to access their critical sections simultaneously, then one will have to wait. In all other respects the program will be unaffected.

The golden rule is always: if in doubt, play safe and make the sections that access shared data into mutually exclusive critical sections.

Archetype Mutual Exclusion Problem

Any program for which mutual exclusion is required between critical sections belonging to just one class can be written as follows, where *initn* denotes any (non-critical) initialisation, *critn* denotes a critical section and *remn* denotes the (non-critical) remainder of the program (where **n** is 1, 2 or 3):

Process 1	**Process 2**	**Process 3**

init1;
WHILE TRUE DO
    crit1;
    rem1
OD
	init2;
	WHILE TRUE DO
	    crit2;
	    rem2
	OD
		init3;
		WHILE TRUE DO
		    crit3;
		    rem3
		OD

and further processes have a similar form. We use this archetype program as a basis for the discussion of solutions to the mutual exclusion problem in later chapters.

Basic assumptions about this archetype mutual exclusion problem are:

1. *init1, init2, init3, crit1, crit2, crit3, rem1, rem2, rem3* may be of any size and may take any length of time to execute. Each may vary from one pass through the WHILE loop to the next.

2. *crit1, crit2, crit3* must execute in a finite time; i.e. each process must leave its critical section after a finite period of time.

3. *init1, init2, init3, rem1, rem2, rem3* may be infinite; i.e. any process may remain indefinitely in its non-critical section and never re-enter its critical section.

With these assumptions, our archetype problem is quite general. You may be inclined to say that many programs would not fit into this form, but a little reflection should convince you that the form we have chosen is general enough to cover all circumstances.

Suppose, for instance, that a process looks like this:

Process

non-critical section 1; *critical section 1;* *non-critical section 2;* *critical section 2;* *non-critical section 3*

It does not look much like the infinite loop of our archetype program as it stands. It is easy to transform to the archetype form, however, by rewriting it as follows:

Process

```
non-critical section 1;
i := 1;
WHILE TRUE DO
    IF i = 1
    THEN critical section 1
    ELSE critical section 2
    FI;
    IF i = 1
    THEN non-critical section 2
    ELSE
        non-critical section 3;
        exit
    FI;
    i := 2;
OD
```

This is clearly the same as Process 1 of the archetype program if we identify the first two statements (before the WHILE) with *init1*; the first IF statement with *crit1*; and the last two statements before the OD with *rem1*.

In a similar manner it is possible to rewrite any process with critical sections into the archetype form. We have introduced this archetype program purely for the convenience of being able to refer to one particular program, but one that is so general that it in no way restricts the applicability of our arguments.

1.2.3   Producer–Consumer Problem

This is an abstraction of a very common class of problems which occur in most real-time systems. Exactly two processes are involved. One process (called the *producer*) generates data and passes it to the second process (called the *consumer*), which receives the data and uses it for further computation.

All that concerns us is the passing of data from producer to consumer. We do not care what the data is, how or where the producer got it from, what form it is in, or what the consumer does with it after it receives it. The whole problem is simply to find a satisfactory mechanism for passing the data from producer to consumer.

We do assume, however, that the data can be regarded as a sequence of items, although we are not concerned about what an item consists of (it could be a single bit or a large and complex data structure, all items may be the same size or they may vary in size). To be acceptable, however, we demand that the solution satisfies the following requirements:

1. The data items must be received by the consumer in the same order as they were sent by the producer.

2. No items may be lost in transit from producer to consumer.

3. No spurious items may be inserted during transit (nor may items be duplicated so that they are received twice).

In other words, precisely the same sequence of items must be received by the consumer as is sent by the producer. Diagrammatically, the producer-consumer problem can be represented as follows:

> *This is a data-flow diagram in which oval (round cornered) boxes denote processes and rectangular boxes denote data. The lines show data flow, the direction being implicitly from left to right and from top to bottom unless shown otherwise. This data-flow diagram should not be confused with a conventional flow chart.*

Any mechanism for passing data from producer to consumer will, itself, impose some synchronisation constraints on the two processes. These are:

1. The consumer process cannot receive data until the producer sends it.

   This is just a special case of what is often called the *law of causality*, which states, in general, that an effect cannot precede its cause.

2. The mechanism which passes data from the producer to the consumer will, in general, have a finite capacity. The producer cannot send more data while the communication channel is full.

   For example, if the letterbox in your house is full, then the postman cannot deliver any more letters until you take the letters out and make room for further deliveries. In this case, the postman is the producer, you are the consumer, and the letterbox is the mechanism for passing data from producer to consumer. The communication mechanism cannot force the consumer to receive data, it must simply hold the data until the consumer is ready to receive it.

The area in which the communication mechanism stores data after being sent by the producer and before being received by the consumer is called a buffer. The special case of no buffer (which can alternatively be thought of as a buffer of zero capacity) is also possible, in which case the producer may send data only at that precise time at which the consumer is ready to receive it (this situation is also called a rendezvous).

More general producer–consumer problems can be defined also. Instead of a single producer and a single consumer, one may have a situation in which there are several producers feeding a single consumer, or a single producer feeding several consumers, or several producers feeding several consumers; in all cases through a single communication channel. Most of the standard solutions to the simple producer–consumer problem are easily generalised to multiple producers and consumers. Our discussion of the producer–consumer problem in later chapters will be based primarily on the simple single producer, single consumer case, however.

Example: Printer spooling in UNIX

In the UNIX operating system, the *lpr* command is used to output a file to the printer. If the printer is already in use, this command queues the file and it will be output later, after all preceding files in the queue have been printed. This is often called *spooling* the files, because on early computers this queue of files was kept on a spool of magnetic tape.

The implementation of this command involves several processes, through which the data is passed in turn. The data-flow diagram for the implementation is shown in Fig. 1.1.

This diagram shows the processes involved, including those that are implemented in hardware as part of the printer itself. As can be seen, the *lpr* command is in two parts. The first part is the command program which is called by the user's program (or by the command interpreter which interprets commands typed by the user on the keyboard) and runs as if it were part of the user process which calls it. The second part is a separate process (called the *printer daemon* in UNIX jargon) which runs concurrently and copies data from the queue of files to the kernel of the operating system for printing. This is done by means of a system call which executes the *printer driver* routine within the kernel.

This second process in the chain acts as a consumer of data sent by the *lpr* command (the first process in the chain), but also acts as a producer of data which will be consumed by the next process.

The printer driver routine in the UNIX kernel separates the data into

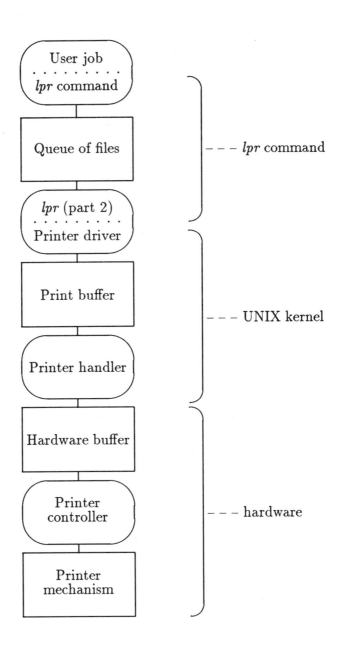

Figure 1.1: Data flow for UNIX printer spooling.

individual characters and puts them into a print buffer. Yet another process (also part of the kernel), called the *printer handler*, is activated by interrupts from the printer (whenever it is ready for another character). This process simply outputs the next character from the buffer to the printer and then goes to sleep until the next interrupt.

The printer itself may be thought of as containing a fourth process which runs in the printer controller hardware (often implemented as a special purpose microprocessor with its dedicated program in ROM). When the printer handler routine in the kernel executes a print instruction, the character to be printed is simply loaded into a buffer in the printer hardware. This character is then read by the controller process. It decodes the character and produces control signals to the mechanical parts of the printer to generate an impression of the character on the paper. Most modern printers actually contain a buffer not for one character, but for several thousand or more, enabling the printer controller to carry out sophisticated optimisations of the mechanical process of printing such as printing alternate lines in the reverse direction to reduce print head motion.

1.2.4   Readers and Writer

Another very important and fundamental class of problems involves several processes accessing a shared data area (often called a *file*, but that does not imply that it is necessarily stored on disc; it may be on any storage medium, including main memory or even CPU registers). A common simple form of this problem has an arbitrary number of processes which read the file and only one process which writes to the file, hence it is called the *readers and writer* problem. The synchronisation requirements of this problem are:

1. Any number of readers may simultaneously read the file.

2. If the writer is writing to the file, no readers may read it.

It is important to note that the readers do *not* also write to the file, *nor* does the writer read the file. This is clearly a much more restrictive situation than the general one of a number of processes all of which may both read and write to the file. Any solution of the general problem will also be a solution of the more restricted readers and writer problem, so why bother with the restricted case at all?

The reason is simply that much more efficient solutions are possible for the readers and writer problem, and in many situations the less efficient solutions to the general problem are unacceptably slow.

Suppose, for instance, that the shared data file was a library catalogue. Ordinary users of the library look at the contents of the catalogue, but do not change it, so they are readers. The librarian may change the catalogue, so he is a writer (in reality, he would probably also be a reader, but that point is not relevant to our argument here). The more general problem would assume all processes can both read and write, so if any process accesses the file, all other processes must be excluded; which boils down to a problem of mutual exclusion as already described. This would mean that two library users would not be permitted to look at the catalogue simultaneously, which is clearly going to impose intolerable delays on users at busy times. There will obviously be a tremendous improvement in performance if users can look at the catalogue simultaneously, and there is no good reason to prevent it.

On the other hand, it is important to prevent any user from looking at the catalogue while the librarian is in the middle of writing to it, otherwise the user may read data from the catalogue which is simply incorrect.

1.2.5 Readers and Writers

A slightly more general version of the readers and writer problem allows any number of writers, instead of just one. As you might expect, this is called the *readers and writers* problem. The synchronisation conditions which must be satisfied are:

1. Any number of readers may simultaneously read the file.

2. Only one writer at a time may write to the file.

3. If a writer is writing to the file, no reader may read it.

As before, readers may not write, nor may writers read.

There are many other similar problems that arise in concurrent programming. For example, one process updates (both reads and writes) the shared data file, and any number of other processes read the file. The example of access to a library catalogue which we described earlier is actually more likely to fall into this category than into the simple readers and writer category. We do not have room in this book to examine every possible situation in detail, so our discussion of these problems will be confined to the simplest and most important cases; i.e. the readers and writer problem and the more general readers and writers problem.

1.2.6 Resource Sharing

The most common and fundamental resource sharing problem is sharing a uniprocessor between a number of processes, which we looked at earlier.

There are, however, a wide variety of other resource sharing problems which arise in operating systems and in many other concurrent programs. The basic common requirement for most of these situations is mutual exclusion on the use of the resource: if one process is using the resource, other processes may not use it at the same time. The problems can become more complex with multiple resources (or resources that can be allocated in part — like memory). In later chapters we consider some of the simpler resource sharing problems; more complex situations are often highly specialised and generally beyond the scope of this book.

Dining Philosophers

One rather artificial but well-known resource sharing problem, which has been used as an example many times in the literature, is the Dining Philosophers Problem. It can be stated as follows.

Five philosophers sit around a large circular table. In the centre of the table is a large bowl of spaghetti which is regularly replenished. Each philosopher has his own plate immediately in front of him on the table. Also on the table are exactly five forks, one placed between each pair of adjacent philosophers. The philosophers spend their time alternately eating and thinking. To eat, a philosopher requires two forks, but he can reach only those two forks which are immediately adjacent to him. If one or both of these are being used, he must wait until they are free. When a philosopher finishes eating he puts the forks back in their original positions so that his neighbours may use them. He then proceeds to think until he gets hungry again.

The problem is to find a protocol (i.e. rules of behaviour) which will ensure that none of the philosophers starves. It is assumed that none of the philosophers will eat continuously, and that starvation occurs only if a philosopher is prevented from eating for an infinite time (he can be prevented from eating for any finite time and still survive).

This is a non-trivial resource sharing problem. The 'processes' in this case are the philosophers, and the resources are the five forks they use for eating. The problem is complicated by the fact that the forks are not equally available to all philosophers.

To show that this problem is more difficult than appears at first sight, consider the following protocol. When a philosopher gets hungry he first looks for the fork on his left. If it is available, he picks it up. He then looks for the fork on his right. If it is available he picks it up and starts eating. If it is in use, he waits until it becomes free (while still holding in his left hand the fork from his left).

The danger with this protocol is that all the philosophers can starve. This happens if, by chance, they all get hungry at the same time. In this case, all five philosophers pick up the forks on their left. Each philosopher now has a fork in his left hand. They all then look for the forks on their right, but none of these is available (each is being held by a neighbouring philosopher). The protocol now states that each waits until the fork on his right becomes available. They will all wait forever, because the protocol says nothing about releasing the fork in a philosopher's left hand if the fork on his right is not free. Instead, all five philosophers doggedly hang on to the forks in their left hands, each waiting for the philosopher on his right to release a fork (but he is waiting for the philosopher on *his* right to release a fork, and so on). Consequently, all five philosophers starve to death!

Because the Dining Philosophers Problem is rather specialised and of very limited applicability, it is not appropriate to spend much time on discussing it here, although we do refer to it in some of the exercises. The interested reader is referred elsewhere for more detail (e.g. Ben-Ari, 1982).

1.3 Basic Parallel Processing Problems

The fundamental question facing the designer of a parallel program is how to partition the task across the processors available. In general, this is a very difficult problem and there is no single strategy that will give an efficient solution in all situations. So, we look for those categories of problems which admit simple solutions, and use these as a basis from which to tackle more difficult problems.

A very large and important class of problems involves the processing of large sets of data. The simplest cases to handle are those in which the elements of the data set may all be processed independently of each other and this is the main category of problems that we consider for parallel processing.

1.3.1 Independent Data Sets

Suppose that we wish to process a large data set in such a way that the processing can be decomposed into an independent process on each element of the data. In other words, the result we wish to compute can be expressed as a set of values, each of which may be expressed as a function of a single element of the original data set. We allow cases in which some of these values do not exist.

This, apparently rather restricted class of problems, is, in fact, applicable to a large number of common situations. Consider, for instance, the problem of searching a library catalogue for all the books in a specified combination of categories (e.g. we may wish to find all the books with 'concurrent program-ming' or 'real-time programming' in their titles). The result will be the set of books which satisfy these criteria. Clearly, one can look at each book in the catalogue independently, the result being either to eliminate it or include it in the result set.

In Chapter 11, various ways of handling this class of problems are described, using both multiprocessing and distributed processing techniques.

1.4   Exercises

Exercise 1.1 Show that interleaving a process that pops a stack with one that pushes the stack can lead to errors unless mutual exclusion is enforced on the sections of the program that access the stack.

Exercise 1.2 Is mutual exclusion necessary between two processes which access a common queue, one to put items onto the queue and the other to take items off the queue?

Exercise 1.3 A computer system is being used to control the flow of traffic through a road tunnel. For safety reasons, there must never be more than approximately N vehicles in the tunnel at one time. Traffic lights at the entrance control the entry of traffic and vehicle detectors at entrance and exit are used to measure the traffic flow.

An *entrance process* records all vehicles entering the tunnel, and a separate *exit process* records all vehicles leaving. Each of these processes can, at any time, read its vehicle detector to determine how many vehicles have passed since the last reading was made. A *traffic lights process* controls the traffic lights at the entrance to the tunnel which are set to red whenever the number of vehicles in the tunnel equals or exceeds N, and green otherwise.

Assuming that shared memory is available and that a mutual exclusion mechanism is provided, write pseudocode programs for all three processes indicating clearly the critical sections.

Chapter 2

Basic Hardware Mechanisms

In this chapter, we examine the basic hardware mechanisms for concurrent programming, as provided on most common computer systems. It is assumed that the reader is familiar with the general instruction-set architecture of conventional computers, including interrupts and related features. The basic concurrency mechanisms that have to be provided are *process switching* and *mutual exclusion*. Once we have implementations for process switching and mutual exclusion, all other synchronisation problems can be solved in terms of these basic mechanisms.

2.1 Process Switching

The operating system is generally responsible for deciding when to stop one process running and start another. It also has to carry out this process switching. One of the essential requirements that must be met when suspending a process is that it must be stopped rather delicately so that nothing is corrupted and it can be resumed later without suffering any ill effects. To do this, the *state* of the process must be saved at the time it is suspended.

Definition   The *state* of a process is the totality of information needed to be saved when the process is suspended, to enable it to resume from the point at which it was suspended, as if nothing had happened (other than some time has passed).

The state of a process on a typical computer is (i) the contents of all registers known to the programmer (including the program counter and program status word or other flags and status registers), (ii) the contents of all areas of memory accessible to the process, and (iii) the contents of all files (on disc, or elsewhere) which are accessible to the process.

In practice, a typical operating system will ensure that the areas of memory accessible to a process will be preserved while that process is suspended after an interrupt. If the operating system needs to use the process's memory for other purposes, it will save the contents on disc and then restore them again later before resuming the suspended process. All files which the process has opened (these are the only files it has access to) will also be preserved unchanged. Hence the only things the operating system actively needs to save when it suspends a process are (i) the contents of all registers, (ii) the addresses of the areas of memory accessible to the process, (iii) the addresses of all open files. There may also be a few other small items of housekeeping information (e.g. the processor time used by the process, which may be used by the scheduler in deciding which process should be run next).

The operating system kernel saves the state of a suspended process in what we call the *process control block* (PCB), usually located in main memory.

2.1.1   Hardware Mechanisms

Nearly all present-day computers provide three basic hardware mechanisms for process switching: the *interrupt*, the *return-from-interrupt* and the *system call* (the last of these is sometimes alternatively called a *software interrupt, executive call, monitor call* or *trap*). Both the interrupt and the system call act much like a subroutine jump instruction on most computers, except that the address of the routine jumped to is not specified explicitly and usually a very limited number of subroutine addresses are available. The two mechanisms differ mainly in that an interrupt is caused by an event completely external to the program, while a system call is an actual machine instruction (i.e. the process itself causes the interrupt).

The return-from-interrupt is a machine instruction that acts much like a subroutine return instruction.

Examples

We consider three computer architectures which form a chronological sequence: the PDP8, PDP11 and VAX (all three by Digital Equipment Corporation). Although the PDP8 and PDP11 are now obsolescent, they are historically significant in that the PDP8 was the first commercially successful minicomputer and the PDP11 was the most widely used and successful minicomputer ever made. Both are now largely superseded by modern microcomputers.

The PDP8 and PDP11 architectures have a simplicity and elegance which is lacking in many present-day computers, although the current fashion for reduced instruction set (RISC) architectures is, in effect, a return to simplicity. The PDP8 was designed to be a very low cost machine in the days before cheap integrated circuits. Hence to keep the cost down, simplicity of central processor design was imperative. The PDP8 was so simple that it was somewhat tedious and inefficient to program. Today, such an extreme degree of simplicity is generally neither necessary nor desirable.

The PDP11 design incorporated an additional degree of sophistication to overcome the limitations inherent in the too simple PDP8. The interrupt mechanism used in the PDP11 has not been significantly bettered today and almost all popular computers (including the latest microprocessors) have interrupt mechanisms using very similar principles. The VAX is the main computer architecture made today by Digital Equipment Corporation. Its design arose from experience with its main predecessors, the PDP8 and PDP11. It is included in the discussion for completeness.

> **PDP8** — On receiving an interrupt, the program counter (which contains the address of the next instruction) is saved in memory location zero, further interrupts are disabled, and the number 1 is loaded into the program counter (so the interrupt handling routine always begins at location one in memory). As background, it is useful to know that the PDP8 has very few registers: a program counter which points to the next instruction to be executed, an accumulator for general use, a one bit link register used for the carry bit in arithmetic, and a one bit interrupt enable register (1 if interrupts are allowed, 0 if they are not). There is no stack pointer register, nor any register available in which to save a return address. A subroutine jump instruction saves the return address in the memory location immediately preceding the first instruction of the subroutine.
>
> Consequently, the interrupt is implemented as a subroutine jump to location zero (the code of the subroutine starts in location one), the only extra feature being that interrupts are automatically turned off. There is no special instruction to return from an interrupt. Instead, an ordinary subroutine return instruction (simply an indirect jump to the address stored in location zero) is used, preceded by an interrupt enable instruction, whose action is always delayed by one instruction so that interrupts are not actually re-enabled until after the subroutine return has been executed.

The PDP8 mechanism is very simple and fast but it has the disadvantage that there is only one interrupt handling routine for all types of interrupts. If several different types of interrupts are possible, this routine must test all possible sources of interrupt in turn to find the one that has actually occurred. This can be very time consuming and limits the speed of interrrupt handling on the PDP8 if a large number of different types of interrupt may occur. For very simple situations, however, this method is fast and easy.

As the contents of the accumulator and link register are not saved automatically when an interrupt occurs, if the interrupt handler needs to use these registers, it must first save their contents and then restore them again before returning to the interrupted program.

PDP11 — On receiving an interrupt, the program counter (PC) and the program status register (PS) are saved on the system stack in main memory. The program status register must be saved as well as the program counter because it contains the processor priority which is automatically changed when an interrupt occurs (hence the old value must be saved or it would be lost). It is convenient to use the system stack as the place in which to save PC and PS because the stack is routinely used to save subroutine return addresses and the PDP11 has one register dedicated to holding the stack pointer (SP).

Interrupts are *vectored* on the PDP11 which means that the device causing the interrupt supplies a parameter which is used by the hardware as the index to a table within the operating system which contains the starting addresses of interrupt handling routines for each different type of interrupt. This table contains two words per entry, one being the start address of the interrupt handler (which is loaded into PC), the other being the new value of the program status word (which is loaded into PS).

There is no automatic disabling of interrupts when an interrupt occurs. PDP11 interrupts are classified into 4 possible priority levels, and the processor has its own priority level which is changeable by program. If the processor priority is set to level n, then only interrupts on levels greater than n are accepted (interrupts at the same or lower levels are effectively disabled). The processor priority level is set when the PS register is loaded (three bits of PS specify the processor priority), so the operating system programmer can choose the priority level to set after each type of interrupt by putting the appropriate values in the program status words of the interrupt vector table. He can, in the same way, choose where to start each interrupt handling routine, they do not have to be located at fixed places.

A return-from-interrupt instruction implements approximately the converse action to an interrupt. It pops the top two words off the system stack and loads them into PC and PS (usually the values saved from those registers when the interrupt originally occurred). The initial values of PC and PS are not saved by the return-from-interrupt instruction, however.

A system call instruction is just like an interrupt, except that the instruction contains an eight-bit parameter which is used as an index to another table in the operating system, from which the new values of PC and PS will be loaded.

Interrupt handlers on the PDP11, as on the PDP8, must be responsible for saving the contents of any register they wish to use, and restoring its original contents before returning to the interrupted process. The PDP11 has seven registers which are not automatically saved, so saving them all can be relatively time consuming and if the very fastest interrupt handling is required, the optimum approach is to use the minimum number of registers possible in the interrupt handler and save only those registers. In some very simple cases, interrupt handlers are written which use no registers at all (except PC and PS).

Of course, if all the registers were automatically saved on an interrupt, this would slow down all interrupt handling (the hardware would still need seven more memory accesses to save the seven extra registers, and seven more memory accesses would be needed to restore them in executing the return from interrupt instruction). This would be in addition to the time already needed to save PC and PS.

VAX — The interrupt mechanism on the VAX is essentially very similar to that on the PDP11, but, in addition, a single machine instruction is available to the programmer to enable him to save the contents of registers not saved automatically by the interrupt; and a corresponding instruction to restore them.

2.1.2   Implementation of Process Switching

The basic process switching algorithm which needs to be implemented is:

> save state of process in PCB;
> load state of new process

The hardware mechanisms described in the previous section do not implement this process switching algorithm. The usual interrupt mechanism does not save the complete state of a process. Instead it saves the absolute minimum it can get away with. This means that it can be made as fast as possible, but the programmer is then responsible for saving all the rest of the state.

Furthermore, it does not save the registers in the process control block of the interrupted process, as we require. Instead, the interrupt mechanism saves the program counter and other essential registers on the system stack.

Thus, the hardware mechanisms implement only part of this algorithm, the rest must be done by software in the interrupt handler. As we have already seen, the hardware is designed primarily to allow very fast interrupt handling to be implemented when required. This will usually not involve switching to a new user process. It is quicker to return to the interrupted process rather than switch to another process. So the hardware mechanism usually saves the minimum necessary on the system stack, *not* in the PCB. This also has the advantage that it allows interrupts to remain enabled even while in an interrupt handler. If a higher priority interrupt comes along, it can be serviced and the return address will be put on the stack (and will not overwrite the previous return address). When the higher priority interrupt handler returns, the original interrupt handler will be resumed from where it was interrupted.

Examples of Fast Interrupt Handling

> **A software clock** can be implemented very simply by arranging a hardware clock to generate interrupts at regular intervals and writing an interrupt handler which simply increments a counter every time it is entered (possibly using suitable modulo arithmetic so that seconds, minutes, hours, etc. are kept explicitly). This probably requires at most one working register, so there is no need to spend time saving and later restoring the contents of other registers. Also, if the interrupt handler does not have any process scheduling function, the process returned to after the interrupt service is complete will always be the interrupted process. So, there is no need to spend time copying the registers saved on the system stack into the PCB of the interrupted process; they

can simply be left on the stack (to be restored automatically by the return-from-interrupt instruction).

Simple pulse counting software is similar, as are some types of very simple peripheral device servicing. Pulse counting is very widely used in embedded systems and for process control of all types. Devices used for measuring velocity, whether it is the velocity of a car or the velocity of water flowing in a pipe, often work on the principle of generating pulses at regular intervals (of distance), so determining the speed involves counting the number of pulses in a known time interval. Many types of measuring device make use of this principle.

It can be argued that interrupt handlers are themselves processes, and this is indeed correct. Their implementation is invariably handled rather differently from ordinary user processes, however. An interrupt handler is initiated only by an interrupt, it is not timeshared in the way that user processes are. Once it starts to run it will run to completion and can only be interrupted by an interrupt of higher priority (there are some systems where this is not the case, but they are the exception rather than the rule). Therefore, it requires no PCB, and the normal scheduling routine that decides which user process to run next need not even be aware of the existence of the interrupt handlers. In fact, for these reasons, it is quite common not to consider interrupt handlers as processes at all. This viewpoint has considerable hidden dangers. Interrupt handlers *are* processes and they run concurrently with user processes. It is certainly not safe to forget about them as they can do things which may interfere with user processes unless the user processes take action to protect themselves.

Chapter 4 contains a more detailed discussion of the interaction of interrupt handlers and ordinary user processes within a conventional multi-user operating system for a uniprocessor machine.

2.2 Mutual Exclusion

Mutual exclusion is implemented on a uniprocessor system basically by controlling the times at which process switching may occur. It is necessary to remember, however, that even a uniprocessor normally contains several *peripheral controllers* which are effectively other processors running in parallel with the central processor. When mutual exclusion is necessary between a process running on the central processor and a peripheral controller (which is generally not programmable but runs a dedicated process), often the only mechanism provided is mutual exclusion on a single memory access. For processes which are timeshared concurrently on the central processor, all of the following mechanisms may be available.

2.2.1   Memory Access

A single memory write is always indivisible, hence mutually exclusive of all other memory accesses. This means that there is no risk that a memory location can ever be found in an intermediate state, it must either contain its value before the write access or its value after it. Also, although memory read is often implemented as a destructive read (which leaves zero in the memory location), followed by a rewrite of the information back into the location from which it has just been read, these two steps are inseparable. Thus memory read and memory write are indivisible operations, or *primitive* operations.

> **Example** — If a memory location contains the value 6 and the next access to that memory location writes the value 39, a peripheral controller running concurrently and accessing that same memory location may read the value 6 or the value 39, depending upon whether it gets in ahead of the central processor or not. It will never read any other value, however (assuming no other instructions write to that location).

At first sight this may appear to be a rather weak and useless property. It is, however, fundamental to many of the algorithms presented later and is, in reality, an important property of all normal hardware memory access mechanisms.

Memory Access in High-Level Languages

Access to variables in high-level languages can be relied upon to be indivisible only if it is known that the variable is stored alone in a single memory location. This is often the case for the basic data types (such as characters, integers and reals) on mainframe computers. It may not be so for double precision numbers, however, and is usually not the case for character strings, arrays and complex data structures.

On some small micro computers, the memory word length is very short (e.g. 8 or 16 bits) and even normal precision integers and reals may be stored in two or more memory locations. Such variables will not be accessed by indivisible operations and programmers of concurrent software must remember this.

Unfortunately, problems can also arise if data items are very short and packed two or more to a word. Many high-level language compilers pack character strings and bit strings, several items per word, to save space. In these cases, write accesses may not be indivisible. For example, if it is required to write a new value into the i-th bit of a particular word of memory, on some computers this would require several machine instructions: read the word from memory into a register; put the new bit into the correct position in the register; then write the register back to memory. To make the situation even more uncertain, some machines do provide single memory access to bits and bytes within a word, and, on these machines, indivisible access to packed data items *is* possible (provided the compiler writers made use of the special instructions to do this).

Regrettably, very few programming languages specify, in the language definition, anything at all about the indivisibility of access to variables. Hence, if a particular compiler is known to implement, say, boolean variables and normal size integer variables in such a way that access to them is guaranteed indivisible, typically this must be regarded as an implementation dependent feature. This is unfortunate because the alternatives to using the indivisibility of memory access are often much less efficient or much less convenient, or both. (In Chapter 5 and later chapters, some of the special primitives for concurrency that may be provided in high-level languages are introduced.)

The programmer of concurrent software is faced with a choice of four main possibilities:

1. **He can use a standard high-level language which provides concurrency primitives.** The program can be written strictly within the language definition and hence it is implementation independent. Direct access to shared variables should not be used unless the language definition explicitly specifies it to be safe. This option should give the greatest reliability and maintainability. The price may be a significant reduction in execution efficiency of some programs (but not all).

   Probably the best general-purpose language to choose for this approach is Ada (see Chapter 9). It has adequate support for concurrent programming, its definition has been made an international standard, and 'validated' compilers (i.e. compilers which have been tested and found to conform closely to the language definition) are widely available. Its main drawbacks are the size and cost of compilers and supporting software, and the fact that Ada does not prohibit some dangerous or system dependent practices in concurrent programming. Ada compilers generally do not even give warnings in these situations.

The main area of danger is in the use of shared variables which Ada permits, yet places the responsibility firmly on the programmer to ensure that access to shared variables is programmed correctly. Section 9.11 in the Ada Reference Manual (ISO 8652, 1987) contains a detailed discussion of the use of shared variables.

2. **He can write an implementation dependent high-level language program** which uses knowledge that the chosen compiler implements certain types of variables so as to make their access always indivisible. This is a very risky approach as few compilers specify unambiguously which types of variables will be accessed indivisibly.

   A very nasty problem that may arise when using shared variables is that in certain circumstances simultaneous access to *different* variables may cause errors (see Exercise 2.3).

3. **He can write assembly code routines** for accessing the shared variables for which indivisible access is needed, and call these routines from the high-level language program. This method incurs only slight loss of efficiency and convenience (both arise from the additional procedure calls), but the resulting software is machine dependent. Also, the programmer must be familiar with the assembly code, in addition to the high-level language.

4. **He can write the whole program in assembly code.** This is an attractive option only if the added overall efficiency that can be achieved justifies the vastly increased costs of program development and the reduction in reliability (owing to the greater amount of assembly code, which gives the programmer more opportunity to make mistakes).

Single Word Readers and Writers

Suppose we have a readers and writers situation (i.e. several processes read a shared variable, and several other processes write to the shared variable, but no processes both read and write) and the shared variable is a single word of memory. Processes which update the variable are not allowed, because they have to both read and write (e.g. if a process wishes to add 1531 to a shared integer variable, this requires first reading the current value of the variable, then adding 1531 and writing the result back into the variable).

   As an example of a true readers and writer problem using a single word shared variable, suppose that a computer is being used to control the operation of a central heating boiler and one of the processes periodically samples the boiler temperature which is written into a global (i.e. shared) variable. Several other processes need to look at the boiler temperature from time to time, which they do by reading the global variable (which always contains the latest temperature reading). Such a situation can be programmed without taking any special precautions to ensure mutual exclusion, provided it is known that the boiler temperature is stored in a single word of memory (on its own, it must not share that word with any other variables). The hardware memory unit will then ensure mutual exclusion for all accesses to that word.

This solution is equally safe whether all the processes are running on the same processor or whether some processes run on different processors (but sharing the same memory, of course).

2.2.2 Individual Instructions

It is conventional for computer hardware to be designed to permit interrupts to occur only *between* instructions. Normally, an instruction may not be interrupted in the middle of its execution. If this was permitted, it would be necessary for the state of the machine, as saved when an interrupt occurs, to include registers which are not directly accessible to the programmer. This would be highly inconvenient and hence it is a general rule that interrupts are accepted only between instructions (an interrupt request that arrives in the middle of an instruction is not lost but merely made to wait). There are a few special exceptions to this (see Exercise 2.1), but they do not diminish the importance of the general rule.

This has the important additional effect that processes being time-shared on a uniprocessor can rely on individual machine instructions (with very few exceptions) being mutually exclusive under all circumstances, because the process switching mechanism is always either an interrupt or a machine instruction such as a system call. In other words, a single machine instruction is guaranteed to be indivisible: once execution of it has begun, no other process can interrupt until it has finished.

Unfortunately this property is of use only to the assembly code programmer. In high-level languages it is very unsafe to rely on knowing that the compiler generates a particular sequence of machine instructions. In assembly code, it is a very useful property that is also exploited in the low-level implementation of many higher level primitives for real-time programming (discussed in later chapters).

Many modern computers provide a number of special instructions that are particularly useful for concurrent programming purely *because* they are guaranteed indivisible (i.e. mutually exclusive with other instructions). The most common are listed below.

Exchange Instruction

In the exchange instruction, the contents of a memory location and a register are exchanged (less commonly, some machines provide an exchange instruction which exchanges two memory locations). We will write:

$$\boxed{r :=: x}$$

which is equivalent to the following, in which t is used purely for temporary storage:

$$\boxed{t := x;\ x := r;\ r := t}$$

We enclose these sections of code in thick-ruled boxes to indicate that they represent single atomic instructions, i.e. they are indivisible.

Test-and-Set Instruction

The test-and-set instruction performs the following action:

$$\boxed{IF\ x = 0\ THEN\ x := 1;\ r := 1\ ELSE\ r := 0\ FI}$$

where r is generally a status flag or other register and x is a memory location.

An alternative form of this instruction, as implemented in some computer architectures, does not load a boolean value into a status register, but instead executes a branch if $x = a$ (where a is a fixed value, usually 0 or 1) and then sets x to a, all in one indivisible operation.

Lock Instruction

This instruction, sometimes called test and switch branch (TSB), is similar to the test and set instruction that we looked at earlier, but it contains a complete wait loop within the instruction. Its action can be written as follows:

$$WHILE\ x = 1\ DO\ OD;\ x := 1$$

where x is a memory location. A separate 'unlock' instruction need not be specially provided as its effect can be obtained simply by $x := 0$.

On a uniprocessor this instruction will inevitably lead to deadlock if interrupts are not permitted during execution of the instruction (as is the rule for other instructions). If x is initially 1, the only way the instruction can terminate is for some other process to reset x to zero. On a uniprocessor the only way to start another process is by an interrupt, hence interrupts must be permitted during this instruction, but only between the DO and the OD in the wait loop. In fact, this instruction is intended primarily for use in a multiprocessing environment.

An essential requirement for its implementation is that it must be safe (the concept of safety will be discussed more fully in Section 3.1.1). In this case, what is required to ensure safety is that, if x is 1 when the instruction starts execution, and then, during execution of the wait loop, another processor sets x to 0 so that the wait loop then terminates, the value of x must be returned to 1 before the 0 value can be read by a third process. This is to ensure that the instruction can be safely used to implement mutual exclusion. If several processors are all waiting for the same x, only one will be allowed to proceed when x returns to 0 (which one depends upon the hardware implementation of the lock instruction: it may be completely unpredictable in some machines, while a fixed priority order may operate in others).

Increment and Decrement Instructions

Many computers provide single machine instructions to increment or decrement a memory location, and load the result into a register as well. These instructions can often be usefully employed in synchronisation algorithms that would not work if the incrementing (or decrementing) was done by separate instructions to read the value from memory, increment it and write it back to memory. On many computers, the incrementing or decrementing of the memory location takes place in a single memory cycle and is therefore mutually exclusive, even with processes running on other processors which share the same memory (such as a peripheral device controller).

We can write the increment instruction in the following way, where x is the memory location and r is the register:

$$\boxed{x := x + 1;\; r := x}$$

> **Example: A Shared Counter** — In some very simple applications, the complete critical section can be implemented as a single instruction, particularly if some of the special instructions described above are available.
>
> Suppose, for example, that several concurrent processes are each, from time to time, incrementing the same counter. Assuming the counter can be stored in a single word of memory (using the normal representation of an integer variable), an increment instruction (in machine code) can be used to increment the counter in one instruction, thus guaranteeing mutual exclusion. If two or more instructions had to be used

(for example, if the counter required more than one word, or if increment instructions were not available), then mutual exclusion would have to be enforced by one of the techniques described later.

It is, of course, equally easy to write a process which reads the shared counter, because reading a single word of memory requires only a single instruction, so the normal mutual exclusion of individual instructions is quite adequate.

There are very many practical applications of such a shared counter. To take just one concrete example as an illustration, suppose that a computer is being used to count the number of people entering a football ground through many different turnstiles, and that a separate process controls each turnstile. A shared variable is used to represent the total number of people that have entered the ground so far. Each process increments this variable whenever another person passes through the turnstile linked to that process.

2.2.3   Disabling Interrupts

The most obvious and direct way of ensuring mutual exclusion between critical sections in processes being time-shared on a uniprocessor is to disable interrupts during the critical section to prevent process switching. Typically, there are special instructions available to disable and enable interrupts. After a *disable interrupts* instruction is executed, no interrupts will be accepted until an *enable interrupts* has been executed (of course, interrupt requests are normally just held up while interrupts are disabled, not lost).

Our archetype mutual exclusion program becomes:

Process 1	**Process 2**
init1; *WHILE TRUE DO* *disable interrupts;* *crit1;* *enable interrupts;* *rem1* *OD*	*init2;* *WHILE TRUE DO* *disable interrupts;* *crit2;* *enable interrupts;* *rem2* *OD*

with the obvious generalisation to n processes.

This solution is very simple and reliable, but suffers from a number of disadvantages:

1. **It is available only in privileged mode.**

   Most computers (except some small microprocessors such as the Z80 and 8086) are designed for multi-user operation and provide a *privileged mode* of operation for the operating system and a *user mode* for all other programs. Certain instructions are designated *privileged instructions* and are only available in privileged mode. These instructions are needed by the operating system, but if available to ordinary user programs could cause potentially disastrous interference with other users or with the operating system itself.

   The instructions to disable and enable interrupts are invariably classed as privileged instructions on such machines. Hence they are not available except in privileged mode.

2. **It is ineffective on multiprocessor systems.**

   Disabling interrupts only prevents other processes on the same processor from running concurrently. It has no effect whatsoever on processes running on different processors. Hence, disabling interrupts during critical sections is totally ineffective unless all the processes involved are running on the same processor.

3. **It is a very heavy-handed approach as it excludes *all* other processes.**

   All we really want to do is exclude critical sections of the same class. Disabling interrupts excludes all other processes, whether or not they are in critical sections at all, let alone of the same class. Some computers allow the selective disabling of interrupts, which can be exploited to allow some processes to interrupt but not others. Such facilities are helpful, but they still do not provide the ability to exclude only those critical sections of the same class, and nothing else.

These disadvantages rule out the use of this method in most normal circumstances. The main areas in which disabling interrupts is a useful way to achieve mutual exclusion are (i) writing operating systems, (ii) dedicated systems on 'bare' machines (i.e. machines run without operating systems), and (iii) on the simpler types of processor which do not support multi-user systems. These areas do include a vast number of important applications, and many real-time systems have been implemented as either (ii) or (iii) above.

The many popular personal computers which run MS-DOS or PC-DOS on
an 8086 or related processor are well known examples of systems which fall
into category (iii). The processor makes no distinction between the operating
system and user processes, so any user process is free to use the instructions
to disable and enable interrupts, along with all other instructions.

2.2.4 Multiprocessor Mechanisms

On multiprocessor computers in which several processors share a common
memory, there are generally some basic mechanisms provided for mutual exclusion at the machine instruction level. The normal indivisibility of machine
instructions does *not* provide mutual exclusion between different processors.
Many instructions involve several memory accesses each. If another processor
shares access to the same memory, there is normally nothing to prevent it from
accessing memory *between* accesses by the first processor. Indeed, it will have
no way of knowing if consecutive memory accesses by another processor are
part of one instruction or several instructions. The memory unit itself will
enforce mutual exclusion on each individual memory access, but beyond this
additional mechanisms are needed to enforce mutual exclusion.

Furthermore, as we have already seen, disabling interrupts is no longer an
effective means of ensuring mutual exclusion once we move to a multiprocessor
environment. New mechanisms are needed.

Memory Locking

Multiprocessor machines sometimes provide a special *memory lock* instruction
(not to be confused with the lock instruction described earlier) which is treated
as a prefix to the instruction immediately following it, and causes a memory
lock to be applied for the duration of that instruction. This means that no
other devices are permitted access to the shared memory during execution of
the locked instruction.

Memory locked instructions are thus effectively indivisible (i.e. mutually
exclusive) on multiprocessor systems, just as all machine instructions are indivisible on uniprocessors.

Digression — Memory Locks in the Intel 8086 Series
The history of computer architecture contains many examples of inelegant de-
signs and patches that have been added rather hurriedly at the eleventh hour.
Nowhere is this more in evidence than in mechanisms to support concurrency.
This is probably because the full implications of these mechanisms are often not

totally appreciated even by software engineers, let alone by computer hardware engineers.

Even after many decades' experience of computer design, there are still cases of this happening today. Intel's highly successful 8086 series architecture is a case in point. The 8086 includes a memory lock prefix instruction which can be used to prefix any other instruction and cause a memory lock to be applied for the duration of that instruction. Now, the 8086 was designed as a single user machine. No special facilities were provided to help prevent one user process from interfering with other processes (in particular, it does not provide memory protection, nor are user processes prevented from using I/O instructions or other instructions which the operating system may prefer to keep for its own use alone).

So, the designers did not worry that the lock instruction could have disastrous effects if misused. The 8086 instruction set includes string instructions which will operate on strings of arbitrary length (possibly many thousands of bytes). These instructions can consequently take a very long time to execute and involve thousands of memory accesses. If memory lock is applied to such instructions, other devices are locked out of memory for relatively long periods of time. This can be a disaster for a fast disc controller, say, which has to read data from a disc rotating at a fixed speed, and store that data in memory at the rate at which it comes off disc. There is typically only a few microseconds in which to write each data word to memory. If access to memory is not obtained within this time, the data is lost and the complete disc transfer has to be aborted.

Under the philosophy that the 8086 is a single user machine, this does not matter. If the programmer chooses to write a program that corrupts his own disc transfers, that is his lookout!

When the 80286 was planned, the philosophy changed. This processor was designed to be a multi-user machine with full memory protection and other features to prevent processes interfering with each other in uncontrolled ways. Clearly, in such an environment, the unconstrained use of memory lock cannot be permitted for ordinary user processes. Instead, unconstrained use of memory lock is permitted for the operating system only, and all other programs can be prevented from using it (the operating system can decide whether or not a user process can use memory lock, but it must either allow its use for all types of instructions or ban its use for all instructions). Nevertheless, so that all processes can obtain some mutual exclusion facilities in a multiprocessor system, memory lock is automatically implemented on all exchange instructions, whether requested or not.

This solution was fine, until the 80386 was designed. The 80386 includes support for paging. This made it impracticable to implement memory lock on some instructions, even though the use of memory lock was confined to the operating system and privileged processes only. The culprit is again the string instruction. Suppose the string crosses a page boundary into a non-resident page. It is impossible to maintain the memory lock while the page is recovered from disc (the disc controller cannot access memory while the lock is on), but if the lock is released, this destroys the mutual exclusion which was the whole point of using the lock in the first place.

The designers, metaphorically speaking, threw up their hands in despair and decided to abandon the 80286 approach. Instead, the 80386 adopts a new approach that totally prohibits any process from using memory lock on specified types of instructions, which include string instructions. Having restricted the use of memory lock to only those instructions for which it is always safe (i.e. those whose execution time is always fairly short), there is no longer any need to prevent ordinary user processes from using it. So, on the 80386, memory lock is no longer regarded as a privileged instruction.

This saga illustrates well the subtle interactions that occur with mechanisms for mutual exclusion. These problems are by no means confined to hardware. Software designers attempting to implement similar mechanisms should also beware!

2.3   Message Passing in Distributed Systems

Distributed processors without shared memory rarely provide hardware mechanisms for mutual exclusion. Instead, all synchronisation and communication between processors is achieved by means of basic message passing mechanisms. These can be at a variety of levels of sophistication according to the characteristics of the physical transmission medium as well as basic factors such as the cost and performance requirements of the communication mechanism. The cheapest, simplest and fastest point-to-point communications over short distances (up to a few metres) can be obtained by a basic parallel interface, described in the next section.

Communications networks, and long distance point-to-point communications generally require much more sophisticated hardware to cater for transmission delays, special transmission media, error detection and correction, routing, etc. The hardware is generally so much more complex that it is a negligibly small extra overhead to provide a somewhat higher level mechanism to the programmer, as described in Section 2.3.2.

2.3.1 Basic Processor-Processor Interface

The hardware used in the simplest processor to processor communication is a unidirectional parallel port with a simple 'handshake' protocol. This typically operates on the following principles:

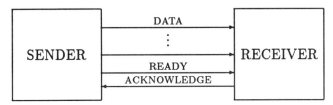

There are n data lines (for the parallel transmission of messages of n bits each) and two control lines: the *ready* line from sender to receiver, and the *acknowledge* line in the reverse direction. Each message conforms to the following protocol:

1. The sender sends the message by putting the message content (n bits) onto the data lines and then sending a *ready* signal. The sender must hold the data on the data lines until it receives an *acknowledge* signal back.

2. The receiver knows that a message is being sent when it receives a *ready* signal. It then reads the data lines and processes the message in whatever way is appropriate. When it has finished reading the message from the data lines, it sends an *acknowledge* signal back to the sender.

This cycle can repeat as soon as the *acknowledge* signal has been received by the sender.

Usually all the lines involved in this interface are electrical circuit connections (e.g. wires) and pass voltages or currents which represent the logic values 0 and 1. These values are held for finite periods of time before they change to new values. The 'signals' on the *ready* and *acknowledge* lines are typically represented as the instantaneous transitions from the value 0 to the value 1. Of course, after a signal has been sent, the line will have the value 1 and it must return to 0 again before the next signal can be sent. Particular hardware will impose detailed timing constraints on when this return to 0 is permitted, but these details are of no concern to us here. It is perfectly reasonable for our purposes to idealise the hardware by regarding the control lines as simply transmitting instantaneous signals.

Simple processor-processor interfaces of this type are often used to connect a central processor to peripheral device controllers, particularly for special devices such as may be used in embedded real-time systems. They may also be used for the cheapest and simplest forms of processor-processor communication in parallel processor systems, although more sophisticated communications interfaces are more usual. The main disadvantages of this simple interface are, firstly, that messages are of a fixed length (usually between 8 and 64 bits), and secondly, that the sender must hold the message on the data lines until the receiver has read it.

2.3.2   High-Level Message Passing Interface

Asynchronous Message Passing

Local area networks such as Ethernet and Cambridge Ring networks are usually interfaced to the computers on the network by a higher level protocol than the one described in the previous section. Typically, such systems provide an interface to the programmer along roughly the following lines. There are two operators available to the programmer, *send* and *receive*, which provide asynchronous message passing.

---

send(message, destination)

This operator causes the *message* to be transmitted to the specified *destination*. If there is only one possible destination, the second argument is omitted. The execution of *send* need not be synchronised with receipt of the message, and messages will be lost if the receiver does not attempt to receive them.

---

receive(message, source)

This operator causes the process to wait until the next message is received. The contents of the message are put in the variable *message* and the address of the device sending the message is put in the variable *source*. If there is only one possible source, the second argument is omitted.

In fact, the mechanism as described is somewhat idealised. Actual hardware is often messier, but close to this in its effect. Sometimes the message is stored directly in memory as it is received and when reception is complete an interrupt is generated. Although the execution time of *send* may not be synchronised directly with *receive*, the execution of *send* may be delayed by traffic on the network. Also, although *receive* may not have to be waiting when a message is sent, messages may be lost if a second message is sent before the first has been received. Actual hardware varies considerably in the details of how these aspects are handled and in other details such as the maximum permitted length of a message.

In later chapters, when we discuss algorithms based on message passing, these will usually be written in terms of the simple *send* and *receive* operators for convenience. It is generally fairly easy to modify these to use the particular message passing instructions available on the computer of your choice.

Synchronous Message Passing

There are some message passing systems (e.g. the interprocessor links of Inmos Transputers) that provide a mechanism similar to *send* and *receive* except that full synchronisation of *send* and *receive* is required for message transmission to take place. Whichever begins execution first will wait for the other. This is called a *rendezvous* and is the message passing mechanism used in several high-level languages for concurrency (see Chapter 9). It is a better mechanism from the programmer's point of view as it gives full control of synchronisation as well as passing the message, and is relatively easy to use.

2.4 Exercises

Exercise 2.1 Many computer architectures have string instructions which can operate on strings of considerable length and may take a relatively long time to execute. It would be unsafe to hold up all interrupts during the execution of these instructions, yet the general rule that tends to be followed wherever possible is that interrupts are permitted only *between* instructions, not in the middle. Find out what is done in architectures such as the Intel 8086 and the DEC VAX (both of which have string instructions) to solve this problem.

Exercise 2.2 On a uniprocessor machine, disabling interrupts effectively prevents all other processes from running until interrupts are enabled again. Would it make sense to provide an analogous facility on multiprocessor machines: i.e. disable all other processors from running until enabled again later?

Exercise 2.3 What errors can occur if two concurrent processes simultaneously try to update a shared variable that is less than one memory word in size and is packed with other objects into a single word of memory?

Can errors ever occur if two processes simultaneously try to update *different* variables?

Chapter 3

Low-Level Mutual Exclusion Algorithms

In Chapter 2, basic hardware mechanisms for implementing mutual exclusion were described. These mechanisms ensure mutual exclusion of single memory accesses and single machine instructions. The only mechanism that is applicable to critical sections of more than one instruction is disabling interrupts.

Unfortunately, disabling interrupts is practicable only in limited circumstances. The problem then arises: how do we ensure mutual exclusion of critical sections of more than one instruction when we are not able, or do not wish, to disable interrupts? One solution is to use an algorithm specially designed for such a purpose. This chapter is devoted to the study of such algorithms and especially to the pitfalls that await the unwary in their use. Although the algorithms given in this chapter all look very straightforward, they contain many opportunities for subtle errors, and much of the discussion will be about how and where such errors can creep in.

Algorithms to implement mutual exclusion consist of two parts: a *pre-protocol* which precedes the critical section, and a *post-protocol* which follows it (some authors call these parts the *prelude* and *postlude*). To illustrate the various algorithms, we will use the archetype mutual exclusion program introduced in Section 1.2.2, for which each process will be expanded as follows:

Process

> *initialisation;*
> *WHILE TRUE DO*
>   *pre-protocol;*
>   *critical section;*
>   *post-protocol;*
>   *remainder*
> *OD*

Some of the programs given in this chapter make use of special machine instructions, while others rely only on the indivisibility of memory access (these can sometimes be implemented in a high-level language). Some incorrect algorithms are given, as well, to illustrate common faults in concurrent programming.

For simplicity, we consider only two processes. Most of the algorithms can be easily generalised to n processes (for any finite n), but great care should be taken that errors are not introduced. If in any doubt at all, refer to the published literature (but check for yourself as well; publications may contain misprints and occasionally more serious errors). The best text on algorithms for mutual exclusion is a recent book by M. Raynal, which also contains extensive further bibliography (Raynal, 1986).

3.1   Algorithms Using Special Instructions

It is relatively easy to write mutual exclusion algorithms if any one of the following is available as a single machine instruction: exchange, test-and-set, or lock. Of course, because single machine instructions are indivisible and mutually exclusive only on uniprocessors, it follows that any algorithms which rely on this property will also be effective only on uniprocessors. This applies to all the algorithms given in this section. On multiprocessor systems which provide memory lock instructions, these can be used to ensure that the instructions which must be indivisible remain so in the multiprocessing environment.

The algorithms all use a single shared boolean variable, which we call *bolt* (named after the bolt on a door, which is used to prevent the door being opened). This variable is initially set to 0 to indicate that no process is currently inside its critical section. Whenever a process enters its critical section it sets *bolt* to 1 and when it leaves the critical section it resets it to 0. A process wishing to enter its critical section while *bolt* is 1 must wait until *bolt* becomes 0 again (*bolt* = 1 is analogous to the door being bolted, while *bolt* = 0 is analogous to it being unbolted).

This basic idea is quite straightforward, so why do we need special instructions at all? Suppose we simply write the algorithm using normal instructions: for instance, as follows.

3.1.1   An Unsafe Algorithm

Consider the algorithm in Fig. 3.1. The program is written with the steps labelled $\alpha1$, $\alpha2$, etc. so we can refer to them later in the discussion.

Although this algorithm will enforce mutual exclusion most times, it can fail occasionally. Consider, for instance, execution of the processes interleaved

	Process 1		**Process 2**
$\alpha1$	*init1;*	$\beta1$	*init2;*
$\alpha2$	*WHILE TRUE DO*	$\beta2$	*WHILE TRUE DO*
$\alpha3$	*WHILE bolt=1 DO OD;*	$\beta3$	*WHILE bolt=1 DO OD;*
$\alpha4$	*bolt := 1;*	$\beta4$	*bolt := 1;*
$\alpha5$	*crit1;*	$\beta5$	*crit2;*
$\alpha6$	*bolt := 0;*	$\beta6$	*bolt := 0;*
$\alpha7$	*rem1*	$\beta7$	*rem2*
	OD		*OD*

Shared: *bolt : 0..1 (initially 0)*

Figure 3.1: An unsafe algorithm for mutual exclusion.

in the sequence: $\alpha1$, $\alpha2$, $\alpha3$, $\beta1$, $\beta2$, $\beta3$. In this case both processes have got past their respective wait loops ($\alpha3$ and $\beta3$), and can now proceed together into their critical sections, so that mutual exclusion is broken. This happens only in the unusual circumstances that Process 1 is suspended between $\alpha3$ and $\alpha4$ (i.e. after the wait loop has been passed, but before the process has had a chance to set the value of *bolt* to 1 to lock out other processes) and Process 2 then runs and is able to proceed into its critical section without being made to wait. Furthermore, for real damage to occur, Process 2 must be suspended while still in the middle of its critical section, and Process 1 resumed so that it proceeds through its critical section (before Process 2 has completed its critical section). The program is *unsafe*.

Definition An algorithm for mutual exclusion is said to be *unsafe* if there is any possible timing of its execution which allows the mutual exclusion to be broken.

The Inadequacy of Normal Testing

This whole scenario is really very unlikely. The chances of an interrupt occurring between $\alpha3$ and $\alpha4$, the operating system then switching to Process 2, another interrupt occurring in the middle of $\beta5$ (the critical section), and the operating system then switching back to Process 1, all seems rather remote!

On the great majority of occasions the algorithm will work perfectly well.

It is the very fact that the algorithm fails so rarely (it could be as infrequently as only one failure in a million runs) that make this fault so serious. Because such failures are rare and unpredictable (they depend upon the chance times at which the operating system switches from one process to another), it can be almost impossible to detect them by normal testing procedures. Even if errors *are* found in test runs, they are normally not reproducible because they depend upon the precise times at which the operating system switches processes and this is something over which the ordinary user generally has no control. Indeed, even the operating system itself rarely has a sufficiently precise knowledge of time and of all the factors that can effect the timing of programs to be able to control the exact position in a program at which an interrupt occurs. The lack of reproducibility of these failures completely invalidates the usual test procedures for tracking down errors (i.e. reproducing the circumstances giving rise to the error in a situation in which extra diagnostic information is generated).

This is a very serious problem for concurrent programming methodologies, and is addressed further in Chapter 12. For the moment, the main lesson to be learnt is that these types of error can best be found by *a thorough analysis of the program*, rather than by relying solely on conventional testing.

3.1.2   Using Exchange Instructions

On computers with a single machine instruction which exchanges the contents of a register and a memory location (or which exchanges the contents of two memory locations), a suitable algorithm for mutual exclusion is shown in Fig. 3.2, in which the single machine instructions are shown enclosed in small boxes (the thick-ruled boxes indicate atomic instructions, the thin-ruled outer boxes simply delineate the processes).

This easily generalises to n processes by replacing $x1$ or $x2$ with xi for the i-th process. Quite often algorithms like this are written in the literature by giving the algorithm in a general form which applies to all processes. In such circumstances, you need to be very clear about which are shared variables and which are local variables, because it will not be clear simply by looking at the variable names. Here we have given $x1$ and $x2$ different names to emphasise the fact that they are distinct. Furthermore, $x1$ is local to Process 1 (i.e. used by Process 1 alone) and $x2$ is local to Process 2. (In fact, this information can be discovered by an examination of the program: $x1$ is referenced only in Process 1 and $x2$ is referenced only in Process 2.)

This algorithm depends upon the exchange instructions being indivisible (hence they are shown enclosed in small boxes). This ensures that when the

Process 1	**Process 2**

x1 := 1;
init1;
WHILE TRUE DO
　　x1 :=: bolt;
　　WHILE x1 = 1 DO
　　　　x1 :=: bolt OD;
　　crit1;
　　x1 :=: bolt;
　　rem1
OD
	x2 := 1;
	init2;
	WHILE TRUE DO
	　　x2 :=: bolt;
	　　WHILE x2 = 1 DO
	　　　　x2 :=: bolt OD;
	　　crit2;
	　　x2 :=: bolt;
	　　rem2
	OD

Shared:　*bolt : 0..1 (initially 0)*

Local:　*x1, x2 : 0..1*

Figure 3.2: Mutual exclusion with exchange instructions.

value of the shared variable *bolt* is copied into the local variable ($x1$ or $x2$), it is set to 1 at the same time. No other process is able to read the value of *bolt* before it is set to 1. Thus it is now no longer possible for both processes to enter their critical sections at the same time.

The last exchange instruction (immediately preceding *rem1* or *rem2*) strictly does not need to be an exchange instruction. The algorithm is still correct if it is replaced by the two separate instructions:

$$bolt := 0;$$
$$x1 := 1$$

3.1.3　Using Test-and-Set Instructions

A mutual exclusion algorithm which uses test-and-set instructions is shown in Fig. 3.3.

In this case, the effect is again to ensure that if both processes try to read *bolt* at the same time, whichever gets there first and reads *bolt* also sets it to 1 before the other process is allowed to read it.

3.1.4　Using Lock Instructions

The algorithm which uses lock instructions is the simplest of the lot. The lock instruction effectively provides the complete pre-protocol, and the post-

Process 1	Process 2

```
init1;
WHILE TRUE DO
    │ x1 := bolt; bolt := 1; │
    WHILE x1 = 1 DO
        │ x1 := bolt; bolt := 1 │
    OD;
    crit1;
    bolt := 0;
    rem1
OD
```

```
init2;
WHILE TRUE DO
    │ x2 := bolt; bolt := 1; │
    WHILE x2 = 1 DO
        │ x2 := bolt; bolt := 1 │
    OD;
    crit2;
    bolt := 0;
    rem2
OD
```

Shared: $bolt : 0..1$ (initially 0)

Local: $x1, x2 : 0..1$

Figure 3.3: Mutual exclusion with test-and-set instructions.

protocol is simply to set *bolt* to 0. The algorithm is shown in Fig. 3.4.

Multiprocessor systems which provide the lock instruction typically define it in such a way that this algorithm is safe. In other words, a memory lock is automatically applied between reading the value of *bolt* and setting it to 1.

3.1.5   Generalisations

All of these algorithms which use special instructions are generalisable to n processes in the obvious ways. Furthermore, most can be used equally well on multiprocessor systems, provided memory lock is applied to all instructions which are required to be indivisible. The exception is the algorithm using the lock instruction. A memory lock must not be applied to this instruction for much the same reasons that interrupts cannot be disabled during the instruction (see the discussion of this point in Section 2.2.2). As mentioned in the previous section, however, multiprocessor systems that provide lock instructions typically define them in such a way that they can be used safely to implement mutual exclusion.

3.1.6   Fairness

For the case of n processes, the question of *fairness* arises. Suppose that several processes are simultaneously wanting to enter their critical sections. Do they

Process 1

```
init1;
WHILE TRUE DO
    ┌─────────────────────────┐
    │ WHILE bolt=1 DO OD;     │
    │ bolt := 1;              │
    └─────────────────────────┘
        crit1;
        bolt := 0;
        rem1
OD
```

Process 2

```
init2;
WHILE TRUE DO
    ┌─────────────────────────┐
    │ WHILE bolt=1 DO OD;     │
    │ bolt := 1;              │
    └─────────────────────────┘
        crit2;
        bolt := 0;
        rem2
OD
```

Shared: *bolt : 0..1 (initially 0)*

Figure 3.4: Mutual exclusion with lock instructions.

all have the same chance of being given permission or are some more favoured than others?

Definition An algorithm for mutual exclusion is said to be *fair* if all processes attempting to enter their critical sections are sure to be treated equally.

This definition is not rigorous: we have not defined what is meant by being 'treated equally'. It is quite adequate for our purposes, however, as we are not going to pursue this question of fairness to any great depth.

The algorithms given earlier in this section are not fair (i.e. they do not guarantee that all processes get an equal chance to enter their critical sections). This does not mean than that the algorithms favour particular processes; in fact, the code is virtually identical for each process. The problem arises because the precise behaviour of the algorithms depends upon the precise details of the interleaving of the concurrent processes. It is possible for a process to be unlucky and miss out on entering its critical section simply because it gets interrupted in a particular place. The fact that it may have been waiting much longer than other processes is not taken into account.

Furthermore, these algorithms are also subject to starvation, which is an extreme form of unfairness in which some processes never get a turn at all (see Section 3.2.3).

3.2   Algorithms Using Ordinary Instructions

We now look at algorithms which do not require special machine instructions. They rely for their correctness only on the indivisibility of individual memory accesses. These algorithms can therefore be implemented on any computer and may even be usable in high-level languages (see Section 2.2.1).

Firstly, we consider several incorrect algorithms. An algorithm which is *unsafe* has already been shown in Section 3.1.1. Unfortunately, this is by no means the only type of subtle error to which concurrent programs are prone. Several more quite plausible algorithms are now introduced to illustrate the other common pitfalls in this type of programming. All are difficult to diagnose in the normal way and they highlight yet again the need for very careful analysis as the only really systematic way of finding certain types of errors in concurrent programs and thereby achieving an acceptable level of reliability.

3.2.1   An Algorithm Subject to Deadlock

Consider the following approach to implementing mutual exclusion for two processes. Two shared variables, *flag1* and *flag2*, are used, both initialised to zero. The first of these, *flag1*, is set to 1 when Process 1 is about to enter its critical section, and reset to 0 after Process 1 leaves its critical section. Process 2 controls *flag2* similarly. Hence, Process 1 can look at *flag2* to tell if Process 2 is in its critical section, while Process 2 can look at *flag1* to tell if Process 1 is in its critical section.

To avoid the problem of lack of safety, we make each process set its own flag before it looks at the flag of the other process. Hence, our algorithm is as shown in Fig. 3.5.

This algorithm can be shown to be safe; i.e. there is no possible timing of the execution of the two processes that will allow both of them to enter their critical sections together. It suffers from a quite different problem, however, that of *deadlock*.

Consider the following execution sequence: $\alpha 1$, $\alpha 2$, $\alpha 3$, $\beta 1$, $\beta 2$, $\beta 3$. At this point, both *flag1* and *flag2* are 1, hence, when they proceed, both processes will be held up at their wait loops ($\alpha 4$ and $\beta 4$). Process 1 will wait until *flag2* becomes 0 and Process 2 will wait until *flag1* becomes 0. Neither *flag1* nor *flag2* can change, however, because the only place that either is reset to zero is at $\alpha 6$ or $\beta 6$, and neither of these instructions can be executed until one of the processes passes through its critical section. But neither process can enter its critical section until the flags are changed. Consequently, both processes wait forever!

	Process 1			**Process 2**
$\alpha 1$	*init1;*		$\beta 1$	*init2;*
$\alpha 2$	*WHILE TRUE DO*		$\beta 2$	*WHILE TRUE DO*
$\alpha 3$	*flag1 := 1;*		$\beta 3$	*flag2 := 1;*
$\alpha 4$	*WHILE flag2=1 DO OD;*		$\beta 4$	*WHILE flag1=1 DO OD;*
$\alpha 5$	*crit1;*		$\beta 5$	*crit2;*
$\alpha 6$	*flag1 := 0;*		$\beta 6$	*flag2 := 0;*
$\alpha 7$	*rem1*		$\beta 7$	*rem2*
	OD			*OD*

Shared: *flag1, flag2 : 0..1 (both initially 0)*

Figure 3.5: An algorithm subject to deadlock.

Definition Two or more processes are *deadlocked* if each is waiting for an event which can occur only after the other process has been allowed to proceed (and will therefore never happen).

Definition A concurrent algorithm is *subject to deadlock* if there is any possible timing of its execution which leads to processes becoming deadlocked.

As with lack of safety, deadlock will be detected in test runs only if very exceptional timing circumstances happen to occur. In the above example, for instance, deadlock occurs only if Process 1 is interrupted between $\alpha 3$ and $\alpha 4$, and Process 2 is run past $\beta 3$ before control is returned to Process 1.

Not only may deadlock be a rare and effectively randomly occurring fault (similarly to lack of safety), but, to make matters worse, it can be easily overlooked in some circumstances, even when it does occur. Suppose that a multiprogramming system is heavily loaded with a large number of processes sharing the machine. Everything will run slowly because of the large number of processes competing for resources. If two processes deadlock, but the rest continue to run as normal, it may well take some time before it is realised that two processes have stopped completely. Even if there are no other processes on the machine, it will generally be apparent that deadlock has occurred only when they fail to produce expected output on time.

Of course, processes that are deadlocked have not really stopped (they have not told the operating system that they want to terminate execution). As far as the operating system is concerned, they continue to run as usual. Each is simply stuck in an infinite loop.

Furthermore, deadlock of just two processes does not mean that the complete system stops. All other processes can continue to run, and the machine may well be fully used despite the two deadlocked processes. Hence it can be far from obvious that there is anything wrong at all. Altogether, it is not an easy situation to cope with, and one that is best avoided by very careful program design.

3.2.2   An Algorithm Subject to Permanent Blocking

Consider now a different approach. A single shared variable, *turn*, is used. When *turn* is 1 then Process 1 is allowed to enter its critical section, and when *turn* is 2 then Process 2 is allowed to enter its critical section. Let us try the algorithm given in Fig. 3.6.

Process 1	**Process 2**
init1; *WHILE TRUE DO* *WHILE turn=2 DO OD;* *crit1;* *turn := 2;* *rem1* *OD*	*init2;* *WHILE TRUE DO* *WHILE turn=1 DO OD;* *crit2;* *turn := 1;* *rem2* *OD*

Shared: *turn : 1..2 (initially 1)*

Figure 3.6: An algorithm subject to permanent blocking.

This algorithm safely enforces mutual exclusion. Process 1 can enter its critical section only if *turn* is 1 and Process 2 can enter its critical section only if *turn* is 2. The variable *turn* is set to 1 only by Process 2, after it has passed through its critical section; and *turn* is set to 2 only by Process 1, after it has passed through its critical section. It is therefore not possible for both processes to be in their critical sections concurrently.

The drawback of this algorithm is that it requires each process to enter its critical section strictly alternately with the other: Process 1, Process 2, Process 1, Process 2, Process 1, ... This is unsatisfactory in general as it holds up the process which wants to enter its critical section more frequently, but, worse still, if one process decides to remain in its non-critical section (*rem1* or *rem2*) for ever (which is perfectly acceptable), the other process remains permanently blocked.

Definition   An algorithm for mutual exclusion is subject to *permanent blocking* if one process (or more) can be permanently prevented from entering its critical section, i.e. it can wait for an event which will never occur.

3.2.3   An Algorithm Subject to Starvation

Consider again the algorithm given in Section 3.2.1. To try to avoid deadlock, let us modify the algorithm by including, within the wait loop, additional statements to temporarily reset the appropriate flag to zero. The purpose of this is to allow one or other process to break out of deadlock if it tries to occur. The algorithm is given in Fig. 3.7.

The *delay* statements denote dummy statements which have no effect on the program variables but take time to execute. The time delay is purely to give an opportunity for the other process to read the flag while it is zero. In fact, even if no delay is included there will still be a chance for the other process to see the flag while it is zero, but the probability of that happening will be quite small.

Analysis of this algorithm shows it to be both safe and deadlock free. It is, however, subject to another form of blocking known as *starvation*. Suppose that execution is interleaved as follows. By chance, Process 1 always gets interrupted while it is inside its critical section and nowhere else. Then Process 2 will always find *flag1* to be 1 and therefore if Process 2 tries to enter its critical section it will get caught in the wait loop ($\beta 4$–$\beta 8$). If, by coincidence, interrupts continue to occur only when Process 1 is in its critical section ($\alpha 9$), and never at any point in the program at which *flag1* is zero, then Process 2 will remain stuck in its wait loop.

Of course, if the point at which Process 1 is interrupted varies randomly, then even if Process 1 spends no time in *rem1*, eventually it will be interrupted at some point where *flag1* is 1, and Process 2 will get a turn. This is not very

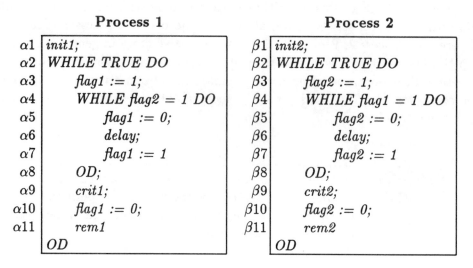

Shared: *flag1, flag2 : 0..1 (both initially 0)*

Figure 3.7: An algorithm subject to starvation.

satisfactory, however, because there is no guarantee that Process 2 will be able to proceed: whether or not it does depends purely upon chance timing.

Definition   An algorithm for mutual exclusion is subject to *starvation* if it is possible for a process to wait for an event which may never occur.

Starvation is the third common type of concurrent programming 'error' that is very difficult to find by normal program testing. It is not always considered to be an error. Some programs which are theoretically subject to starvation may be tolerated because it can be shown that the probability of a process being blocked for an unacceptable length of time is negligibly small.

Starvation is only subtly different from permanent blocking. A permanently blocked process is waiting for an event which cannot happen, while a process suffering starvation is waiting for an event which may or may not happen; it is just a matter of chance that the event does not occur. The effect is very similar.

Starvation is viewed with less concern than deadlock because, in situations in which the timing varies in an unpredictable and effectively random way, a process which is blocked through chance timing should eventually become unblocked simply by waiting long enough. The times when starvation is a really serious problem are if (i) real-time constraints may be infringed if a process is held up for an unpredictable length of time, or (ii) the timing is not unpredictable, but it is possible for interrupts to become synchronised with the execution of a process, so that interrupts always occur at the same place in a loop (hence the process may not become unblocked simply by waiting long enough). The first of these situations is very common in real-time applications. The second situation, which is a characteristic of the implementation rather than the problem, although rather rarer, is by no means unknown. Simply because it is rare, it can be an unexpected trap for the unwary. It is always wise to demand that programs be starvation free unless it can be demonstrated that such a requirement really is unnecessary.

Liveness

Normally it is desirable to use algorithms which are not subject to deadlock, starvation or permanent blocking. Such algorithms are said to be *live*.

Definition   An algorithm for mutual exclusion is *live* if any process attempting to enter its critical section will be delayed for at most a finite length of time; i.e. it is not possible for any process to be kept waiting for ever.

3.2.4   Peterson's Algorithm (1981)

It turns out to be surprisingly difficult to find an algorithm for mutual exclusion that is both safe and live (not subject to either deadlock or starvation). Solutions are invariably considerably more complex than the simple algorithms we have given which suffer from deadlock, starvation or other problems. Nevertheless, correct solutions have been known for many years. Many texts on concurrency follow E.W. Dijkstra in giving Dekker's Algorithm (Dijkstra, 1965).

In recent years there has been increasing research interest in real-time and parallel algorithms, and G.L. Peterson has given a simpler algorithm (Peterson, 1981). Its simplicity makes it the preferred choice for general use. Peterson's Algorithm is shown in Fig. 3.8.

Process 1	Process 2

```
init1;                          init2;
WHILE TRUE DO                    WHILE TRUE DO
    flag1 := 1;                     flag2 := 1;
    turn := 1;                      turn := 2;
    WHILE flag2 = 1 AND             WHILE flag1 = 1 AND
            turn = 1 DO OD;                 turn = 2 DO OD;
    crit1;                          crit2;
    flag1 := 0;                     flag2 := 0;
    rem1                            rem2
OD                              OD
```

Shared: *flag1, flag2 : 0..1 (both initially 0)*
          turn : 1..2

Figure 3.8: Peterson's Algorithm for mutual exclusion.

This protocol may be viewed as the 'union' of two simpler protocols, obtained by (i) eliminating *flag1* and *flag2*, or (ii) eliminating *turn*. Each of these simpler protocols is safe, but subject to deadlock or permanent blocking. By combining them as shown above, an algorithm is obtained which is safe and live.

Although this algorithm is both short and simple, like most concurrent algorithms based upon shared memory, it is surprisingly difficult to find a totally convincing argument that it will always work (i.e. that it is safe and live). As we have already seen, normal testing is quite inadequate for such programs, and careful and thorough analysis is essential to achieving a high degree of confidence in a program's correctness. A proof of Peterson's Algorithm is given later in Chapter 13, in which proof techniques are discussed more generally.

Although we favour the use of Peterson's Algorithm for most normal situations, there may be special circumstances that require an algorithm with particular properties. Other algorithms do exist which may have significant advantages in special circumstances. The interested reader should refer to the research literature for such algorithms. The book by M. Raynal is a good starting point (Raynal, 1986).

3.3   Generalisation to n Processes

So far, we have considered only the case of two processes with critical sections. The algorithms given earlier which use special instructions all generalise to n

processes in obvious ways. The generalisation of Peterson's Algorithm is less obvious, although it can be done. The resulting algorithm is more complex and difficult to understand. The interested reader is referred to Raynal's book or to Peterson's original paper (Raynal, 1986; Peterson, 1981).

3.4 Distributed Algorithms

For multiprocessor machines with a shared memory, all the algorithms described already will work correctly (all shared variables must be located in the shared memory). There is a danger that these algorithms may become subject to starvation, however. The reason for this is that they are usually dependent upon the hardware mechanism for accessing shared memory being starvation free. If this mechanism is subject to starvation then any process which accesses the shared memory could become starved if other processes access the shared memory sufficiently frequently.

Unfortunately, shared memory hardware is often subject to starvation because the simplest way to design the hardware is generally to give access to the shared memory according to a fixed priority order rather than on a first-come-first-served basis. This is certainly an unwelcome complicating factor for algorithms on multiprocessor systems, but it is often a less serious problem in practice because in most circumstances the load on the shared memory is not so high as to cause continuous contention for the memory.

In fully distributed systems, shared memory is not available and the algorithms discussed so far are not directly applicable. Two main approaches are possible. Firstly, shared memory can be emulated on most distributed systems without too much difficulty (see Section 11.3.3), and may be useful for other purposes as well as for implementing mutual exclusion. It is then possible to use a shared memory algorithm such as those already described. Secondly, an algorithm specially designed for distributed systems may be used. The simplest of these are based on token passing, which is the technique discussed next.

3.4.1 Token-Passing Algorithms

The idea of token passing is similar to that used in hardware 'daisy chaining'. Suppose a number of processors are linked by a unidirectional message-passing ring. A single token is passed around the ring from processor to processor. A processor is only permitted to enter its critical section when it has possession of the token, which it retains until it leaves the critical section.

The idea is very simple, and a possible implementation of it is as follows. The processors are labelled 0 to $n - 1$ and the i-th processor contains two processes: *P[i]* is the user process in which the mutual exclusion is required, and *L[i]* is an extra process to handle the message passing. We write *send(x)* to denote the operation of sending the message x (a message sent by processor i will be received by processor $i + 1$, modulo n), and *receive(x)* to denote the operation of receiving a message, which is put in the variable x. We assume that the execution of *send* does not wait for receipt of the message, and that *receive* reads the last message sent, or waits for the next message if the last message has already been received.

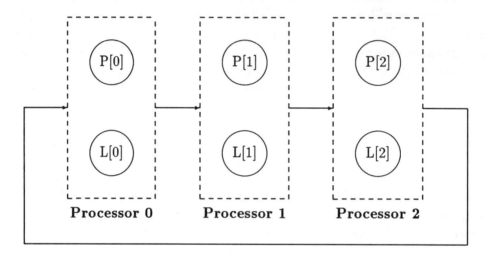

The diagram above shows the case of three processors (each represented by a dashed box), each containing the two processes *P* and *L*, and linked by a message-passing ring. The solid lines represent the message channels. Assume that *P[i]* and *L[i]* can communicate with each other via shared memory (but not with *P[j]* and *L[j]*, where $i \neq j$). A suitable algorithm for these two processes is shown in Fig. 3.9, using only ordinary instructions to synchronise *P[i]* and *L[i]*. If semaphores or other synchronisation primitives are available, it will often be preferable to use these (purely within each separate processor), as we will see in later chapters.

The whole system must be started by sending exactly one token to any processor. That will start the token circulating around the ring. This algorithm remains correct if the operators *send* and *receive* are redefined to include rendezvous waiting; i.e. whichever is executed first will wait for the other: the message is sent only when both are ready.

This simple token-passing mechanism is both safe and live. In addition, if there is heavy contention for mutual exclusion, it is *fair*: processes are able to enter their critical sections in the order in which they occur around the ring.

P[i]	L[i]

initialisation;
 WHILE TRUE DO
     waiting := TRUE;
     WHILE NOT critical DO OD;
     critical section;
     waiting := FALSE;
     critical := FALSE;
     remainder
 OD
	WHILE TRUE DO
	     receive(token);
	     IF waiting THEN
	        critical := TRUE FI;
	     WHILE critical DO OD;
	     send(token)
	 OD

Shared: *waiting : boolean (initially FALSE)*
              critical : boolean (initially FALSE)

Figure 3.9: A simple token-passing algorithm for a ring of processors.

The token may be represented by any message (it may be empty, or of arbitrary content). Often the message-passing channels will be needed for other messages as well, in which case the token for mutual exclusion may be any uniquely identifiable message. If several different classes of critical sections are required, a distinct token may be used for each, and the algorithm modified accordingly.

Token passing is very efficient if there is heavy contention. In the most extreme case of all processes trying to enter their critical sections at the same time, the token is passed just once for each critical section entered. On the other hand it is very inefficient if processes rarely enter their critical sections. Then the token gets passed around the ring continually, putting an effectively useless load on the message channels.

Token Passing with Token Requests

A variation on simple token passing which gives good message-passing efficiency in the case of infrequent execution of critical sections is as follows. Two types of messages are distinguished: the *token*, as before, which must be possessed by a process while in its critical section; and a *tokenrequest*, which is sent out by a process wanting to enter its critical section. The token is not passed on after use, but retained by the processor which used it last, until a token request is received. The token is then forwarded in place of the token request. The algorithm is in Fig. 3.10, using the same labelling of processes as previously.

P[i]

```
initialisation;
WHILE TRUE DO
     send(tokenrequest);
     waiting := TRUE;
     WHILE NOT critical DO OD;
     waiting := FALSE;
     critical section;
     critical := FALSE;
     remainder
OD
```

L[i]

```
WHILE TRUE DO
     receive(message);
     IF message = token THEN
          IF waiting THEN
               critical := TRUE;
               WHILE critical DO OD;
               tokenhere := TRUE
          ELSE
               send(token)
          FI
     ELSE {message = tokenrequest}
          IF tokenhere THEN
               tokenhere := FALSE;
               send(token)
          ELSE
               send(tokenrequest)
          FI
     FI
OD
```

Shared: *waiting, critical, tokenhere : boolean (initially all FALSE, except tokenhere is initialised to TRUE in exactly one processor)*

Figure 3.10: A token-passing algorithm for a ring of processors, using explicit token requests. The text enclosed in curly brackets {} is merely a comment.

A weakness of these token-passing algorithms is their lack of fault tolerance. If a failure anywhere causes the token to get lost (or an additional token to be created) then the system breaks down. More complex algorithms have been devised to introduce a degree of tolerance to various types of hardware faults. The interested reader is referred to more specialised texts for such algorithms (see Further Reading). One simple approach to fault tolerance is introduced in Exercise 3.5.

3.5 Exercises

Exercise 3.1 A real-time system contains five distinct processes. One process is dedicated to reading a temperature from a digital thermometer at regular times, while a second is dedicated to reading a pressure from a pressure transducer. The temperature and pressure are stored as floating point numbers at fixed locations in shared memory (new values simply overwrite the earlier values, so only the latest are kept). The remaining three processes read the latest values of temperature and pressure from shared memory and use them for further computation.

The complete system is implemented on a simple 8-bit microprocessor, with all five processes time-shared on the same processor. Floating point numbers are represented by four bytes, and require four memory accesses to read or write. Discuss possible approaches to safe implementation of the access to the shared temperature and pressure variables.

Exercise 3.2 Examine the algorithm for mutual exclusion given in Fig. 3.11. Is it (i) safe, (ii) live? Give arguments to justify your answer.

Exercise 3.3 The algorithm for mutual exclusion using the exchange instruction, as given in Fig. 3.2, is safe and deadlock free. Show that it is subject to starvation, however.

Exercise 3.4 Show that the algorithm for mutual exclusion using the test-and-set instruction, as given in Fig. 3.3, is also subject to starvation.

Exercise 3.5 The simple circulating token algorithm for mutual exclusion given in Fig. 3.9 suffers from a lack of resilience to communication failures that cause the loss of the token. A degree of resilience can be obtained by the introduction of a second token (a dummy not used for mutual exclusion) which circulates behind the real token, never overtaking or being overtaken. If either token is lost in transmission between processors, this loss can be detected by any processor that finds it has received the same token twice in succession, without the other token having been received in between. It can then regenerate the lost token.

Process 1	**Process 2**

```
init1;
WHILE TRUE DO
    disable interrupts;
    WHILE bolt = 1 DO
        enable interrupts;
        disable interrupts
    OD;
    bolt := 1;
    enable interrupts;
    crit1;
    bolt := 0;
    rem1
OD
```

```
init2;
WHILE TRUE DO
    disable interrupts;
    WHILE bolt = 1 DO
        enable interrupts;
        disable interrupts
    OD;
    bolt := 1;
    enable interrupts;
    crit2;
    bolt := 0;
    rem2
OD
```

Shared: bolt : 0..1 (initially 0)

Figure 3.11: A proposed algorithm for mutual exclusion.

Write an algorithm to implement this technique, making sure that the following requirements are satisfied: (i) neither token can overtake the other; (ii) only one token is effective for permitting a process to enter its critical section; (iii) the loss of a single token will be detected within one complete cycle round the ring by the other token; (iv) a lost token will be regenerated by only one processor.

Chapter 4

Synchronisation in the UNIX Kernel

In this chapter, we look at the application of low-level concurrent programming techniques to the design of a typical operating system. The system chosen is the highly successful UNIX system. UNIX began life around 1970 as a small and economical, interactive, multi-user operating system for minicomputers. It was originally developed as a purely in-house system by Ken Thompson, Dennis Ritchie and others in the Computing Science Research Centre at Bell Telephone Laboratories, which is part of AT&T. At this time AT&T was not permitted to market computer products for legal reasons arising from its monopoly position in the telephone market. Hence, UNIX was initially developed without any intention to distribute it outside Bell Laboratories.

Nevertheless, interest from computer scientists in universities, with encouragement from the authors of UNIX, persuaded AT&T to license its use for non-profit educational and research purposes at a nominal charge. The system was distributed with the full source code, although without any support or maintenance. Many computer science departments in universities and colleges acquired UNIX in the mid to late 1970s under this policy. Undoubtedly, the low cost of UNIX to educational establishments, coupled with the availability of source code, were the major factors in its rapid rise in popularity.

Since then it has grown considerably in size, and has been ported onto a wide variety of computer architectures, including networked workstations and other distributed and multiprocessor systems. It is now marketed by AT&T on a fully commercial basis. Nevertheless, the basic simplicity, elegance and coherence of the UNIX concept remains in the latest versions and, to a great extent, accounts for the widespread success of UNIX in very varied circumstances.

The part of UNIX which interests us here is the kernel. This is the central part of the operating system which remains permanently resident in main memory and is responsible for managing the use of the major machine resources: central processor time, main memory, and all the main input/output (I/O) devices (discs, keyboards and screens, etc.).

So that the basic structure and philosophy of the kernel can be presented clearly and concisely, much of the finer detail will be glossed over and some simplifications made. More specialised references on the UNIX kernel should be consulted for a more complete and precise design description (see Further Reading).

4.1   Process Structure in the Kernel

Ordinary user programs are run by the kernel as processes that are timeshared to give each a fast response to the user sitting at his terminal. A few UNIX commands are implemented within the kernel itself, but most are implemented as ordinary programs which are treated as processes and run in exactly the same way as any other process. The kernel cannot distinguish processes which implement commands from those which are user programs. Commands obtain any special privileges they need by having access to system files (or devices) which are not accessible to other processes.

Processes communicate with the kernel by means of system calls. System calls exist for such purposes as: open or close a file; read or write to an open file; create a new process; kill a process; get the time of day and date; etc. There are no special system calls for input and output to particular devices because UNIX treats all I/O devices as if they were files. Every device known to the kernel has a file name somewhere in the file system (conventionally in the directory */dev*). Whenever a process asks the kernel to read or write to the 'file' of that name, the kernel actually performs a transfer to the physical device associated with the name, instead of carrying out an ordinary file access.

System calls in UNIX are entries to the kernel. The code in the kernel is executed almost as if it were simply a library routine. The only essential difference is that the kernel is executed in privileged mode because it must be able to access parts of memory (and peripheral devices) to which the user process does not have access directly. Even though the code being executed is within the kernel, it is still treated as part of the process which gave the system call. Hence every process has two modes of operation: user mode while it is executing its own code, and kernel mode while it is executing a system call.

In most programming languages, use is made of a system stack for storing local variables, parameters and return addresses each time a subroutine is called. Each user process has its own system stack which is located in the

PCB associated with each process.

Definition A *Process Control Block* (PCB) is an (abstract) data object associated with each process, which contains essentially the complete state of the process, together with whatever accounting, budgeting, scheduling and other information about the process that the system requires. The state of the process includes the addresses in main memory of the process code and data, space to save the registers when the process is suspended, open file descriptors, the system stack for the process, and other items which can affect the functional behaviour of the process (parameters for I/O transfers, the file system environment of the process, signals sent to the process, the owner of the process, permissions given to the process, etc.). Another way of looking at it is that the PCB contains all the operating system data associated with a process which is not in the normal code and data segments.

The PCB must not be directly accessible by the process (i.e. the programmer of the process cannot write code to arbitrarily change parts of the PCB), because that would enable the process to defeat the operating system's control over resource allocation.

The address of each PCB is stored in the *Process Table*, defined as follows.

Definition The *Process Table* is a table in the kernel that contains an entry for each user process. Logically, it is simply a mechanism for finding all processes which exist in the system and where the PCB of each is located (from which all further information about the process can be obtained).

The kernel also contains some means of identifying the *Current Process*, which is the process currently running, or which has been most recently interrupted. The implementation of this may be simply a variable which points to the PCB of the Current Process, or alternatively the runnable processes may be ordered, with the Current Process first in the ordering.

When the scheduler routine wishes to switch to another process it will save the current register values in the PCB of the Current Process and load the registers with values from the PCB of the new process to be run. The new process will also be identified as the Current Process. Although there is only one Current Process at any one time, there may be many runnable processes and many other non-runnable processes (processes become non-runnable for reasons that will become clear later).

Note — In UNIX literature, the term 'Process Control Block' is not used; and the information which we consider to belong in the PCB is somewhat scattered in a typical UNIX implementation. That information which is required most immediately by the kernel is actually kept in the Process Table, in an entry which contains much more than just a pointer to the PCB. Typically, it contains scheduling and accounting information, addresses of the various segments of the process, and several other parameters used frequently by the kernel. Much of the less immediately required information is kept in what is known in UNIX jargon as the u-block or u-area. The system stack is often implemented as two distinct stacks: a user stack and a kernel stack. When the process is running in user mode it uses the user stack, when it executes a system call and enters privileged state it uses the kernel stack. Each of these stacks may be implemented in a separate segment of main memory.

For our purposes, however, it is a convenient abstraction to think of the PCB as a single object, and the Process Table as simply a set of pointers to PCBs.

Re-entrant Routines

Several different user processes may give the same system call at approximately the same time and if the normal time-sharing mechanism causes the time-slice of one user process to end while it is in the middle of a system call, then that system call could be invoked again by a different process before the original execution is complete. The code within the kernel that implements system calls must therefore be *re-entrant*.

Definition   A *re-entrant* routine is one which may be executed concurrently by more than one process. A separate copy of the arguments, return address and working space (i.e. the local variables) must be made for each process calling the routine.

To ensure re-entrancy, the kernel programmer must take care to follow certain rules when writing those parts of the kernel. Re-entrant code must never use global variables for working space, because only one copy of global variables is kept, whereas local variables are allocated on the stack when the routine is entered. As there is a separate stack for each process, there will also be a separate set of local variables (including the arguments of the routine, and the return address) for each process which uses that routine.

Furthermore, when access is required to global variables, it must be remembered that such variables can be shared by all processes and hence the normal rule about implementing access to shared data only within critical sections applies.

It is often necessary for the routine which implements a system call to be able to find out which process gave the system call. This process is easily identified because it is always the Current Process. In most implementations, even during a system call several machine registers will remain loaded with addresses referencing the Current Process.

4.2 Synchronisation in the Kernel

It is necessary to provide synchronisation between the interrupt-driven part of the kernel routines for doing I/O transfers to a peripheral device and the system call part of the same device routines. We will distinguish these two parts by calling them the *interrupt handler* and *device driver* respectively. The device driver is a re-entrant routine in the kernel which is entered when a process gives a system call requesting an I/O transfer to the device concerned. Therefore it is executed as part of the process which gave the system call.

On the other hand, the interrupt handler is logically a completely distinct process. A confusing feature of normal UNIX terminology is that interrupt handlers are not regarded as processes at all. Here we do not follow that convention: instead, interrupt handlers *are* considered to be processes. They are, however, treated differently from other processes (which we will call *user processes*). An interrupt handler has no PCB, no entry in the Process Table and is completely unknown to the scheduler. The so-called Current Process is never an interrupt handler, always a user process. Hence, interrupt handlers are, indeed, rather special processes (but processes, nevertheless).

It is not necessary to attach all the paraphernalia of a PCB to interrupt handlers because they are always small routines, located at fixed known places in the kernel, and they are never timeshared with each other or with user processes. When an interrupt occurs, the corresponding interrupt handler is entered automatically (by the hardware interrupt mechanism) and will normally run to completion, terminating itself by executing a return-from-interrupt instruction which resumes the interrupted process.

The only exception to this is that sometimes another interrupt may be permitted to interrupt the handler of a lower priority interrupt. In that case, the higher priority handler runs to completion, whereupon control returns to the interrupted lower priority handler, which runs to completion and returns control to the user process which was running when the first interrupt occurred (i.e. the Current Process).

Interrupt handlers do not need to have even a stack of their own. Of course, they must have somewhere to put any local variables that they require. In fact, the stack of the Current Process is often used. As interrupt handlers must always be small and fast, they do not use very much working space, so it is reasonably safe to borrow some from the user process. An alternative approach is to use a global interrupt stack which is shared by all interrupt handlers (not because they want to communicate with each other, but simply to save space).

4.2.1   Sleep and Wakeup Routines

The device driver and interrupt handler must communicate with each other (usually as producer and consumer: one sends data to the other). Both these processes can access global variables in the kernel, so data is generally passed through buffers in the global data space of the kernel. Synchronisation is needed also, however, and there are two routines provided for this purpose in the UNIX kernel. These are ordinary procedures, not system calls, so they are not directly callable by user processes.

The two procedures are called *sleep* and *wakeup*, specified as follows:

> *sleep(event)*
> ___
> This causes the Current Process to go to sleep (i.e. it is marked as non-runnable and, consequently, the scheduler will not run it) until the specified *event* occurs, at which time it will be made runnable again. The argument *event* is simply an integer value (not a variable).

---
wakeup(event)

This causes all processes currently sleeping on *event* to be
made runnable again. Again, *event* is an integer value. This
routine has no effect on the calling process (which may be
the Current Process or an interrupt handler).

There is no memory of events after a wakeup call, only processes that were
sleeping on the event at the time of the wakeup will be woken up. If a process
goes to sleep just after a wakeup, it does not get woken up (until the next
wakeup on that event). Note also that there is no guarantee that a process
that is woken up starts to run again immediately. Instead, it simply joins the
set of runnable processes from which the scheduler will select the next process
to run.

Race Conditions

Great care must be taken when using *sleep* and *wakeup* that a process never
goes to sleep on a lone event that may already have occurred. This situation is
commonly called a race condition, because there is logically a race between the
process calling *sleep* and that calling *wakeup*, with the embarrassing outcome
that if the process calling *wakeup* wins, the other process will sleep forever
because the event (signalled by the call to *wakeup*) has already occurred.

The normal way of avoiding such a race condition is to test directly for
the actual event that must be waited for, and go to sleep only if it has not
yet occurred. This piece of code must be implemented as a critical section
by disabling interrupts beforehand and enabling them again afterwards. For
example, suppose a process which is putting data into a print buffer finds the
buffer full. It must sleep until space becomes available in the buffer. The
section of code to do this may look like this:

```
.  .  .  .  .  .
disable interrupts;
IF print buffer is full THEN sleep(PrBufNotFull) FI;
enable interrupts;
.  .  .  .  .  .
```

The interrupt handler that copies data from the print buffer to the printer
will call *wakeup(PrBufNotFull)* to signal the fact that there is now room for

more data to be put into the print buffer. In practice, it is often possible for more than one process to put data into a buffer, and this can happen with a print buffer. In that case, the sleeping process may be woken up, yet when it starts to run, the buffer may already be full again (because another process has been run before it and filled the buffer). To handle this situation, we need to modify the code as follows:

```
. . . . . .
disable interrupts;
WHILE print buffer is full DO sleep(PrBufNotFull) OD;
enable interrupts;
. . . . . .
```

The typical use of *sleep* in the UNIX kernel is embedded in code like this. The event parameter, *PrBufNotFull* may be any integer value. The only requirement is that different events used by different device drivers must not use the same integer value.

4.2.2   Real-Time Delays

It is sometimes necessary to wait for a specified length of time before taking some action. A routine, called *timeout*, is provided for this purpose. Like *sleep* and *wakeup*, it is an ordinary procedure available only for internal use within the kernel.

timeout(p, a, t)

This procedure has no effect on the Current Process, but it causes an entry to be made in a special Callout Table in the kernel that is inspected by the clock interrupt handler and causes the following action. At some point in time at least *t* units of time after timeout was called, the procedure *p(a)* is executed. This procedure is called by the clock interrupt handler, so it must abide by the rules for writing interrupt handlers.

The main purpose of *timeout* is to program real-time delays which may be required when handling peripheral devices. For example, if controlling an autodial telephone line, after dialling the number, you need to wait a few seconds for the call to be made and the dialled number to answer. If no answer is received after several seconds then the attempt should be terminated. Applications such as this can be easily programmed with *timeout* (see Exercise 4.5).

In many UNIX systems, the unit of time used in *timeout*, and elsewhere, is a sixtieth of a second. UNIX is not intended to handle real-time situations that require more accurate timing than this.

The procedure *p(a)* is called by the clock interrupt handler, so it is effectively part of the clock interrupt process. Hence, it must be small and fast, because all interrupt processes must run to completion very quickly, and not use too much stack space. If it is required to put a real-time delay on some action which cannot be performed quickly, then the following approach should be used.

The real-time delay can be inserted in the kernel code of any system call (which is executed as part of the Current Process), using *timeout, sleep* and *wakeup* in the manner shown below:

system call code

```
. . . . . .
disable interrupts;
timeout(wakeup, TimeUp, Delay);
sleep(TimeUp);
enable interrupts;
. . . . . .
```

The effect of this code is simply to put the Current Process to sleep for at least *Delay* units of time. It is, of course, necessary to disable interrupts while calling *timeout* and *sleep* because otherwise an interrupt may occur between the two allowing the scheduler to run another process, causing the timeout to expire before *sleep* is called, with fatal consequences for the Current Process.

4.3 Device Drivers

Device drivers in most operating systems are complex and vary considerably according to the type of device and the type of I/O operation required. UNIX is simpler than many others because it treats all devices as either *character* devices or *block* devices. Character devices (e.g. keyboard, printer) are accessed serially in units of one character, the characters being buffered in the kernel.

A block device is accessed as if it is an array of blocks (typically 1K characters per block) in which direct access to each block is possible by supplying its index in the array as an address. Two types of access are generally implemented for block devices: (i) the *block* device interface, in which each block accessed is separately buffered in the kernel (which contains a cache of one-block buffers which are allocated as required); and (ii) the *raw* device interface, in which the data is not buffered in the kernel but transferred directly between the device and the address space of the user process.

As a specific example, let us consider the case of an I/O transfer to or from a block device by the raw device interface. This may be appropriate, for instance, for transfers to a disc which is being used for some purpose other than as a filestore (accessing files is normally done via the block device interface). The structure of the device driver will be roughly as shown in Fig. 4.1.

The first action of the device driver is to check that the request is acceptable (the user's permission to access the device will have been already checked when the device was opened, which must precede any attempt to read or write). The type of request must be valid for this device and if the device is addressable (e.g. a disc) the address supplied must be within the allowed range. Typically, the device address will also need translating into the format required by the device controller hardware. The address for the data in main memory must also be checked to see that it is within the address space of the Current Process. On most machines the user process supplies a virtual address which must be translated into a physical address for the device controller.

Details of the I/O request are then entered into a queue of requests for that device (the order of requests in this queue may be altered to optimise usage of the device, if that is acceptable). If the queue is full, however, the process must go to sleep until space becomes available.

If the device is not already busy carrying out an I/O request, the transfer requested can be started. Then, the process must sleep until the request has been completed (which can be indicated by a flag in the queue entry for the request or alternatively in the PCB). It is important that the process goes to sleep until the I/O transfer has been completed otherwise the system call may return to the user process before the data has been fully transferred into (or out of) the buffer in the user process. If the user process tried to use this buffer while the transfer was still in progress, data corruption could occur.

After the I/O transfer has been completed, some final housekeeping is done (deleting the entry from the queue, etc.), and the system call is complete. Notice that interrupts are disabled for most of this routine. It is important not to disable interrupts for much longer than really necessary, but any access to global data structures (such as the queue of I/O requests for the device) must be inside a critical section for safety.

Device Driver

(entered on system call requesting I/O)
initial housekeeping and checks;
disable interrupts;
WHILE queue is full DO sleep(QueueNotFull) OD;
put request into queue;
IF device is not busy THEN initiate I/O transfer FI;
WHILE request not completed DO sleep(RequestComplete) OD;
final housekeeping;
enable interrupts;
return to user mode

Interrupt Handler

(entered on interrupt from device)
read device status register;
IF end of transfer THEN
      set request completed flag;
      wakeup(RequestComplete);
      IF queue is not empty THEN
          select next request from queue;
          initiate I/O transfer
      FI;
      IF queue is not full THEN wakeup(QueueNotFull) FI
ELSE
      take appropriate action (e.g. retry failed transfer)
FI;
return to Current Process

Figure 4.1: Structure of the kernel routines for a raw device.

Consider now the interrupt handler part of the code. It is entered when an end-of-transfer interrupt occurs, or if an error interrupt occurs (indicating that the transfer has failed). The interrupt handler must first determine the precise reason for the interrupt by reading the status register in the device controller. In the usual case of an end-of-transfer interrupt, the action required is to mark the transfer request as complete, wake up the process that issued the request and start the next transfer.

Logically, the event number *RequestComplete* should be unique to the particular request. Some implementations find this inconvenient and the same event number may be used for several requests. This is not a problem, however, provided the call to *sleep* in the device driver is inside a WHILE loop as shown, and the request-completed flag is unique to each request. Of course, the event number *QueueNotFull* is distinct, but there is only one of these per device driver.

In many UNIX implementations, the queue of requests is implemented as a linked list with the links kept in the PCB of each process. In that case, there is no upper limit to the length of the queue (i.e. if a process exists it will always be possible to link it into the queue), so the section of code that checks for a full queue is unnecessary.

No explicit disabling of interrupts is shown in the interrupt handler because it is usual for the hardware to automatically disable further interrupts whenever an interrupt is received, and the instructions that return to the Current Process at the end of the interrupt handler will normally automatically re-enable interrupts.

4.4   Clock Interrupt Handler

The structure of the clock interrupt handler is more-or-less as shown in outline in Fig. 4.2.

The hardware must be set up to generate clock interrupts regularly after every unit of time. The unit of time is an implementation dependent parameter (typically one sixtieth of a second). On some computers the hardware clock must be reset after each clock interrupt, in which case the code to reset the clock must also be included in the clock interrupt handler.

Process switching is carried out when necessary by the scheduler (step 4 in the algorithm). Usually this involves not only changing the global variable which points to the PCB of the Current Process, but also changing various context registers such as the stack pointer and memory management registers. The code for carrying out this context switch requires care to ensure that all context dependent registers are changed correctly and safely.

Clock Interrupt Handler

(entered on a clock interrupt)

1. Increment the global variables that give the real time and date.

2. Feed timing information to accounting and profiling routines in the kernel.

3. Examine the Callout Table and execute any procedures for which the time delay has now expired, then remove them from the table.

4. Scheduler — If the Current Process has completed its allocated time slice, save its state in its PCB, then look in the Process Table to determine which process should be run next, and load the state of that process, making it the new Current Process.

5. Return to the Current Process.

Figure 4.2: Kernel routine for the clock.

The final step of the clock interrupt handler is to terminate itself by returning to the Current Process. If the scheduler has switched to a new Current Process, then this will not be the same user process that was running when the clock interrupt occurred.

4.5 Implementation of sleep and wakeup

Within the kernel, a global Sleep Table contains an entry for each event upon which processes are sleeping. Each entry consists of two parts: the event number and a set of processes sleeping on that event. All sleeping processes are non-runnable. When a process calls sleep or wakeup, the action that takes place is shown in Fig. 4.3.

Both *sleep* and *wakeup* are ordinary procedures so they are entered and return like any other procedures. The scheduler routine is called from within *sleep* and *wakeup*, and operates in the same way as it does in the clock interrupt handler described in the previous section. The scheduler may change the Current Process, so that the user process running on completion of *sleep* or *wakeup* may not be the same process that was running on entry to the routine!

sleep(e)

1. Save the state of the Current Process in its PCB.

2. Disable interrupts.

3. Search the Sleep Table for the event number, e. If e is already present, add the Current Process to the set of processes waiting for e. If e is not present, add a new entry for e, with the Current Process as the only process waiting for e.

4. Mark the Current Process as non-runnable.

5. Scheduler (as in the clock interrupt handler).

6. Return to the Current Process.

wakeup(e)

1. Save the state of the Current Process in its PCB.

2. Disable interrupts.

3. Search the Sleep Table for event e. If it is not found, go to step 5.

4. Remove the entry for e from the Sleep Table and make all the processes sleeping on e runnable again.

5. Scheduler (in case any of the processes just woken up is of higher priority than the Current Process).

6. Return to the Current Process.

Figure 4.3: Kernel routines for *sleep* and *wakeup*.

4.6 Exercises

Exercise 4.1 It appears to be in error to call the kernel procedure *sleep* inside a critical section (when interrupts are disabled). Why is this not the case?

Exercise 4.2 It is a serious error to call the kernel procedure *sleep* in an interrupt handler, yet it is quite acceptable to call the procedure *timeout*. Why is this so?

Exercise 4.3 The procedure given as an argument to *timeout* may not itself call *sleep*. Why not?

Exercise 4.4 Using pseudocode, show how you would write the kernel routines for handling input from an analogue to digital converter with the following characteristics. When a reading is required, an I/O instruction to start conversion must be issued, then at least 10 milliseconds must elapse before the converted value is read (by another I/O instruction). The A/D converter does not generate interrupts.

Exercise 4.5 Using pseudocode, show how you would write kernel routines for initiating a telephone call on an autodial modem with the following characteristics. The user process gives a system call to initiate the telephone call, supplying the telephone number as a parameter. The telephone call is begun by an output instruction with the telephone number as data. An interrupt is generated when the called party answers, or if the engaged signal is obtained. If no answer is obtained within 15 seconds the call should be aborted (by giving another output instruction). A parameter indicating success or failure should be returned to the user process finally.

Exercise 4.6 The kernel of an operating system contains an array of buffers *block[1..N]*, where each *block[i]* is the same size as a block on disc. All disc I/O is done to or from these buffers. The disc driver is required to be implemented as two procedures:

$$readdisc(blockno, discaddr)$$
$$writedisc(blockno, discaddr)$$

which transfer data between the buffer *block[blockno]* and the disc, where *discaddr* is the address on disc.

Write algorithms for *readdisc* and *writedisc*, assuming that critical sections are to be implemented by disabling interrupts. A routine may be linked to the disc end-of-transfer interrupt (ignore disc errors). Assume that routines *sleep, wakeup* and *timeout* are available if required (with specifications as given earlier).

Schedule the disc accesses by the following means. An array *transfer[1..N]* is set up, where *transfer[i]* has one of three values: (i) WAITREAD, (ii) WAITWRITE, or (iii) NOTWAITING; denoting that *block[i]* is (i) waiting to be read from disc, (ii) waiting to be written to disc, or (iii) not waiting for a transfer, respectively. Another array *transferaddr[1..N]* stores the disc addresses for the transfers. Assume that a parameterless function *nextdisctransfer()* is already written: it scans the arrays *transfer* and *transferaddr* to select the optimum transfer to carry out next, and returns its index.

Chapter 5

Semaphores

The concept of a semaphore was introduced by E.W. Dijkstra (Dijkstra, 1965). The purpose served in introducing semaphores was threefold. Firstly, they provide a synchronisation mechanism independent of any particular computer architecture. Secondly, they avoid the inefficiencies inherent in wait loops when a process is running but doing nothing useful because it is cycling round an empty loop. Thirdly, semaphores are designed to be easy to use and hence to simplify the solution of many concurrent programming problems. In fact, the UNIX kernel routines, *sleep* and *wakeup*, introduced in Chapter 4, satisfy the first two of these requirements. Semaphores have close similarities with these UNIX routines, but were designed with ease of use as a major aim whereas with *sleep* and *wakeup* ease of implementation was foremost.

Several different variants of the semaphore concept are common in the literature on concurrent programming. Here we define *boolean* and *integer* semaphores, as well as distinguishing *weak* and *strong* semaphores.

5.1 Boolean Semaphores

A boolean semaphore is in some respects an ordinary boolean variable, but the difference is that it may be used in only a few well specified ways to provide synchronisation between processes. Naturally, it must be shared by the processes being synchronised. A boolean semaphore also possesses close similarities with the event argument of the routines *sleep* and *wakeup*, but whereas event arguments are just values, semaphores are variables (i.e. there is a memory associated with a semaphore).

Definition A *boolean semaphore* is a boolean variable upon which the
following three operations are allowed and no others (no direct assignment to, or use of, the value is allowed). All operations on a particular semaphore are mutually exclusive.

---

init(s,b)

This initialises the semaphore *s* to the boolean value *b*.

P(s)

This procedure has the following effect:
>   *WHILE s=0 DO run other processes OD;*
>   *s := 0*

Mutual exclusion is suspended while in the body of the loop
(i.e. when other processes are being run).

V(s)

This simply sets the value of *s* to one.

The *P* and *V* operators on a semaphore are analogous to the *sleep* and
wakeup operators on an event (*P* and *V* are the initial letters of the Dutch
words for 'wait' and 'signal'). If a process executes *P(s)* when *s* has the value
zero, that process goes to sleep until another process executes *V(s)*. One main
advantage of semaphores is that this cannot lead to a race condition. If the
process that executes *V(s)* does so sooner than expected (i.e. before *P(s)* is
called), it sets *s* to one which means that the process subsequently executing
P(s) will not be put to sleep at all (but *s* will be set to zero). So we no longer
have to worry about the possibility of going to sleep for ever if the event we
are sleeping on has already occurred.

A further important feature of semaphores is that if several processes are
sleeping on the same semaphore (i.e. all have executed *P(s)* when *s* was zero)
and another process executes *V(s)* for the same *s*, then only one of the sleeping
processes will be woken up and allowed to proceed. The rest will continue to
sleep until another *V(s)* is executed. This property makes programming easier
in many cases and avoids the necessity to put calls to *P* inside a loop as we
often had to do with *sleep*.

Just as was the case for *sleep*, the *P* operator uses any waiting time to run other processes. This suggests that semaphores are intended as a synchronisation mechanism for multiprogrammed uniprocessor computers. This is indeed the case, but they may also be used in multiprocessor systems, with the semaphore implemented in shared memory. They are less appropriate for fully distributed systems without shared memory (although it is always possible to emulate shared memory).

5.2   Mutual Exclusion with Semaphores

The semaphore is designed as a convenient tool for implementing mutual exclusion and other synchronisation problems. Our archetype mutual exclusion algorithm is very simply coded as shown in Fig. 5.1, using a single semaphore which we call *mutex*. The critical sections are simply enclosed between pairs of statements: *P(mutex)* and *V(mutex)*.

```
        Process 1                      Process 2

init1;                          init2;
WHILE TRUE DO                   WHILE TRUE DO
    P(mutex);                       P(mutex);
    crit1;                          crit2;
    V(mutex);                       V(mutex);
    rem1                            rem2
OD                              OD
```

Shared: *mutex : boolean semaphore (initially 1)*

Figure 5.1: Mutual exclusion with semaphores.

This solution to the mutual exclusion problem immediately generalises to n processes, all being similar to the two shown.

5.3   Integer Semaphores

Integer semaphores are like boolean semaphores except that they can have any non-negative integer value. The P operator decrements the value (but not below zero) and the V operator increments the value.

Definition An *integer semaphore* is an integer variable upon which only the following three operations are allowed. All operations on a particular semaphore are mutually exclusive.

---

init(s,i)

This initialises the semaphore s to the non-negative integer value i.

P(s)

This procedure has the following effect:
> *WHILE s=0 DO run other processes OD;*
> *s := s−1*

Mutual exclusion is suspended while in the body of the wait loop (i.e. when other processes are being run).

V(s)

This procedure adds one to the value of s.

Integer semaphores can be used to implement mutual exclusion in exactly the same way as can boolean semaphores. The algorithm given in Fig. 5.1 remains correct when s is changed to an integer semaphore. Integer semaphores can also be used for more general resource allocation problems (the mutual exclusion problem can be thought of as a simple resource allocation problem with one indivisible unit of resource: permission to enter a critical section).

5.4   Resource Allocation with Semaphores

If the program for implementing mutual exclusion with an integer semaphore is changed so that the semaphore is initialised to another value, say n, then this program now solves a more general problem: that of allowing at most n processes to concurrently execute specified sections of code.

This is particularly useful for a wide range of resource allocation problems. Suppose n units of some resource are available. Initialise semaphore s to n. Then every time a process wishes to use another unit of resource it executes $P(s)$, which will decrement the value of s, causing the process to wait if s is zero. The value of the semaphore denotes the number of unallocated units of resource, and processes will be made to wait only if the resource is fully used. Every time a process finishes using a unit of resource, it calls *V(s)* to indicate that its unit of resource is free to be reallocated.

Consider a situation in which three magnetic tape units are available to be shared by three concurrent processes. Each process requires one tape initially, but subsequently requires two tapes. So each process is of the following form:

Process

```
. . . . . .
use one tape;
use two tapes;
. . . . . .
```

A simple way of ensuring the synchronisation of the three processes is to use an integer semaphore *tapes*, initialised to 3 (the number of available tapes):

Process

```
. . . . . .
P(tapes);
use one tape;
P(tapes);
use two tapes;
V(tapes); V(tapes);
. . . . . .
```

Shared: *tapes : integer semaphore (initially 3)*

This solution is clearly subject to deadlock. If all three processes progress to using their first tape, all three tapes are in use and no process can proceed. But, until one or other process can proceed, no tapes will be released. So we have deadlock.

5.4.1   Deadlock Avoidance

One of the main areas of difficulty in complex resource allocation problems is trying to avoid deadlock. A general strategy that will always work in problems like the three tapes example is to ensure that all the resources that a process will ever need are claimed right at the start of the process and released only when all are no longer required. The process for the three tapes example becomes:

Process

```
. . . . . .
P(mutex); P(tapes); P(tapes); V(mutex);
use one tape;
use two tapes;
V(tapes); V(tapes);
. . . . . .
```

Shared: *mutex : boolean or integer semaphore (initially 1)*
         tapes : integer semaphore (initially 3)

The additional semaphore *mutex* is needed purely to ensure that the two calls to *P(tapes)* cannot be separated (as that would allow deadlock).

Unfortunately, this general strategy of claiming all resources at the start is often very wasteful of resources. In the example, because each process requires two tapes, and only three are available altogether, the processes are forced to run sequentially, one at a time. This defeats the whole object of concurrency!

There are situations in which the simple strategy works well, but in many cases a more sophisticated approach is desirable. Many other deadlock avoidance strategies have been devised for resource allocation. More detailed discussion of this problem can be found in many texts on operating systems (e.g. Maekawa, Oldehoeft and Oldehoeft, 1987).

5.5   Weak and Strong Semaphores

So far we have not specified fully what happens if several processes are simultaneously waiting in *P* operations for the same semaphore. When another process executes a *V* operation on that semaphore, only one of the waiting processes will be allowed to proceed (because as soon as one proceeds it will put the semaphore back to zero again which will prevent other processes from proceeding). Which is the lucky process?

Often the definition of semaphores leaves this question unresolved. This approach is valid: we are perfectly entitled to leave some things unspecified if we wish. Semaphores defined in this way are termed *weak* semaphores.

Definition   A *weak* semaphore is one in which all processes waiting on the same semaphore proceed in an unspecified order (i.e. the order is unknown, or *indeterminate*).

Alternatively, semaphores may be defined so that the order in which the waiting processes are run is fully specified. Many different orders are possible, but that usually specified is the order in which they began waiting (i.e. the order in which they executed *P*). This treats every process equally and so is the fairest solution. It is also easy to implement. Such semaphores are termed *strong*.

Definition A *strong* semaphore is one in which all processes waiting on the same semaphore are queued and will eventually proceed in the same order as they executed *P* operations (FIFO order).

For the mutual exclusion algorithm given in Fig. 5.1, strong semaphores guarantee freedom from starvation, but weak semaphores do not. It is possible (although non-trivial) to find an algorithm for mutual exclusion which is starvation free yet uses only weak semaphores. Morris's Algorithm (Morris, 1979; also in Raynal, 1986) was the first published solution to this problem. This algorithm uses three weak semaphores to emulate the action of a single strong semaphore. We will usually assume strong semaphores as they are both more convenient and more commonly provided (on uniprocessor systems).

5.6   Implementation of Semaphores

Implementation of semaphores is essentially similar to the implementation of *sleep* and *wakeup* in UNIX, except that semaphores are variables and a memory location must be associated with each, as for any other variable. The problem is where to locate these. Two main approaches to the implementation of semaphores are considered: (i) in a programming language, and (ii) in an operating system.

5.6.1   Implementation in a Programming Language

In this case, the language should be extended to include a new data type, which may be called simply type *semaphore*. The programmer declares the semaphores he wishes to use as if they were ordinary variables, but of the type *semaphore*. The compiler can check that they are used only in *init*, *P* and *V* operations. The main difficulty with this approach is that the compiler only knows about processes within the one program and has to do its own scheduling between these, which is inefficient because it is often in addition to the scheduling already done in the operating system.

A programming language which provides semaphores should also provide the other facilities likely to be required by concurrent programs. Real-time applications commonly require access to special peripheral devices and the program may need to be able to link to interrupts from these devices if fast response is needed. This is possible only if the operating system in use permits it, and the mechanism for linking to the interrupts is likely to be more dependent upon the architecture of the computer and the operating system than it is on the programming language. Hence the implementation of such 'concurrent' languages is often machine dependent and operating system dependent.

5.6.2   Implementation in an Operating System

This has the advantage that P and V can be fully integrated into the normal scheduling mechanism. The implementation is similar to that for *sleep* and *wakeup* in the UNIX kernel, except that P and V must be provided as system calls so as to be accessible to user programs. There are some problems, however.

Firstly, the storage of the semaphores themselves: if space is allocated in the kernel itself, it will usually be very limited, which in turn limits the number of semaphores available. This raises the further problem of how to allocate these semaphores to processes wishing to use them; additional routines to 'open' and 'close' semaphores are required. If a process uses a lot of semaphores and forgets to close them when it has finished with them, those semaphores remain unavailable for others.

Secondly, whereas *sleep* and *wakeup* are routines for use only by other parts of the kernel, semaphores are intended for use directly by user processes and so must be linked to system calls. This raises security problems: how do we stop one process interfering with a semaphore which belongs to another process? We need to keep and check access information with semaphores, much as we do with files. This increases the memory requirements of each semaphore and also the time needed to carry out P and V operations.

The ideal solution may be an integrated one in which semaphores are implemented partly within the programming language and partly within the operating system. This is rarely done because programming languages and operating systems are usually quite separate. It is feasible in some parallel languages which are designed for particular parallel processor systems and often integrate operating systems facilities into the programming language.

5.6.3   Implementation on Parallel Processors

On multiprocessor machines with shared memory accessible by all the processors, the implementation of semaphores presents no special problems. The value of the semaphore can be stored in the shared memory, together with the queue of processes waiting on that semaphore (if that method of implementation is used). The method used is effectively the same as on uniprocessor machines.

For distributed systems without shared memory, implementation is less straightforward. Of course, one method is to emulate shared memory and use the same technique as before. More genuinely distributed implementations are possible, however, although they are not particularly common. Most distributed systems provide other primitive mechanisms for communication and synchronisation so that semaphores are not needed.

5.7   Exercises

Exercise 5.1 Show how semaphores could be implemented in the UNIX kernel (and only for use within the kernel) by making use of *sleep* and *wakeup*. Give pseudocode for the routines *init*, *P* and *V*.

Exercise 5.2 Give a pseudocode implementation of *init*, *P* and *V* within an operating system kernel in which each process is, at any one time, in exactly one queue: the active queue (of runnable processes) or one of the semaphore queues. Assume that each queue is implemented as a doubly linked list, the pointers being kept in the PCB and pointing to the PCB of the next process in the chain. The last PCB in a chain contains a null pointer. The process at the head of the active queue is the Current Process. Assume that the memory associated with each semaphore is kept as global data in the kernel. Give two versions of your implementation: one for strong and the other for weak semaphores.

Exercise 5.3 Write programs in pseudocode for the two parts of a printer driver in an operating system kernel, using semaphores for synchronisation.

Exercise 5.4 Write programs in pseudocode to implement the UNIX kernel procedures *sleep* and *wakeup* using semaphores as the basic synchronisation mechanism.

Exercise 5.5 Write a program in pseudocode to implement the Dining Philosophers Problem (see Section 1.2.6), using semaphores for synchronisation. Give the most obvious and direct solution (which will be subject to deadlock).

Exercise 5.6 In the Dining Philosophers Problem, show that if no more than four philosophers are trying to eat at the same time, at least one will succeed always. Use this result to obtain a deadlock-free program for the Dining Philosophers.

Is starvation possible with your program?

Exercise 5.7 On occasion, it would be useful to have an operator which allowed a process to wait for either of two semaphores, say $P(s1\ OR\ s2)$. The idea is that if only one of $s1$ and $s2$ is 1, that one should be chosen to avoid the process waiting longer than necessary. Functionally, it is unspecified which of $s1$ and $s2$ is chosen, because it will depend upon the circumstances of the implementation. Unfortunately, no such operator on semaphores is available. Write a program to achieve a similar effect, using ordinary semaphores (assume that $s1$ and $s2$ are boolean semaphores).

[Hint: You will need to use additional semaphores and additional processes.]

Can your program be generalised to implement $P(s1\ OR\ldots OR\ sn)$ for any positive integer **n**?

Chapter 6

Buffering Techniques

We now examine another fundamental problem of concurrent programming: how to organise the transmission of an ordered stream of data items from one process to another. This is the producer–consumer problem introduced in Section 1.2.3.

There are two main aspects to the producer–consumer problem. Firstly, a mechanism is required to store the data items while in transit from producer to consumer (maintaining their order correctly). Secondly, producer and consumer must be synchronised appropriately.

We call the temporary storage area a *buffer*, and the techniques for organising this storage are naturally called *buffering techniques*.

Definition A *buffer* is an area of memory (on any physical medium) used for the temporary storage of data while in transit from one process to another.

The buffering techniques introduced in this chapter are of importance for both uniprocessor and multiprocessor systems. The multiple buffering techniques discussed are designed to increase the speed of systems in which producer and consumer run on separate processors. They do this by minimising the amount of synchronisation needed between the producer and consumer and hence allowing them to run in parallel with minimum delays to both.

Such techniques are important even on uniprocessors, which, despite their name, still contain peripheral device controllers which are processors in their own right (although normally running dedicated processes stored in ROM). Autonomous input/output transfers (often referred to as direct memory access or DMA) are carried out by a process in the device controller. This process is one half of a producer–consumer pair, the other half being the process running on the central processor which controls the I/O (typically this process will be the interrupt handler for the device). The buffering techniques described in this chapter are routinely used in operating system kernels for handling I/O to peripheral devices, as well as in many other real-time programs, whether they run on uniprocessor or parallel processor machines.

As speed of execution is the main reason for choosing the more complex buffering methods, detailed timing analyses will be given for most of the algorithms.

Synchronisation of the producer and consumer is largely distinct from the organisation of the buffers. In this chapter we are primarily interested in the buffering techniques themselves, and generally we choose the simplest method of synchronisation (of those introduced so far) which is to use semaphores. In Section 6.8 a purely algorithmic representation (not using primitives or special instructions) is given for comparison. Other synchronisation methods for the producer–consumer problem are discussed in later chapters and in the solutions to the exercises.

6.1 Archetype Producer–Consumer Program

Without any loss of generality, we can assume that any producer–consumer program has the form shown in Fig. 6.1.

Producer
WHILE TRUE DO
compute(data);
write(data)
OD

Consumer
WHILE TRUE DO
read(data);
use(data)
OD

Local: *data : anytype*

Figure 6.1: Archetype producer–consumer program.

The routine *write* contains all the instructions which transfer one data item out of the producer. One item may be one bit or a large data structure. If it requires many separate instructions to transfer it, all of them will be inside *write*, possibly with some computation between the separate instructions. The routine *compute* is all the rest of the producer process. The only requirement on *compute* is that it must contain no instructions which transfer the data item from the producer. Within these constraints, the division of the producer into *compute* and *write* is arbitrary. We will see later, however, that sometimes performance will be improved if we can keep *write* as short as possible, putting as much of the program as possible into *compute*.

Similarly, the routines *read* and *use* are an arbitrary division of the consumer, the only proviso being that all instructions to transfer a data item into the consumer are contained within *read*.

We do not care what computation takes place in either producer or consumer, all that concerns us is the transfer of data out of the producer and into the consumer. The execution times for the four routines *compute*, *write*, *read* and *use* will need to be known for the timing analyses of the various buffering methods, but what they do in other respects is irrelevant.

Example: Producing Random Arrays

As an example of how a producer process may be divided into *compute* and *write*, consider the following situation. A single data item is an array of 1000 random 16-bit integers. The producer generates each random number and immediately outputs it, repeating this process 1000 times for the complete data item. After supplying one data item of 1000 random numbers, it will repeat the whole process, supplying a stream of these data items:

Producer of random 1000-number arrays

```
WHILE TRUE DO
      FOR i := 1 TO 1000 DO
            generate next random number;
            output random number
      OD
OD
```

In this case, *compute* is empty, and *write* is:

write(data)

```
FOR i := 1 TO 1000 DO
      generate next random number;
      output random number
OD
```

This is because we have said that the complete array of 1000 random integers is being regarded as one data item for the producer–consumer communication (it is entirely our choice as to what constitutes a single data item). The routine *write* must contain all the output statements for a single data item.

It is equally possible to rewrite this program so that all the computation is done before any of the output. (We refer to it as output, but it may not be 'real' output to a printer or other peripheral device: we simply mean that the data is being transferred out of the producer process.) We could write:

Producer of random 1000-number arrays

```
WHILE TRUE DO
    FOR i := 1 TO 1000 DO
        generate next random number in x[i]
    OD;
    FOR i := 1 TO 1000 DO
        output x[i]
    OD
OD
```

In this case, *compute* is the first FOR loop, and *write* is the second. When we discuss the various buffering techniques, it will be seen that this could be preferable in some cases, but the price we have had to pay is that the producer process now needs an additional 1000 words of local storage (the array *x[1..1000]*).

6.2   Single Buffering

6.2.1   The Algorithm

As the name implies, *single buffering* is the use of a buffer that is large enough for exactly one data item in the stream of data being sent from producer to consumer. This is the simplest form of buffering, and a typical algorithm, using semaphores for synchronisation, is given in Fig. 6.2.

The semaphore *write* is 1 when the buffer is empty and 0 when it is not empty. The semaphore *read* is 1 when the buffer is full and 0 when it is not full.

The algorithm is very simple: semaphore *write* is used to prevent the producer from writing into a non-empty buffer, and semaphore *read* is used to prevent the consumer from reading a non-full buffer. Note that non-full is *not* the same as empty and that non-empty is not the same as full. The buffer may be non-empty and non-full at the same time, in which case it is either being filled or being emptied. Of course, reading is generally non-destructive, so the use of the phrase 'emptying the buffer,' meaning reading it, should not be taken too literally. The data remains in the buffer after the consumer has read it, but the buffer is empty in the sense that the data it contains is no longer required and can therefore be overwritten without loss.

Producer	Consumer

WHILE TRUE DO
    compute (data);
    P(write);
    buffer := data;
    V(read)
OD
	WHILE TRUE DO
	    P(read);
	    data := buffer;
	    V(write);
	    use (data)
	OD

Shared: *write : boolean semaphore (initially 1)*
        read : boolean semaphore (initially 0)
        buffer : anytype

Local: *data : anytype*

Figure 6.2: Single buffering algorithm, with semaphores.

6.2.2 Timing Analysis

Let T_c be the time to execute *compute*, let T_f be the time to fill the buffer, let T_e be the time to empty the buffer (i.e. read the buffer) and let T_u be the time to execute *use*. Assume for the moment that these times remain constant for each cycle of the WHILE loops. Then if the producer is never held up waiting for the consumer it will execute a complete cycle in time $T_c + T_f$, and if the consumer is never held up it will execute in time $T_e + T_u$ per cycle. The elapsed time to completely process one record (i.e. one cycle of the producer and one cycle of the consumer) is $T_c + T_f + T_e + T_u$. This is the execution time per record if producer and consumer are time-shared on a single processor (assuming no other processes are competing for the processor time, and ignoring scheduler overheads).

If producer and consumer are running on different processors, however, they will be running in parallel for much of the time, but not all of the time because the synchronisation requirements mean that some time will be wasted while one process is waiting for the other. There are three distinct cases to consider.

Case 1: $T_c + T_f > T_e + T_u$ and $T_c > T_e$

The producer cycle takes longer than the consumer cycle, so the consumer is ready for the next record before the producer has finished putting it into the buffer. Thus, the consumer has to wait for the producer. The producer never has to wait for the consumer, however, because the time the consumer takes to empty the buffer is less than the time spent by the producer in computing the next record, so the buffer is always empty when the producer is ready to write the next record.

Two complete cycles of producer and consumer are shown on a time scale below:

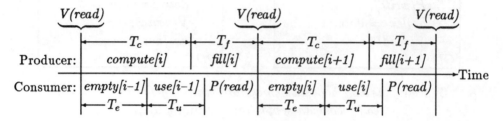

The indices in square brackets after *compute, fill,* etc. refer to the record number (i.e. the number of times round the WHILE loop in producer or consumer). From the diagram it can be seen that the producer is working on the *i*-th record while the consumer is still processing the *(i–1)*-th. Synchronisation occurs when the producer completes filling the buffer and executes *V(read)*. The consumer will have been waiting in *P(read)* and is then able to proceed.

The *write* semaphore is ineffective in this case because when the producer executes *P(write)* after completing execution of *compute*, the consumer has already executed *V(write)* after emptying the buffer, so the producer is not made to wait at all. Hence the operations on *write* are irrelevant to the timing and have been omitted from the diagram above.

The effective cycle time in this case is $T_c + T_f$.

Case 2: $T_e + T_u > T_c + T_f$ and $T_u > T_f$

This is the converse case. The consumer cycle takes longer than the producer cycle, so the producer is ready to put the next record into the buffer before the consumer has finished reading the last. Thus, the producer has to wait for the consumer. The consumer never has to wait for the producer, however, because the time the producer takes to fill the buffer again is less than the time spent by the consumer in using the last record, so the the buffer is always full when the consumer wants to read the buffer.

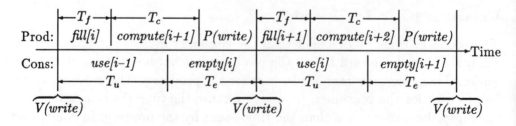

In this case the *write* semaphore is effective in causing synchronisation whereas the *read* semaphore is irrelevant to the timing, and omitted from the diagram.

The effective cycle time in this case is $T_e + T_u$.

Case 3: $T_f > T_u$ and $T_e > T_c$

In this case the consumer uses the last record faster than the producer fills the buffer with the next, so the consumer has to wait for the producer. Also, the producer computes the next record faster than the consumer reads the last record from the buffer, so the producer has to wait for the consumer.

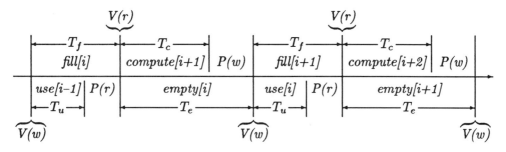

The semaphores *read* and *write* have been abbreviated to r and w repectively to fit them on the diagram more easily. Notice that both semaphores are effective at causing waiting in this case as each process has to wait for the other at different points in the complete cycle.

The effective cycle time for this case is $T_f + T_e$.

Summary

For all three cases, the effective cycle time may be expressed as

$$\max(T_c + T_f, T_e + T_u, T_f + T_e).$$

This is easily proved by considering each of the three cases in turn and using simple algebra to show that the cycle time is given by the above expression. For example, in Case 1 it is easy to show that

$$\max(T_c + T_f, T_e + T_u, T_f + T_e) = T_c + T_f$$

from the conditions

$$T_c + T_f > T_e + T_u \text{ and } T_c > T_e.$$

6.2.3   Applications

Single buffering is very simple to implement and widely used for this reason
alone. In many circumstances it is also sufficiently efficient that there is little
justification for using a more complex method. Input and output to and
from all types of peripheral devices is most simply implemented using single
buffering, and this method is often used in dedicated programs running on bare
machines (i.e. without an operating system). On the other hand, operating
systems have to cater for a very wide variety of situations and generally use
more complex buffering techniques which can offer better performance across
the board.

Example: Output to Disc

Suppose a particular program carries out a large amount of computation to
generate a data record which is written to disc and then the whole process
repeated 1000 times so that altogether a sequence of 1000 records is put on
the disc. Suppose, furthermore, that this program runs on a bare machine
so that all disc output must be done by the program itself; it cannot just be
passed across to an operating system.

A suitable program structure, using single buffering, is as follows:

Disc output process

```
FOR i:=1 TO 1000 DO
      compute next record;
      WHILE disc is busy DO OD;
      put record into buffer;
      write buffer to disc
OD
```

This is effectively a producer process, with the disc controller acting as the
consumer process. Disc transfers are usually carried out autonomously (asynchronously) so that the instruction to write the buffer contents to disc merely
initiates the data transfer, which then proceeds in parallel to the execution of
the rest of the program. Hence the loop which waits while the disc is busy
is essential before putting the next record into the buffer. This wait loop is
the equivalent of the instruction *P(write)* in the algorithm of Fig. 6.2. If it
is omitted there is a danger that the next record will overwrite the current
record while it is in the middle of being written to disc. If this happens, an indeterminate mixture of the current record and the next record will be written
to disc, which is not what we want!

The necessity of including this explicit test to see if the disc is still busy
(i.e. still carrying out the last I/O transfer) only arises in programming I/O

transfers directly. In most circumstances there will be an operating system present to handle I/O and in that case the operating system does all the necessary synchronisation so that the user program does not have to worry. If a user program requests I/O through the operating system kernel, typically the kernel will not allow that user process to proceed until the transfer is complete (the kernel simply finds another process to run in the meantime). On the other hand, if the user process chooses to handle the I/O itself by giving direct instructions to the peripheral device, that user process must also include explicit instructions to wait for completion where appropriate.

In single buffering of output to a peripheral device, as described above, the timing parameters introduced earlier are as follows. T_u is zero (the peripheral controller does nothing between one transfer and the next), T_e is the time taken by the peripheral device to do the output, T_f is the time taken by the program to put the record into the buffer, and T_c is the time taken by the program to do all the computation before it starts to put the record into the buffer.

A program is said to be *compute bound* if the central processor time used is greater than the I/O time, i.e. $T_c + T_f > T_e$ in the example above. It is said to be *I/O bound* if the I/O time is greater than the central processor time, i.e. $T_e > T_c + T_f$ in our example.

If $T_f \ll T_e$ (i.e. the time to put the record into the buffer is negligible in comparison to the output time), then single buffering gives as good a performance as any buffering method, the execution time per record being approximately $\max(T_c, T_e)$, because the only times that are significant now are T_c and T_e. In this case, the computation is done totally in parallel with the output and there is no further improvement possible. The only waiting that takes place is due to the compute time and output time not being exactly equal. If the program is compute bound, processing takes longer and so the peripheral controller clearly must spend some idle time waiting for the next output instruction; while if it is I/O bound, the output takes longer and the processor will complete its work before the peripheral controller and have to wait for the output to catch up.

Input can be handled similarly by single buffering, the difference being that the peripheral controller now runs the producer process, while the program on the central processor is the consumer. In other respects the situation is very similar.

6.3   Double Buffering

6.3.1   The Algorithm

The use of two buffers often reduces the waiting time and increases the effective speed of execution. As might be expected, this is called *double buffering* and is equivalent to a queue with space for at most two items. Each buffer holds exactly one record and the buffers are used alternately. The algorithm, using either boolean or integer semaphores, is given in Fig. 6.3.

Producer	**Consumer**
b := 0; *WHILE TRUE DO* *compute(data);* *P(write[b]);* *buffer[b] := data;* *V(read[b]);* *b := b + 1 MOD 2* *OD*	*b := 0;* *WHILE TRUE DO* *P(read[b]);* *data := buffer[b];* *V(write[b]);* *use(data);* *b := b + 1 MOD 2* *OD*

Shared: *write : ARRAY [0..1] OF semaphore (initially both 1)*
          read : ARRAY [0..1] OF semaphore (initially both 0)
          buffer : ARRAY [0..1] OF anytype

Local: *b : 0..1*
          data : anytype

Figure 6.3: Double buffering, using semaphores.

The index b references the two buffers. As well as two buffers, there are twice as many semaphores as before, one set for each buffer: *write[b]* is 1 when *buffer[b]* is empty (ready for writing); *read[b]* is 1 when *buffer[b]* is full (ready for reading).

The producer computes the first record and puts it into *buffer[0]*, then computes the second and puts it into *buffer[1]*, then computes the third and puts it into *buffer[0]* again, and so on. The consumer follows a similar pattern: it picks up the first record from *buffer[0]*, the second from *buffer[1]*, the third from *buffer[0]*, and so on.

6.3.2   Timing Analysis

Double buffering often involves less waiting than is the case with single buffering. Initially both buffers will be empty, so the producer cannot be held up at all in the first two cycles. It can be filling up the second buffer while the consumer is still emptying the first. The first occasion on which it can wait is if it is ready to put the third record into *buffer[0]* before the consumer has finished reading the first record from *buffer[0]*.

There are just two cases we need to distinguish for the timing analysis.

Case 1: $T_c + T_f > T_e + T_u$

In this case the producer cycle takes longer than the consumer cycle, so the consumer must periodically wait for the producer to catch up (the consumer cannot read a record from a buffer before the producer puts it there).

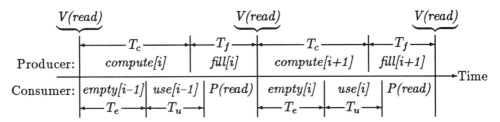

For clarity, the buffer index has been omitted. As before, the index i refers to the record number. Suppose i is even: then *fill[i]* will put the i-th record into *buffer[0]* and *fill[i+1]* will put the $(i+1)$-th record into *buffer[1]*. Similarly, *empty[i−1]* will empty *buffer[1]* and *empty[i]* will empty *buffer[0]*. The semaphores also alternate, with the leftmost V operation shown being on the semaphore *read[1]*.

The effective cycle time in this case is $T_c + T_f$.

Case 2: $T_e + T_u > T_c + T_f$

This is the converse case and the effective cycle time is now $T_e + T_u$.

Summary

In both cases, the time per cycle may be expressed as

$$\max(T_c + T_f, T_e + T_u).$$

Clearly, double buffering gives an improvement over single buffering only if $T_e > T_c$ and $T_f > T_u$. Maximum benefit occurs if $T_e = T_f$ and $T_c = T_u = 0$ in which case double buffering is twice as fast as single buffering.

In all cases, double buffering gives the maximum possible efficiency for the producer–consumer problem provided the timings are the same for each cycle.

If the times vary from record to record, then the bounded buffer described in Section 6.4 may be preferable.

6.3.3   Applications

Double buffering is of value in any producer–consumer situation in which the record being transferred is constructed from a number of component parts which are generated and written into the buffer in turn. In other words, situations in which the computation of the data is interspersed with filling the buffer (or use of the data is interspersed with reading the buffer), such as the first program for the random array example given in Section 6.1.

An alternative form of double buffering is to transfer the data in sequence through the two buffers. So, data is always initially written by the producer into the first buffer, then copied to the second, from which the consumer reads it. Because of the additional data movement, this is not generally favoured, but there may be special circumstances in which it is convenient; for example, if there is insufficient shared memory for two buffers. One buffer may be located in each process, the producer buffer must then be readable by the consumer, or the consumer buffer must be writable by the producer. For optimum performance, it may be necessary to use a third process to transfer the data between the two buffers.

6.4   Bounded Buffer

In cases where the execution times vary considerably from cycle to cycle there may be advantages in having more than two buffers available. Thus, if the producer generates ten records, say, in quick succession and then is very slow in generating the next few records, these variations in speed can be evened out if we have a buffer with room for at least ten records. This allows the consumer to proceed at its own pace, except that the average speed of producer and consumer must eventually work out the same.

The algorithm for a buffer of n records (which are organised as a queue because we require the records to be received by the consumer in the same order that they were sent by the producer) is shown in Fig. 6.4.

The value of the integer semaphore *write* denotes the number of free places in the buffer and the value of the semaphore *read* denotes the number of occupied places in the buffer. After each record is added to the queue, *V(read)* is called, and after each record is removed from the queue, *V(write)* is called. The producer executes *P(write)* before it adds another record to the queue, which will cause it to wait if the queue is full. The consumer executes *P(read)*

Producer	Consumer

<table>
<tr><td>

tail := 0;
WHILE TRUE DO
    compute (data);
    P(write);
    buffer[tail] := data;
    tail := tail + 1 MOD n;
    V(read)
OD

</td><td>

head := 0;
WHILE TRUE DO
    P(read);
    data := buffer[head];
    head := head + 1 MOD n;
    V(write);
    use (data)
OD

</td></tr>
</table>

Shared: *write : integer semaphore (initially n)*
              read : integer semaphore (initially 0)
              buffer : ARRAY [0..(n − 1)] OF anytype

Local: *head : 0..n−1*
              tail : 0..n−1
              data : anytype

Figure 6.4: Bounded buffer, using semaphores.

before it takes a record from the queue, which causes it to wait if the queue is empty.

A general timing analysis of the bounded buffer algorithm is not particularly helpful as the overall performance is heavily dependent upon the variations in the timings from cycle to cycle, and there are so many different possibilities. The easiest way to characterise the performance is to observe that with a buffer for n records, the producer can run up to n records ahead of the consumer. If it tries to run more than n records ahead it will be made to wait because the buffer will be full. So, provided the variations in speed average out over runs of n records, a buffer with space for that number of records will perform well.

6.4.1 Applications

Serial input and output streams are buffered this way in many operating systems. UNIX maintains queues of characters for input and output on all serial character devices such as keyboards, printers and screens (when used in serial character mode; windowing and graphics is rather different).

Devices for which the unit record is much larger than one character are not often buffered with simple bounded buffer queues of more than one or two buffers (i.e. single or double buffering) because of the large amounts of memory that would have to be reserved for the buffers if a separate array of buffers were kept for each device. With disc transfers in an operating system, for example, it is generally inappropriate to think of these as a simple producer–consumer situation. More typically, the disc transfers are initiated by many different processes, and they need not be carried out in the order in which the requests were made (see also Section 6.7).

6.5   Infinite Buffer

It is quite common for the case of an infinite buffer to be discussed in the literature. This is, of course, not possible in reality — all buffers must have a limit on the number of records they can hold. All it means for algorithm design is that we can ignore the check on the buffer becoming full (because an infinite buffer is never full), so it is a convenient way to simplify one aspect of the algorithm when other aspects of it are being studied.

It also has practical applications in that there are some circumstances in which it is known with certainty that a producer can never get more than a known number of records ahead of the consumer. Any buffer larger than that number is effectively infinite and so we can dispense with the checks for a full buffer. Beware, however; such checks should not be removed lightly! You must be able to prove that your program really is incapable of overfilling the buffer. It may be that the check has been done a little earlier in the program for some quite different purpose, in which case there is clearly no point in repeating it if none of the relevant variables have changed.

6.6   Zero Buffer

The case of no buffer at all is an interesting one. In that case, the producer cannot write the data until such time as the consumer is able to receive it. The producer's instruction to write the data and the consumer's instruction to read it are effectively merged into the same instruction (i.e. the data is written directly from the producer to the consumer), and the two processes must be exactly synchronised during the execution of this transfer. This is the *rendezvous* mechanism which was introduced in Section 2.3.2 and is also used in several high-level languages (see Chapter 9). For processes which have access to shared memory, there is rarely any reason to totally exclude the use of buffers, although it is not difficult to write such an algorithm (see Exercise 6.3). For distributed systems, however, data transfer without buffers is often easier to implement and tends to be the preferred mechanism in languages intended for distributed processing.

6.7 Buffer Pool

Buffers are useful in many situations other than the simple producer–consumer problem. Often buffers are filled and emptied at arbitrary times, not in simple first-in first-out order. In such situations a set of buffers, often referred to as a *buffer pool*, is maintained. When another buffer is required, any free buffer in the pool is allocated. Buffers may be be retained for as long as required and freed in any order.

UNIX maintains a pool of single-block buffers. A block is typically 1K bytes and is the unit record for all block device transfers. The UNIX filestore is always on a block device, generally a disc. Whenever a file is accessed, the transfer is buffered in the kernel. One or more buffers (of one block each) are allocated from the pool. If the user process is wanting to read from disc, the kernel will immediately initiate the disc read into the buffer and put the user process to sleep until it is complete. When complete, the required data is copied from the buffer into the user process which is then able to proceed.

If a disc write is requested, the data is merely transferred from the user process into a buffer in the kernel. No disc write takes place. Instead, the data remains in the buffer for the time being. If any process requests to read the same block of that file, a disc read is not needed as the data is still in the buffer. Also, further writes to the same part of the file will simply overwrite the data in the buffer: nothing will be written to disc.

The buffer is finally written to disc only when that buffer is needed for another purpose. Normally all buffers in the pool are allocated and when another buffer is needed, one of the allocated buffers must be freed. If that buffer has been used in a write operation its contents must first be written to disc (if it has been used only for read operations, its contents will be a copy of the block on disc, so it can be freed immmediately, without the need to write it to disc).

This means that buffers may remain in use for arbitrarily long periods of time. It also means that the number and order of real disc transfers is not necessarily the same as that of the requests for file access issued by user processes. The advantage of this type of buffering is that the number of disc accesses is reduced and so the operating system performance is improved. The disadvantage is that the files on disc do not always contain the most up-to-date information. The data written to a file may not actually be written to disc until much later. This can have serious consequences if there is a system crash and the data in memory is lost. To minimise the effects of this, UNIX provides a special command, called *sync*, which writes all buffers to disc, thus bringing the filestore on disc completely up-to-date. This is normally done at regular intervals (typically every few seconds) and just before stopping or reconfiguring the system.

6.8   Bounded Buffer Without Using Primitives

It is not difficult to find an algorithm that does not require synchronisation
primitives or special instructions and hence can be implemented in any language on any computer system. One such algorithm (Peterson and Silberschatz, 1983) is shown in Fig. 6.5.

Producer

```
tail := 0;
WHILE TRUE DO
    compute(data);
    WHILE (tail + 1 MOD n)
            = head DO OD;
    buffer[tail] := data;
    tail := tail + 1 MOD n;
OD
```

Consumer

```
head := 0;
WHILE TRUE DO
    WHILE head = tail DO OD;
    data := buffer[head];
    head := head + 1 MOD n;
    use(data)
OD
```

Shared: $head : 0..n-1$
$tail : 0..n-1$
$buffer : ARRAY [0..(n-1)]$ of anytype
Local: $data : anytype$

Figure 6.5: An algorithm for a bounded buffer without using primitives for
synchronisation.

A queue is particularly easy to handle in the producer–consumer situation
because the producer puts items on the tail of the queue while the consumer
takes them off the head of the queue. There is no direct interaction between
the two, so mutual exclusion of access is unnecessary (see also Exercise 1.2).
The only checks are if the producer tries to put a record onto a full queue or
the consumer tries to take a record off an empty queue.

6.9   Exercises

Exercise 6.1 Processes A and B form a producer–consumer pair, as do processes C and D (independently). A shortage of memory space means

that only a single buffer is available to be shared by these two independent communication channels (A to B and C to D). Write pseudocode programs for all four processes, using semaphores to ensure correct synchronisation.

Exercise 6.2 Write a program (in pseudocode) for a procedure *putchar(c)* which outputs the character *c* on an output device for which the raw output instruction is of the form *output(line)* where *line* is an array of exactly 256 characters. If less than 256 characters must be output, the array should be padded out with null characters.

Your routine should buffer up the characters received, using double buffering, until it has a full buffer to output, or until the end-of-file (EOF) character is received (which is not output). The output device interrupts when it completes a transfer, so you should include an interrupt handler as part of your program. Use semaphores for synchronisation between the interrupt handler and the user process which calls *putchar*.

Exercise 6.3 Write an algorithm for the producer–consumer problem using no buffers; i.e. the data is copied directly from producer to consumer. Use semaphores for synchronisation.

Exercise 6.4 An automated factory contains a number of merging production lines which are configured as shown in Fig. 6.6.

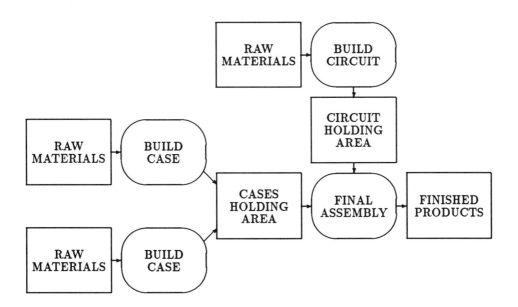

Figure 6.6: Merging production lines in a factory.

One production line is used to construct electronic circuits which are then temporarily stored in a holding area which has space for at most 25 circuits. Two production lines are devoted to the construction of cases. The finished cases are temporarily stored in a holding area with room for 10 cases. The final assembly stage puts the electronic circuit into its case to produce the finished product.

Write an algorithm to simulate the operation of this factory, using semaphores to express the synchronisation needed between the production operations. Assume an infinite supply of raw materials and an infinite storage area for the finished products.

Chapter 7

Readers and Writers

7.1 The Problem

The readers and writers problem was introduced in Section 1.2.4. It is a special case of the more general problem of a number of processes accessing a shared data object. In the readers and writers case, some processes only read the shared data (and never write it), while other processes only write the data (and never read it). As a consequence, the data contains no indications of whether or not it has been read (because readers do not write to the file). Similarly, what is written to the file is in no way affected by the previous contents of the file (because writers do not read the file).

A trivial solution to the readers and writers problem is simply to use the straightforward solution to the more general problem. This enforces mutual exclusion on all accesses to the shared data, irrespective of whether or not they really need it. In many circumstances this solution is completely satisfactory, and there is no reason to seek any other.

In many other circumstances, however, this trivial solution is unacceptably inefficient. Because readers do not change the shared data, there is no reason for them to be mutually exclusive with each other. The inefficiency of a solution which enforces mutual exclusion of readers is particularly noticeable in the readers and writer case, in which there are many readers but only one writer. It is only when the writer tries to access the shared data that mutual exclusion need be enforced, at other times the readers can be permitted to access the data simultaneously. In fact, the trivial solution is inefficient whenever reading is much more frequent than writing.

In this chapter, we look at a variety of different solutions which permit concurrent reading, but enforce mutual exclusion between reading and writing (and between writing and writing, of course).

7.1.1   Archetype Readers and Writers Program

The archetype program for the readers and writers problem is shown in Fig. 7.1.

Writers	**Readers**

WHILE TRUE DO
    compute(data);
    write(data)
OD
	initialisation;
	WHILE TRUE DO
	    read(data);
	    use(data)
	OD

Shared: *buffer : anytype*
          (accessed by *read* and *write*)

Local: *data : anytype*

Figure 7.1: Archetype readers and writers program.

As in the producer–consumer problem, the only constraints on the routines *compute* and *use* are that they must not contain any instructions which access the shared data. All access to the shared data file is contained within the routines *read* and *write*, although these may also contain further computation interspersed between accesses to the shared data. Just as with the producer–consumer case, it is always possible to the put everything into *read* and *write*, so *compute* and *use* disappear. It is not advantageous to do this, however, because the efficiency of most readers and writers algorithms is best if *read* and *write* are kept as short as possible.

It is assumed that the execution of the operations *read* and *write* will always terminate in a finite time, but *compute* and *use* may be infinite.

7.1.2   One Word Data

If the data object being shared by the readers and writer is a single word of memory, the program in Fig. 7.1 needs no synchronisation protocols adding to it. By the basic mutual exclusion of individual memory accesses imposed by the hardware, mutual exclusion of all processes is enforced. Note that this is really much more than required: we needed only to enforce mutual exclusion between the writer and other processes, not between the readers also. The time spent in a single memory access is very short, however, so the unnecessary additional mutual exclusion is not likely to be a worry. In any event, there is generally nothing that the software can do to change this situation as mutual exclusion of memory accesses is built into the hardware and operates all the time, whether it is required or not.

In very special situations, it may be necessary to build hardware to implement *multi-port* memory so that n simultaneous memory accesses can take place, where n is the number of ports (n is rarely greater than two). Such memory units are much more expensive than normal memory and used only if the need is extreme. They are used for applications such as the 'memory mapped' screen output commonly used in personal computers and workstations. The screen controller hardware runs a process which continuously reads sequentially through a block of memory and displays its contents on the screen. This controller typically accesses the memory via a second port so as not to interfere with normal program access to this memory from the central processor.

With such hardware, concurrent access to the same location is possible, sometimes without indivisible access being implemented. In this situation, the screen controller may occasionally read invalid data because of the lack of mutual exclusion. The data will probably be read correctly on the next scan, so the error in the screen display will last for only a fraction of a second and is not serious for most applications.

7.1.3   Applications

At this stage it is timely to consider further the practical applications of what we are studying. These synchronisation problems, such as the readers and writers problem, can easily appear to be very artificial and of largely academic interest. This impression is probably strengthened by the dry and formal way in which we have expressed the problem. It is occasionally worth stepping back from the mathematical formulation of the problem to remind ourselves that it does have very real and important applications. In fact, all of the problems discussed in this book have arisen from difficulties experienced by practising programmers, not from abstract mathematical theory.

Consider, for example, an air traffic control system in which one process (the writer) receives data from radar scanners, carries out some preliminary processing of this data and then uses it to create a map of the sky at a particular instant in time. This map (the shared data object) contains the detected positions of all aircraft at the one instant in time. Other processes (the readers) independently read the map to process it for various purposes such as producing screen displays for the air traffic controller, checking for possible collision courses, etc.

It is important to ensure that any reader sees a consistent map, not one that is in the middle of being re-written (the writer will be regularly receiving data from the radars and will update the map at frequent intervals). If, for instance, a reader sees the position of one aircraft at one point in time and another aircraft at a different time, it makes it much more difficult to determine whether or not those aircraft are on a collision course. Hence the need to ensure that readers never read data that is part way through updating. The situation may be even worse than this in that some data structures can give very gross errors if read while in the middle of being rewritten and this could easily be the source of major program errors if permitted to occur.

To take a very simple illustration, suppose the speed of the aircraft is stored as a 16-bit integer on a machine with an 8-bit memory word. If the current speed is 256 (in whatever units are being used), that will be stored as 1 in the first byte and 0 in the second. If the next speed measurement gives 255, this will be stored as 0 in the first byte and 255 in the second. Suppose that the first byte is stored first chronologically and a reader then reads both bytes before the new value of the second byte can be stored. It will read the speed as 0 (both bytes are 0), a gross error which could have serious consequences.

Indeed, in almost any situation in which a file is being updated concurrently with it being read by other processes, it is much easier for the readers if they can safely assume that they always see the file in a consistent state. If the file is very large and updating it is slow, it may cause unacceptable inefficiencies if we ensure that readers always see a totally consistent file (as we will see, either some processes must be delayed, or extra copies of the file made so that readers may read an old copy while the writer is writing a new one). Under these circumstances, the usual solution is to consider the file as a set of records (or subfiles), and ensure that readers always see each record as being self-consistent, but allow limited inconsistencies in the file as a whole.

For instance, an airline ticket booking system will normally ensure that when the record of bookings for a specified flight is looked at, it is self-consistent and up-to-date. On the other hand, when the managing director looks at the computed cash-flow figures based on the current state of bookings it is unlikely to be totally consistent with the current bookings. The reason is simply that it is inefficient and unnecessary to recompute these figures every time a new booking is made or one cancelled. Instead, such figures are probably computed only on a daily or weekly basis. In effect, all that has been done is to redesign the program so that what we initially considered as one data object is logically considered as a number of smaller data objects. It is worth remembering that the synchronisation techniques we are studying are nearly all applicable to any size objects from one bit to many gigabytes, and the time scales for accessing them may vary from nanoseconds to days. The fundamental techniques are the same whatever the scale and whatever the memory media used.

7.2 Solutions Based on Mutual Exclusion

We consider now two classic solutions to the readers and writers problem. Both are suitable for use with data objects of any size, and implement mutual exclusion between the writers and readers, but not between readers alone. Both of these algorithms are presented in a general form which is suitable for implementation in a wide variety of circumstances: in low-level or high-level languages, and on uniprocessor or multiprocessor systems. The mutual exclusion required by these algorithms may be implemented using any convenient protocol for the circumstances. The particular protocol used is not specified in the algorithms given. Instead, the routines *preprotocol* and *postprotocol*, which are placed before and after the critical sections, denote the chosen protocol.

7.2.1 First Algorithm

The first commonly used algorithm is shown in Fig. 7.2.

Writer i (for i=1..n)

```
WHILE TRUE DO
     compute(data);
     preprotocol(write);
     write(data);
     postprotocol(write);
OD
```

Reader i (for i=1..n)

```
WHILE TRUE DO
     preprotocol(read);
     numread := numread + 1;
     IF numread = 1 THEN
          preprotocol(write) FI;
     postprotocol(read);
     read(data);
     preprotocol(read);
     numread := numread - 1;
     IF numread = 0 THEN
          postprotocol(write) FI;
     postprotocol(read);
     use(data)
OD
```

Shared: *numread : 0..n (initially 0)*
buffer : anytype
(accessed by *read* and *write*)

Local: *data : anytype*

Figure 7.2: First readers and writers algorithm based on mutual exclusion.

It uses two separate classes of mutual exclusion. The first class of mutual exclusion is denoted by the protocol *preprotocol(write)* and *postprotocol(write)*. This is used to ensure that writers are mutually exclusive when they access the file.

Readers need not be mutually exclusive with each other but they must be mutually exclusive with the writers. This is done by making the first reader to start reading call *preprotocol(write)* to lock out the writers. The last reader to finish reading then calls *postprotocol(write)* to release the lock. Readers know whether they are first to start and last to finish by always maintaining a count, *numread*, of the number of readers reading the file. The second class of mutual exclusion, denoted by the routines *preprotocol(read)* and *postprotocol(read)*, is used to ensure mutual exclusion during manipulation of *numread*, which is clearly necessary to avoid incorrect values of *numread* being generated when simultaneously updated by two or more readers.

This solution suffers from the weakness that it is subject to writer starvation because requests to read are always permitted if there is another reader reading the file, despite the fact that writers may be waiting to write. Thus, although any individual reader takes only a finite time to read the file, an infinite sequence of overlapping reads will lock out all the writers for ever.

The algorithm is not subject to deadlock and in other respects is sound, provided that the mutual exclusion protocols used are well behaved.

7.2.2   Second Algorithm

The second common readers and writers algorithm based on mutual exclusion has the basic structure shown in Fig. 7.3.

Writer i (for i=1..m)

```
WHILE TRUE DO
    compute(data);
    ┌─────────────────────────────┐
    │ wait until reading[i] = 0    │
    │           for all i;         │
    │ writing := 1;                │
    └─────────────────────────────┘
    write(data);
    writing := 0
OD
```

Reader i (for i=1..n)

```
initialisation;
WHILE TRUE DO
    ┌─────────────────────────────┐
    │ wait until writing = 0;      │
    │ reading[i] := 1;             │
    └─────────────────────────────┘
    read(data);
    reading[i] := 0;
    use(data)
OD
```

Figure 7.3: Basic structure of the second readers and writers algorithm based on mutual exclusion.

The sections shown in the thick-ruled boxes must be mutually exclusive. The boolean flag *writing* is 1 while any writer is writing to the file and 0 otherwise. The flag *reading[i]* is 1 while the *i*-th reader is reading the file, and 0 otherwise. A separate flag must be used for each reader because several readers may access the file concurrently.

The algorithm is shown in more detail in Fig. 7.4 (only one class of mutual exclusion is used so we omit the argument from *preprotocol* and *postprotocol*).

Writer i (for i=1..m)

```
WHILE TRUE DO
    compute(data);
    preprotocol();
    WHILE
        reading[1] ≠ 0 OR
        reading[2] ≠ 0 OR
        . . . . . . . . . OR
        reading[n] ≠ 0
    DO OD;
    writing := 1;
    postprotocol();
    write(data);
    writing := 0
OD
```

Reader i (for i=1..n)

```
WHILE TRUE DO
    preprotocol();
    WHILE writing≠0 DO OD;
    reading[i] := 1;
    postprotocol();
    read(data);
    reading[i] := 0;
    use(data)
OD
```

Shared: *reading : ARRAY [1..n] OF 0..1 (initially all 0)*
        writing : 0..1 (initially 0)
        buffer : anytype
        (accessed by *read* and *write*)

Local: *data : anytype*

Figure 7.4: Second readers and writers algorithm based on mutual exclusion.

The liveness properties of this algorithm depend upon the corresponding properties of the mutual exclusion protocol used. As soon as one process enters its wait loop (which is inside the critical section delimited by *preprotocol* and *postprotocol*), other processes wishing to access the shared file will be held up by the mutual exclusion protocol. The order in which they are eventually allowed to proceed will depend solely on the mutual exclusion protocol used (readers and writers are treated completely equally in this respect). Thus, the algorithm is as well behaved (or as badly behaved) as the mutual exclusion protocol it uses, upon which it is totally dependent. In particular, it is not subject to starvation (of either readers or writers) provided the mutual exclusion protocol is starvation free.

Using Semaphores

Both algorithms given above can be used either with purely algorithmic implementations of mutual exclusion or by using semaphores or any other primitives for mutual exclusion. If semaphores are used then *preprotocol* and *postprotocol* are the operators P and V respectively. For example the second algorithm based on mutual exclusion is shown with semaphores in Fig. 7.5.

Writer i (for i=1..m)   **Reader i (for i=1..n)**

```
WHILE TRUE DO                  WHILE TRUE DO
    compute(data);                 P(mutex);
    P(mutex);                      WHILE writing≠0 DO OD;
    WHILE                          reading[i] := 1;
        reading[1] ≠ 0 OR          V(mutex);
        reading[2] ≠ 0 OR          read(data);
        . . . . . . . . . OR       reading[i] := 0;
        reading[n] ≠ 0             use(data)
    DO OD;                     OD
    writing := 1;
    V(mutex);
    write(data);
    writing := 0
OD
```

Shared: *mutex : boolean semaphore (initially 1)*
reading : ARRAY [1..n] OF 0..1 (initially all 0)
writing : 0..1 (initially 0)
buffer : anytype
(accessed by *read* and *write*)

Local: *data : anytype*

Figure 7.5: Second readers and writers algorithm based on mutual exclusion, using semaphores.

7.2.3 Timing Analysis

Suppose the readers and writers form part of an air traffic control system, the application mentioned earlier in this chapter. A single writer receives data from radar scanners, constructs a map giving the speeds and positions of all aircraft and writes this map to the shared data file. It repeats this process at regular intervals. Some of the readers are responsible for looking for impending collisions between aircraft. Clearly, such analysis is of little use if the detection of an impending collision can be delayed for such a time that the collision may already have taken place!

In this application and in many others, the time that is important is the 'age' of the data when it is used by the reader. As we are not concerned with the internal structure of the *compute* routine in the writer and do not know precisely when the raw data becomes available, we assume that the data is 'born' when the writer completes execution of *compute* (i.e. at the point at which the writer is ready to start writing the data into the file).

In the First Algorithm (Fig. 7.2) the writer can be subject to starvation, thus the maximum possible age of the data available to the readers is infinite. This algorithm is clearly unsatisfactory for such an application (unless it is known that the readers cannot create an overlapping sequence of reads to delay the writer).

The Second Algorithm is more suitable, provided the mutual exclusion protocol is sufficiently well behaved. Consider the case in which semaphores are used (Fig. 7.5) and suppose they are strong semaphores, so processes which are waiting are permitted to proceed in strictly FIFO order. The timing diagram is as follows.

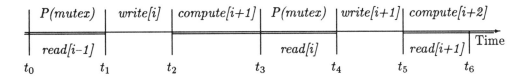

The indices shown in square brackets indicate the record number concerned, while the double line along the time axis indicates periods in which the shared data file is valid and readable. The time on the extreme left (t_0) is the time at which the i-th record is born (i.e. it has just been computed by the writer which is now ready to write it). The diagram shows the worst case timing, in which read accesses begin at t_0 and again at t_3, just when the writer is ready to start writing new data into the file. Hence, the writer is held up until those read accesses are complete (at t_1 and t_4 respectively). Also shown is a reader commencing to read the *(i+1)*-th record at t_5 (the earliest time at which this record is available for reading), which completes at t_6. So t_6 is the latest time at which the changeover from the *i*-th record to the *(i+1)*-th record occurs for the *use* routine in the reader.

Therefore, up until time t_6, the latest data available to a reader is the *i*-th record, which was born at t_0. So, the greatest age of the data available to the reader at the start of the *use* routine (i.e. before fresh data becomes available) is

$$t_6 - t_0 = 3T_r + 2T_w + T_c$$

where T_r is the maximum *read* time, T_w is the maximum *write* time, and T_c is the maximum *compute* time.

7.3   Reducing the Maximum Delays

In the algorithms given in Section 7.2, considerable delays to reading and writing can be caused if there is heavy contention for the shared data file. Algorithms have been published which eliminate delays altogether (Peterson, 1983), but they achieve this at the price of using large numbers of buffers and both reading and writing the data more than once so that multiple copies of the data are available, and at least one of them will always be valid when a reader accesses it. Although processes never wait in an idling loop, the extra work they have to do often means that the age of the data when it gets to the *use* routine in the reader can be greater than in simpler algorithms which do involve waiting.

A simpler and, in many circumstances, a more efficient approach is as follows.

7.3.1   Double Buffered Readers and Writer

We consider first the case of a single writer for simplicity. The algorithm presented here uses the technique of double buffering, modified to suit the readers and writers problem. The idea is that the writer writes to the two buffers alternately (it is assumed that the writer writes a complete new data object every time it writes, not just updating part of the data object) and the readers read from the last buffer that was written to.

The algorithm can use any basic readers and writer algorithm that is not subject to starvation of the readers (but may be subject to writer starvation), so either of the two algorithms given in Section 7.2 would be suitable. Two independent instances of such an algorithm are required, one for each of the two buffers. The read access part of the algorithm for *buffer[bn]* is denoted by *readaccess(bn,x)*, which reads data from *buffer[bn]* into the local variable *x*. The write access part of the algorithm is denoted by *writeaccess(bn,x)* which writes *x* into *buffer[bn]*. The algorithm is given in Fig. 7.6.

<table>
<tr><th style="text-align:center">Writer</th><th style="text-align:center">Reader i (for i=1..n)</th></tr>
<tr><td>

WHILE TRUE DO
    compute(data);
    bn := latestbuf + 1 MOD 2;
    writeaccess(bn,data);
    latestbuf := bn
OD

</td><td>

initialisation;
WHILE TRUE DO
    bn := latestbuf;
    readaccess(bn,data);
    use(data)
OD

</td></tr>
</table>

    Shared: *latestbuf : 0..1 (initially 0)*
               buffer : ARRAY[0..1] OF anytype
               (accessed by *readaccess* and *writeaccess*)
    Local: *bn : 0..1*
               data : anytype

Figure 7.6: Double buffered readers and writer algorithm

As the basic readers and writer protocol used in this algorithm is assumed to be free from reader starvation, this algorithm must be free of reader starvation also, because there is nowhere that starvation can occur except in the *readaccess* routine (there are no explicit wait loops in the algorithm).

The writer is free of starvation because during the whole time that the writer is trying to access its buffer, any new readers will read from the other buffer. Only readers that started reading *before* the writer started trying to write can be accessing the buffer which the writer is trying to use. These readers will all complete reading within a finite time, so writer starvation is not possible.

Timing Analysis

We assume that the minimum *compute* time is greater than the maximum *read* time so that the writer is never held up because a reader is still reading from the previous buffer. The timing diagram is then as follows for the worst case:

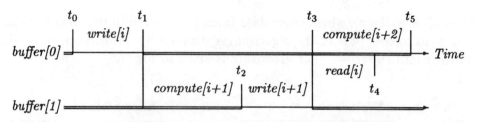

The i-th record is born at t_0 and immediately written into buffer[0], the writing being completed at t_1. The writer then proceeds to begin to *compute* the $(i+1)$-th record and subsequently write it into buffer[1]. This completes at time t_3, and buffer[1] then becomes the latest buffer. Suppose that a reader starts reading buffer[0] fractionally before it is superseded at t_3, and finishes reading it at t_4. This will take place in parallel to the computation of the $(i+2)$-th record. The latest buffer is buffer[0] between t_1 and t_3 and buffer[1] before t_1 and after t_3. The double lines along the time axes indicate the periods during which the buffers contain valid data.

The maximum age of data available to the *use* routine in the reader is:

$$t_4 - t_0 = T_r + 2T_w + T_c$$

where the T_r, T_w and T_c are defined as before. This is a significant saving on the maximum age for the previous algorithm (assuming the *read* time is significant) and is also the lowest possible value for the maximum age; no algorithm can improve upon this time, provided that the minimum *compute* time is not less than the maximum *read* time. This follows because the algorithm suffers no delays whatsoever in this case. The only possible way to speed it up further is to speed up the basic components of the algorithm: *compute*, *read* and *write*.

In the case when the minimum *compute* time is less than the maximum *read* time, the writer may be held up waiting for a reader to finish reading. Such delays can be eliminated by using additional buffers. The algorithm is easily generalised to use any number of buffers in cyclic order.

7.3.2   Double Buffered Readers and Writers

The previous algorithm can easily be generalised to the case of more than one writer by using a separate pair of buffers for each writer. The algorithm is shown in Fig. 7.7.

The i-th writer uses buffer[2*i - 2] and buffer[2*i - 1]. Again, we assume that each writer writes the complete data object every time it writes, rather than just updating parts of the data. A reader always reads the latest buffer (no matter which writer wrote it).

| **Writer i (for i=1..m)** | **Reader i (for i=1..n)** |

```
bn := 2*i - 2;
WHILE TRUE DO
    compute(data);
    writeaccess(bn, data);
    latestbuf := bn;
    bn := bn + 1;
    IF bn = 2*i THEN
        bn := 2*i - 2 FI
OD
```

```
initialisation;
WHILE TRUE DO
    bn := latestbuf;
    readaccess(bn, data);
    use(data);
OD
```

Shared: *latestbuf : 0..(2*m − 1)*
            buffer : ARRAY[0..(2*m − 1)] OF anytype
           (accessed by *readaccess* and *writeaccess*)

Local: *bn : 0..(2*m − 1)*
         data : anytype

Figure 7.7: Double buffered readers and writers algorithm.

7.4 Exercises

Exercise 7.1 Can the producer–consumer problem be considered as simply a special case of the readers and writers problem with a single writer (the producer) and a single reader (the consumer)?

Exercise 7.2 Show that the attempted solution to the readers and writer problem given in Fig. 7.8 is *unsafe*. Suggest a simple means of making it safe.

Exercise 7.3 Show that the attempted solution to the readers and writer problem given in Fig. 7.9 is subject to *deadlock*.

Exercise 7.4 When would it be advantageous to extend the double buffered readers and writer algorithm to use more than two buffers? Rewrite the algorithm to incorporate this generalisation.

Writer	**Reader i (for i=1..n)**

WHILE TRUE DO
    compute(data);
    preprotocol();
    WHILE reading≠0 DO OD;
    writing := 1;
    postprotocol();
    write(data);
    writing := 0
OD
	initialisation;
	WHILE TRUE DO
	    preprotocol();
	    WHILE writing≠0 DO OD;
	    reading := reading + 1;
	    postprotocol();
	    read(data);
	    reading := reading – 1;
	    use(data)
	OD

Shared: *reading : 0..n (initially 0)*
            writing : 0..1 (initially 0)
            buffer : anytype (accessed by *read* and *write*)

Local: *data : anytype*

Figure 7.8: Attempted solution to the readers and writer problem.

Writer	**Reader i (for i=1..n)**

(as in Fig. 7.8)	*initialisation;*
	WHILE TRUE DO
	    preprotocol();
	    WHILE writing≠0 DO OD;
	    reading := reading + 1;
	    postprotocol();
	    read(data);
	    preprotocol();
	    reading := reading – 1;
	    postprotocol();
	    use(data)
	OD

Shared: *reading : 0..n (initially 0)*
            writing : 0..1 (initially 0)
            buffer : anytype (accessed by *read* and *write*)

Local: *data : anytype*

Figure 7.9: Another attempted solution to the readers and writer problem.

Chapter 8

Synchronisation in Modula-2

The programming language Modula-2 was designed by Niklaus Wirth (Wirth, 1985). It evolved from an earlier language known simply as Modula, which itself was based on Wirth's very successful and well known language, Pascal. The main features of Modula-2 not present in Pascal are: (i) the program structuring facility known as a *module*; and (ii) facilities for concurrent programming.

In this chapter, we examine some of the basic synchronisation mechanisms provided in Modula-2. There is no attempt to give a complete description of the language or even of all its concurrency features. The interested reader should consult the many published textbooks and manuals on Modula-2 for a more thorough introduction to the language. The two mechanisms that concern us in this chapter are known as *monitors* and *signals*. Monitors provide mutual exclusion directly, while signals are low-level synchronisation primitives somewhat akin to the *sleep* and *wakeup* routines in the UNIX kernel.

Some implementations of Modula-2 also give access to the basic machine code mechanisms available via special instructions and hardware interrupts (both very machine dependent). Those mechanisms will not be described here.

8.1 Monitors

The concept of a *monitor* in Modula-2 is based upon the programming language concept of a *module* which is introduced first. Modules have nothing to do with concurrent programming as such, but are purely a language mechanism for helping the programmer to structure his program in terms of data abstractions.

8.1.1   Modules

A *module* in Modula-2 (a similar construct in Ada is called a *package*) is
a collection of procedures and global declarations packaged together so that
only specifically declared names can be accessed from outside the module. A
module can be written in two parts: the definition and the implementation.
The definition simply declares the name of the module and the names within
the module which may be accessed externally. These are called the *exports*
of the module and are names of procedures which may be called from outside
the module or names of global variables which may be accessed from outside
the module. The definition may also contain *imports* which are the names of
exports from other modules which are used by the module being defined.

The implementation part of the module has basically the same structure
as a complete program. It consists of global declarations, procedures and a
main program. The main program is typically just for the initialisation of the
global variables used in the module, however.

We are not going to worry too much about all the precise details of Modula-
2 syntax, but the general appearance of a module is as shown in Fig. 8.1.

Module definition

```
DEFINITION MODULE name;
     {export declarations}
     {import declarations}
END name.
```

Module implementation

```
IMPLEMENTATION MODULE name;
     {global declarations}
     PROCEDURE p1...
                 ⋮
     PROCEDURE p2...
                 ⋮
BEGIN
     {initialisation of globals}
END name.
```

Figure 8.1: Syntactic structure of a module in Modula-2.

The only identifiers within the module which are accessible outside the
module are those declared as exports. Thus a module is simply a mechanism

for *information hiding*. It enables both procedures and global variables to be declared whose names are not known outside that module. Thus, with care, it is possible to design modules so that they can be used only according to their specification: direct access to internal parts of the implementation is impossible from outside the module.

For instance, a good implementation of a stack would allow the user to call routines to push and pop the stack, but not allow him to put data directly into the storage area used for the stack or otherwise interfere with the implementation mechanism. This could be done by writing the stack routines in a module for which the only exports were the push and pop routines (and any others required by the specification). The array used for the stack, and the head and tail pointers would be declared as global variables in the module, but would not be exported. This means that they are completely inaccessible from outside the module (except indirectly via the push and pop routines).

The advantage of this approach is that the programmer of the stack module is then free to change his implementation method without having to worry that programs which make use of his stack routines will no longer work. Provided the exported names are the same and have the same functionality as before, changes to the implementation details should not affect the functional behaviour of programs which use the module. Of course, they may well affect the performance.

It is important to realise that a module is a totally different concept from a process. A module, unlike a process, has no existence whatever once the program has been compiled. It is purely a syntactic structure in the source code to help the programmer control the use of identifiers. It enables him to write the program in such a way that some identifiers can be accessed only within a well-defined region of the program (i.e. within a module). Of course, most high-level languages have always provided such a limitation on access to local variables declared in procedures, but the module concept allows this limitation to be extended to global variables and procedure names as well.

8.1.2 Processes

A Modula-2 program may run as a single process (as is always the case in Pascal) or it may run as several processes. There is no special syntactic structure in the language to denote a process. Instead standard library procedures are provided to create new processes out of ordinary Modula-2 procedures. Thus processes do not correspond to any particular structures in the source program. Two different procedures in the same module could be made into two distinct processes, or even the one procedure could be used twice to create two identical processes (because a procedure is used for one process does not mean that it is not available for use by other processes). A process is simply a thread of execution. Two processes may execute the same code, and processes may jump around from procedure to procedure (only when one procedure calls another, of course) and from module to module (again only when a procedure in one module calls a procedure in the other module), just like any other program.

Modula-2 was designed for implementation on conventional uniprocessor computers only and not for parallel machines of any sort. Implementations vary widely in how comprehensively the concurrency features are implemented and therefore in how effectively the language can be used for real-time multiprogramming. On those implementations for which true real-time multiprogramming is possible, the machine independent synchronisation mechanisms provided in Modula-2 are monitors and signals, which we now describe.

8.1.3   Monitors

A *monitor* is simply a module over which mutual exclusion is implemented. That is, at any one time only one process may be in the middle of executing any procedure in the module. In other words, every procedure exported by the module is implemented as a critical section (all of the one class). So, if one process calls a procedure within the module and before that procedure completes execution another process calls the same or another procedure from that same module, the second process will be held up until the first call has completed.

Syntactically, a module is designated to be a monitor by appending an integer in square brackets after its name in the heading of both definition and implementation parts:

> *DEFINITION MODULE name[p];*
> *IMPLEMENTATION MODULE name[p];*

where p is the priority of the monitor. The precise meaning of the priority parameter is system dependent. For our purposes, we can assume that the value of p is irrelevant, but its presence serves to make the module into a monitor.

Monitors provide a very simple and safe way in which the programmer can obtain mutual exclusion. They are of little other use on their own, however, hence discussion of a detailed example is delayed until after we have introduced signals, which are generally used in conjunction with monitors.

The main disadvantage of monitors is that they provide a rather crude facility for mutual exclusion. As we have already seen, a module is a program structuring facility that is independent of concurrency. To use this structure as the program unit upon which to implement mutual exclusion is simple and convenient, but not always the most appropriate from the point of view of run-time efficiency. Often only a small part of the code of a monitor really needs to be mutually exclusive.

8.2   Signals

A signal is a special type of variable which is declared in the usual way (as type *SIGNAL*), but may be operated upon only by the following routines:

WAIT(s)
_____

This procedure causes the calling process to go to sleep until another process sends the signal *s*. If *WAIT* is called from a monitor, mutual exclusion is suspended while the process is asleep (i.e. other processes are free to execute monitor routines during this time).
_____

SEND(s)
_____

If there is a process waiting on the signal *s*, this procedure causes the calling process to be temporarily suspended while the waiting process is resumed. If several processes are waiting on the same signal, only *one* of them is resumed. If no process is waiting on the signal, the procedure has no effect.
_____

Init(s)
_____

This procedure initialises the signal *s*. It must be called before the first use of *s*, but has no other significance.
_____

Usually signals are used within monitors, in which circumstances they override the mutual exclusion of monitors. Suppose that a process calls a procedure in a monitor which then calls *WAIT(s)*. The process will be put to sleep. Suppose then that another process calls a procedure in the same monitor (it is allowed to do this while the first process is asleep in *WAIT*), and this procedure calls *SEND(s)*, with the same signal *s* as before. Control is switched from the process calling *SEND* to the one asleep in *WAIT*, which now proceeds to

run. The process calling *SEND* is now held up until the other process exits
from the monitor thus releasing the mutual exclusion. Indeed, it is perhaps
more appropriate to think of signals as implementing a synchronised process
switch rather than thinking of them as being similar to semaphores.

Notice that signals, unlike semaphores, are not remembered. Although
the signal is declared like a variable, it has no 'value'. *WAIT* and *SEND*
are similar to *sleep* and *wakeup* in the UNIX kernel, but there are important
differences here too. If *WAIT* and *SEND* are used (on the same signal) within
the one monitor, the condition on which the *WAIT* occurred is assured when
the waiting process resumes. This is because only one process is woken up by
SEND, and that process resumes immediately, while the *SEND*ing process is
temporarily suspended. Hence it is usually unnecessary to put WAIT inside a
loop in the way that was needed with *sleep* in the UNIX kernel.

8.3   Producer–Consumer in Modula-2

As an example of the use of monitors and signals, we consider the implementation of the bounded buffer algorithm for the producer–consumer problem.
The buffer and the procedures to access it are packaged together in a monitor
module. The only exports from the module are the access procedures (called
append and *take,* say) so other parts of the program can access the buffer but
cannot interfere with the implementation of the buffer. The buffer itself is a
global data structure in the module, but not exported. As the module is a
monitor, mutual exclusion is enforced on the access procedures, so the buffer
can never be found in an inconsistent state.

The producer and consumer are shown in Fig. 8.2. The buffering mechanism is not coded directly into the producer or consumer, which simply call
the routines *append* and *take.*

Producer	**Consumer**
WHILE TRUE DO	*initialisation;*
compute(data);	*WHILE TRUE DO*
append(data)	*take(data);*
OD	*use(data)*
	OD

Local: *data : anytype*

Figure 8.2: Producer and consumer processes.

Module Definition

The module definition part of the bounded buffer module is shown as the upper box in Fig. 8.3. The priority parameter after the module name shows that it is a monitor.

You can see in the definition part that the only exports are *append* and *take*. These are both procedure names declared more fully a few lines below. These later definitions are needed not only to specify that *append* and *take* are procedures, but also to specify the types of their arguments and results. The definition part of the module also contains a list of imports, which are names of objects which are used by the implementation part of the module and which must be obtained from other modules. In the example given, the type *anytype* is assumed to be defined externally and hence must be imported, along with the integer constant *sizeofbuffer*. Also, the type *SIGNAL* and the procedures that can be used on signals (*SEND, WAIT* and *Init*) are not built into the Modula-2 compiler, but supplied as part of the standard library and hence must be explicitly imported.

In essence, the definition part of the module contains everything that the compiler needs to know to be able to compile the rest of the program (without having to refer to the implementation part). The exports (and the declarations of the exported names) give all the essential information needed to be able to use the module in the rest of the program. Of course, the information given is purely that needed by the compiler: essentially only type information. The programmer will need a lot more information (in particular, the function of the procedures *append* and *take*) but this must be supplied through normal program documentation (which could be included as comments in the Modula-2 program).

The list of imports is required so that the compiler can check that everything needed is available. The types of imported objects are not needed because, once their names are known, the compiler will find where these objects are defined and their definitions will include all the necessary type declarations.

Module Implementation

The implementation part of the module is shown in the lower box in Fig. 8.3. This algorithm is given in a pseudocode which is very close to Modula-2, but not exactly the same. To avoid confusion, the *IF... THEN... ELSE... FI* construct has been retained instead of the Modula-2 equivalent which does not have the *FI* part, but uses *END* instead (in Modula-2, *END* is used as a terminator for *WHILE, CASE* and various other constructs also).

The buffer memory is represented by the global variables *buffer, head, tail* and *occupancy*. The array *buffer* is memory for the actual data items, integers

Module Definition

```
DEFINITION MODULE boundedbuffer[1];
    EXPORT
        append, take;
    IMPORT
        anytype, sizeofbuffer, SIGNAL, SEND, WAIT, Init;
    PROCEDURE append(data : anytype);
    PROCEDURE take(VAR data : anytype);
END boundedbuffer.
```

Module Implementation

```
IMPLEMENTATION MODULE boundedbuffer[1];
    VAR
        buffer : ARRAY [0..sizeofbuffer – 1] OF anytype;
        head, tail : 0..sizeofbuffer – 1;
        occupancy : 0..sizeofbuffer;
        nonfull, nonempty : SIGNAL;

    PROCEDURE append(data : anytype);
        IF occupancy = sizeofbuffer THEN WAIT(nonfull) FI;
        buffer[tail] := data;
        tail := tail + 1 MOD sizeofbuffer;
        occupancy := occupancy + 1;
        SEND(nonempty)
    END append;

    PROCEDURE take(VAR data : anytype);
        IF occupancy = 0 THEN WAIT(nonempty) FI;
        data := buffer[head];
        head := head + 1 MOD sizeofbuffer;
        occupancy := occupancy – 1;
        SEND(nonfull)
    END take;

BEGIN
    occupancy := 0;
    head := 0;
    tail := 0;
    Init(nonfull);
    Init(nonempty)
END boundedbuffer.
```

Figure 8.3: Definition and implementation of the bounded buffer monitor.

head and *tail* index the positions of the head and tail of the queue (*buffer[tail]* is where the next item will be put and *buffer[head]* is the next item to be removed from the queue), and the integer *occupancy* is the number of items currently in the queue.

The operation of the monitor is quite straightforward. Consider the procedure *append*, which puts a data item into the queue. If the buffer is full (*occupancy=sizeofbuffer*), it waits until an item is removed by the consumer, indicated by the signal *nonfull*. Then the data item is put into the next free location and the values of *tail* and *occupancy* updated to take account of the new item. Finally, the signal *nonempty* is sent in case the consumer is asleep in *WAIT(nonempty)*.

The procedure *take* is very similar. It waits if the buffer is empty, then takes the item from the head of the queue and updates *head* and *occupancy*. Finally, it sends the signal *nonempty* in case the producer is asleep in *WAIT(nonempty)*.

The 'main program' part of the module is purely initialisation, which sets the variables *head, tail* and *occupancy* to represent an empty queue. The two signals *nonfull* and *nonempty* must also be initialised.

Particular points to note are:

- Because mutual exclusion is automatically enforced within the monitor module, it is quite safe to have a variable *occupancy* instead of using *head* and *tail* to determine if the buffer is empty or full. Of course, it would be quite acceptable to remove *occupancy* and use *head* and *tail*, provided we adopted the usual trick of always keeping one free location in the buffer.

- Because switching occurs immediately on execution of SEND, this implementation in Modula-2 is really quite efficient and it is possible to use Modula-2 to implement the kernel of an operating system or other dedicated real-time programs which may otherwise be written in a language such as C or even assembly code. Because some Modula-2 systems provide a means of linking to interrupts and giving special machine instructions (such as raw I/O instructions), it may be possible to do this without writing any assembly code whatsoever.

Further to the latter point above, one of the main aims that Wirth had in mind when designing Modula-2 was that it should be possible to write operating systems, compilers and other systems software entirely within the language. It was this requirement that led directly to the incorporation of machine dependent low-level features (such as linking to interrupts and using special machine instructions) and the emphasis on run-time efficiency. Unfortunately, many Modula-2 compilers do not implement all these features.

8.4   Exercises

Exercise 8.1 In a real-time system, mutual exclusion of various classes of critical sections is to be implemented via routines called *pre* and *post*, which are used to bracket the critical section as follows:

Any process

```
      ⋮
pre(s);
critical section;
post(s);
      ⋮
```

where *s* denotes the class of critical sections.

Write algorithms in Modula-2 pseudocode to implement the procedures *pre* and *post*, using monitors and signals as the only synchronisation primitives. Allow at least *N* different classes of critical sections to be handled simultaneously. The argument *s* may be any type of object that you choose.

Exercise 8.2 It is required to implement a simple mailing system between processes. Any process can send a message to any other process by calling the procedure

$$send(source,\ dest,\ message)$$

where *source* is the process identifier (PID) of the calling process, *dest* is the PID of the destination process, and *message* is the message itself. If no buffers are currently free to hold the message, the procedure waits until a buffer is available. It returns to the calling process as soon as the message has been put in a buffer.

A process reads the messages sent to it by calling the procedure

$$receive(source,\ dest,\ message)$$

where *dest* is the PID of the calling process, and the other two arguments are irrelevant on entry, being used to return values. A waiting message for this process will be returned in *message* with the PID of the process which sent it put in *source*. If there is no waiting message, the procedure does not wait, but returns immediately with *source* set to -1.

Write programs in pseudocode for *send* and *receive*, using a pool of *N* buffers and using the monitor construct for synchronisation.

Exercise 8.3 A real-time system is designed to use a procedure *delay(t)* which causes the current process to be put to sleep until the real time is later than *t*.

Write an algorithm in Modula-2 pseudocode to implement *delay* using monitors and signals as the synchronisation primitives. You may also assume that a global variable called *timenow* always contains the current time (in the same units as used for *t*). You may also assume that a parameterless procedure *tick* (which you must write) is called at regular intervals of time by the hardware clock interrupt. Your implementation should allow up to *N* processes to be asleep simultaneously in *delay*.

Chapter 9

Rendezvous in Ada

The programming language Ada is intended not only for use in conventional programming but also for real-time embedded systems and for distributed processing. Hence Ada includes concurrency mechanisms as a fundamental part of the language. Unlike Modula-2, Ada is a registered trademark (of the U.S. Government) which is not permitted to be used for implementations of subsets or supersets of Ada. Hence every Ada implementation contains all the concurrency features described in this chapter.

Also unlike Modula-2, Ada aims to be reasonably efficient when implemented on distributed systems (without shared memory) as well as on uniprocessors and multiprocessors (with shared memory). (It is fair to point out, however, that implementations of Ada on distributed systems are still quite few in number, and the long-term viability of Ada as a completely machine-independent language for efficient distributed processing remains unproven.) The monitor and signal mechanisms used in Modula-2 for interprocess communication and synchronisation are not convenient on distributed systems because, if the processes using a monitor are running on different processors, there is no satisfactory place to locate the monitor. It should ideally be located on every processor that uses it, but that is both difficult and inefficient.

Instead, Ada uses a synchronous message passing mechanism as introduced in Section 2.3.2 and commonly referred to as a *rendezvous* mechanism. In Ada, the rendezvous is treated like a procedure call, but this is a purely syntactic device and we shall see later that some other languages use a totally different form of syntax to express the rendezvous. There are two special types of statement in Ada which are associated with rendezvous. They are the *ACCEPT* and *SELECT* statements, each of which is described in this chapter.

Processes in Ada are referred to as *tasks*. Depending upon the particular implementation in use, these may run on distributed processors, multiprocessors or with interleaving on a uniprocessor. There is a special syntax for defining a task, which is structurally also like a module in Modula-2 (the equivalent Ada construct is called a *package*). We omit the syntactic details as they are of no particular interest to us here: it suffices to know that concurrent processes can be defined in an Ada program. What does interest us are the mechanisms by which such processes communicate and synchronise, and we look at these mechanisms in some detail.

9.1   ACCEPT Statement

The *ACCEPT* statement is syntactically similar to a normal procedure definition, except that it occurs within the code of a task. Its position is significant, whereas the position of a normal procedure definition is largely insignificant.

The *ACCEPT* statement defines not a normal procedure, but a rendezvous in the task in which it occurs. The form of the statement is as follows:

ACCEPT entryname(arguments) DO body END entryname;

where *entryname* is the name of the entry point defined by this statement, *arguments* is a list of formal arguments just like the formal arguments of a procedure definition, and *body* is a sequence of statements just like the body of a procedure definition. In Ada, all the formal arguments must be declared as either input or output arguments (by the keywords *IN* and *OUT*, respectively).

The entry name may be called by another task just as if it were a procedure name:

entryname(arguments)

where *arguments* is now a list of actual arguments. We refer to this as an 'entry call', although to the calling routine it looks just like an ordinary procedure call in its functional behaviour.

Execution of ACCEPT

The execution of these statements takes place as follows:

1. If a process reaches an entry call before an *ACCEPT* statement with the same entry name is reached in another process, the calling process is suspended.

2. If a process reaches an *ACCEPT* statement before any other process reaches a call to the entry name defined by the *ACCEPT*, the accepting process is suspended.

3. Only when both the calling process has reached the entry call and the accepting process has reached the *ACCEPT* statement defining that entry will the rendezvous take place, the following sequence then being executed.

   (a) The values of all input arguments are copied from the calling process to the accepting process.

   (b) The accepting process then executes the body of the entry definition.

   (c) The values of the output arguments are then copied from the accepting process to the calling process.

   (d) Finally, the calling and accepting processes now proceed independently (i.e. concurrently or pseudo-concurrently). The calling process continues with the statements following the entry call and the accepting process continues with the statements following the *AC-CEPT* statement.

4. Another rendezvous can occur at the same entry point only when the accepting process returns to that *ACCEPT* statement and either the same calling process or another calling process reaches a call to that entry name (it could be the same calling statement as before, or another one, as long as the entry name matches that in the *ACCEPT*).

5. If several processes call the same entry name before a process accepts that entry (i.e. reaches an *ACCEPT* statement for that name), they are queued in order of arrival and accepted in that order. Each time the accepting process reaches the relevant *ACCEPT* statement, only one of the calling processes will be permitted to complete its rendezvous.

Notice that the code in the body of an *ACCEPT* statement is executed just as if it were a normal part of the process in which it occurs. It is executed only when control arrives at the *ACCEPT*. This is quite different from a normal procedure definition which is not placed in the middle of other code but will be effectively jumped into when it is called elsewhere in the same process. Control does not jump into an *ACCEPT* statement in the same way.

Instead, the *ACCEPT* is more like a *sleep* or *wait* instruction, that may cause the process to be suspended at this point until another process calls that entry. Then a message (consisting of the input arguments) is passed from the calling process to the accepting process, and the accepting process proceeds. The completion of the body of the *ACCEPT* has no significance for the accepting process. It simply proceeds to the following statement without delay. It does have significance for the calling process, however, which has been suspended until this time. Now a message (consisting of the output arguments) is sent back from the accepting process to the calling process, and the calling process is allowed to proceed on its own way once again.

So, whereas the two processes run concurrently both before and after the rendezvous, whichever process arrives first has to wait for the other and then, during the rendezvous, the calling process waits while the accepting process executes the body of the *ACCEPT* statement.

Points to Note

Some major points to note about Ada rendezvous are the following (these largely summarise the above discussion except for the last two points which are additional features of the syntax):

- **Symmetrical waiting:** Whoever arrives first (at ACCEPT statement or at calling statement) will wait for the other.

- **Mutual exclusion:** Only one calling process at a time is allowed to rendezvous with the accepting process. Other calling processes must wait for subsequent rendezvous.

- **Liveness and fairness:** Because processes calling the same entry name are queued in strictly chronological order, deadlock and starvation of calling processes cannot occur and, furthermore, all calling processes are treated fairly with respect to the rendezvous.

- **Similarity to procedure calls:** To the calling process (only), a rendezvous looks just like a procedure call. In fact, the calling process need not know whether a particular call is implemented as a normal procedure (i.e. executed as part of the same process) or as a rendezvous with another process.

- **Multiple definition:** The same entry name may be defined in more than one *ACCEPT* statement (all must be in the same process, however). A particular definition becomes effective only when that *ACCEPT* statement is reached during execution of the process.

- **Arrays of entry names:** An array of entry names may be declared, in which case an *ACCEPT* statement defines only one element of this array. The particular element is specified by the array index value supplied, which is computable and so may vary from execution to execution.

9.2 SELECT Statement

The *ACCEPT* statement on its own is of limited usefulness. What is often needed is to be able to specify that the accepting process should *not* wait in an *ACCEPT* statement if no-one is calling that entry name. The *SELECT* statement provides a mechanism for doing just this, and more. Its form is shown in Fig. 9.1.

```
SELECT
     WHEN condition1 =>
          ACCEPT name1(arguments1) DO body1 END name1; extra1
OR
     WHEN condition2 =>
          ACCEPT name2(arguments2) DO body2 END name2; extra2
OR
     ⋮
ELSE
     extra
END SELECT;
```

Figure 9.1: Form of the Ada *SELECT* statement.

The condition following the keyword *WHEN* is any boolean expression and is called a 'guard' on the *ACCEPT* statement. Each of the tokens *extra1*, *extra2*,..., *extra* denotes any sequence of statements. The parts of the *ACCEPT* statement itself are as defined earlier.

Execution of SELECT

The semantics of the complete *SELECT* statement are as follows:

1. If there is no *ACCEPT* statement for which both (i) the guard is true and (ii) there is a calling process waiting for that rendezvous, then execute the *ELSE* part (i.e. the sequence of statements following the *ELSE*, denoted by the token *extra*).

2. The *ELSE* part is optional. If it is not present, and at least one of the guards is true, then wait until one of the *ACCEPT* statements (following a guard which is true) can be executed. If there is no *ELSE* part and none of the guards is true, then an execution error is generated (Ada specifies how such errors are handled, but we do not give details here).

3. If there is exactly one *ACCEPT* for which both (i) the guard is true and (ii) there is a calling process waiting for that rendezvous; then execute that *ACCEPT* followed by the *extra* after it.

4. If there are two or more *ACCEPT* statements for which both (i) the guard is true and (ii) there is a calling process waiting for that rendezvous, then select any one of these and execute it, followed by the *extra* after it. It is not specified which of these rendezvous is selected.

Thus the *SELECT* statement is a means of selecting one or none of several rendezvous for execution, depending upon given conditions and whether or not any processes are calling those rendezvous. Never more than one rendezvous is executed within a single execution of the *SELECT* statement. The *extra* following the rendezvous (or in the *ELSE* part) is not part of the rendezvous and runs concurrently with the calling process. The *WHEN condition* => part of the syntax which precedes an *ACCEPT* statement is optional. If omitted, *WHEN TRUE* => is assumed (i.e. the guard is always true).

9.3   Producer–Consumer with Rendezvous

As an example of the use of rendezvous in Ada, consider once again the producer–consumer problem using a bounded buffer algorithm. As in Modula-2, we define procedures *append* and *take*, only these are now implemented as entries to a third process which is used solely to handle the buffering. The use of *append* and *take* (i.e. the way they are called) remains the same as if they were normal procedures, however.

Typically this process would be made into a package (i.e. module) of its own with the only exports being the procedures *append* and *take*, just as we did in Modula-2. The three processes are shown in Fig. 9.2 in a pseudocode which is very close to Ada.

The bodies of *append* and *take* are somewhat similar to the Modula-2 pseudocode given in Fig. 8.3. The main differences are to do with the syntax of the tests for the buffer being full or empty and the wait statements. The buffer process starts running concurrently with the producer and consumer processes, but only to carry out its initialisation statements which set the buffer variables to represent an empty buffer. This initialisation occurs at the beginning of the process, in contrast to the Modula-2 solution, in which it occurred textually at the end of the monitor.

The main part of the process is an infinite loop which consists of a single *SELECT* statement which will allow one of two rendezvous to be selected (there is no other possibility as there is no *ELSE* part). The *append* rendezvous

Producer Task

```
WHILE TRUE DO
    compute(data);
    append(data)
OD
```

Consumer Task

```
initialisation;
WHILE TRUE DO
    take(data);
    use(data)
OD
```

Buffer Task

```
buffer : ARRAY [0..sizeofbuffer – 1] OF anytype;
head, tail : 0..sizeofbuffer – 1;
occupancy : 0..sizeofbuffer;

occupancy := 0;
head := 0;
tail := 0;
WHILE TRUE DO
    SELECT
        WHEN occupancy < sizeofbuffer =>
            ACCEPT append(data : IN anytype)
            DO buffer[tail] := data END append;
            occupancy := occupancy + 1;
            tail := tail + 1 MOD sizeofbuffer
    OR
        WHEN occupancy > 0 =>
            ACCEPT take(data : OUT anytype)
            DO data := buffer[head] END take;
            occupancy := occupancy – 1;
            head := head + 1 MOD sizeofbuffer
    END SELECT
OD
```

Figure 9.2: Producer–consumer in Ada pseudocode using a bounded buffer algorithm.

can be selected only if the buffer is not full (*occupancy<sizeofbuffer*) and the producer is waiting at a call to *append*. The *take* rendezvous can be selected only if the buffer is not empty (*occupancy>0*) and if the consumer is waiting at a call to *take*. If both these conditions hold then either the *append* or the *take* rendezvous may be executed and it is not specified which will be selected (the implementation may choose either). If neither condition holds, then neither rendezvous can be executed. As there is no *ELSE* part, the buffer process will go to sleep until one or other rendezvous can be executed (an error condition cannot arise because it can never be the case that both guards are false).

Points to Note

- Because *append* and *take* are both part of the same process, they are automatically mutually exclusive (two parts of the same process can never be executed concurrently). Hence the updating of *head, tail* and *occupancy* need not be put inside the body of the *ACCEPT* statements to make them mutually exclusive. The copying of the data into or out of the buffer must be included in the body of the *ACCEPT* only because that is the only place in which the variable *data* is in scope (as in a procedure definition, the formal arguments are accessible only within the body of the *ACCEPT*).

- The Ada solution may be slightly less efficient on non-distributed systems than the Modula 2 solution, because of the additional process.

- On a distributed processor system, the programmer will normally be required to specify on which processor each process will run. The buffer process could share a processor with either producer or consumer, or it could be put on a processor of its own. The relative merits of these three configurations will depend upon the hardware performance characteristics (and on the Ada compiler).

9.4   Other Concurrency Features in Ada

Ada has several less important constructs to aid in concurrent programming, over and above those already described. These include a delay statement that causes a process to be suspended for a given real-time delay (or longer). There are also two other forms of the *SELECT* statement that are used with entry calls instead of with *ACCEPT* statements. The first of these enables an entry call to be made conditional upon the rendezvous being possible immediately. The second enables an entry call to be made conditional upon the rendezvous being accepted within a specified time.

There are also statements to terminate and abort processes and to allocate priorities to processes. The interested reader is referred to texts on Ada for detailed descriptions of these and other Ada features (see Further Reading).

9.5 Rendezvous in Other Languages

A different form of rendezvous is used in CSP and Occam. CSP (Hoare, 1978 and 1985) is an acronym for Communicating Sequential Processes and is a language introduced for the theoretical purposes of expressing, analysing and verifying concurrent programming algorithms using message passing for communication and synchronisation. CSP has had and continues to have a considerable influence on the theory of concurrent programming, although it has never been used for significant practical applications. A large amount of theoretical work is done in CSP and the language is mathematically well-founded (i.e. the definition of the language is mathematically precise and complete enabling rigorous mathematical analysis of CSP programs).

The language Occam (Inmos Ltd., 1988a), on the other hand, was designed specifically for use with distributed systems in general and the Inmos Transputer (Inmos Ltd., 1988b) in particular. It uses a rendezvous mechanism which is very closely modelled on that in CSP.

In both these languages, rendezvous are expressed quite differently from the procedure-like rendezvous of Ada. Instead, the Occam (or CSP) programmer must declare a *channel* between two processes which wish to communicate with each other. Each channel is given a name. Many different channels may be declared, but each is unidirectional (the process at one end of the channel always sends messages while the process at the other end always receives). Of course, bidirectional communication between processes is easily implemented by creating two channels, one in each direction. Special statements are used to send and receive messages. These statements specify the channel down which the message is to be sent (or received) and the content of the message (or the variable in which the message will be placed). Communication is fully synchronous in that the message is not actually sent until both sender and receiver are ready; i.e. whichever of the send and receive statements is reached first must wait for the other so both can execute simultaneously.

Although the underlying rendezvous mechanism is basically the same in Occam as it is in Ada, the appearance of Occam programs can be somewhat different from Ada programs that do the same thing, simply because of the different syntax for the rendezvous.

9.6   Exercises

Exercise 9.1 In a real-time system, mutual exclusion is to be implemented via routines called *pre* and *post*, which are used to bracket the critical section as follows:

```
      ...
pre();
critical section;
post();
      ...
```

Write algorithms in pseudocode to implement the procedures *pre* and *post*, using the Ada rendezvous as the only synchronisation primitive.

How can your solution be extended to allow at least N different classes of critical sections to be handled simultaneously?

Exercise 9.2 A real-time program contains an instance of the readers and writers problem which is programmed using procedures *startread*, *stopread*, *startwrite* and *stopwrite* to implement the appropriate synchronisation protocol on the read and write accesses to the shared data, as follows:

Readers	**Writers**
WHILE TRUE DO	WHILE TRUE DO
startread();	compute(data);
read(data);	startwrite();
stopread();	write(data);
use(data)	stopwrite()
OD	OD

Write pseudocode programs for the four procedures *startread*, *stopread*, *startwrite* and *stopwrite*, using the Ada rendezvous mechanism for synchronisation.

Is your program subject to starvation of either readers or writers?

Exercise 9.3 A number of processes compete for the use of magnetic tape drives. Each process calls *claim(d)* to claim a tape drive. The logical device number of a free tape drive is returned in *d* (the procedure does not return until a drive is available). When the process finishes using that tape drive it calls *release(d)*, with the same value of *d*, to release the drive for use by other processes.

Write pseudocode implementations of *claim* and *release*, using the Ada rendezvous for synchronisation.

Exercise 9.4 Write an Ada pseudocode program for the Dining Philosophers Problem, avoiding deadlock.

Is starvation possible with your program?

Chapter 10

Mascot Real-Time Design

This chapter is rather different from the preceding ones in that its subject is neither a particular concurrent programming problem such as the producer–consumer problem, nor a programming language such as Ada or Modula-2. Instead, it is concerned with the higher levels of program design, glossing over many implementation details. There are many different approaches to software design, the particular method that we will study here is one which is aimed especially at the design of real-time embedded systems.

Mascot was developed by the U.K. Ministry of Defence and is their preferred method for real-time software development. Mascot is an acronym for 'Modular Approach to Software Construction, Operation and Test'. It is intended to aid not only software design in the narrow sense, but also the complete software life cycle including aspects of the overall management of large real-time software projects. Nevertheless, the central core of the Mascot method is a set of conventions for drawing design diagrams, and we devote most of this chapter to describing those conventions. The other parts of the method are specified in much less detail and are less specifically orientated to concurrent programming.

The latest version is known as Mascot 3 (U.K. Ministry of Defence, 1987) when necessary to distinguish it from the earlier versions. This is the version that will be described in this chapter.

Although Mascot has sometimes been described as a formal method, it is really best classed as semi-formal. It defines only a framework in which to work and is by no means a complete design language, but gives the user considerable latitude over many details of the approach and style he wishes to use. Nevertheless, as with any formal system, it does impose constraints upon what the designer can and cannot do.

Mascot itself is programming language independent, although the software tools that have been developed for use with it are often implemented for particular languages only (with early versions of Mascot the language was usually

Coral 66, with Mascot 3 it is usually Ada).

10.1 The Mascot Method

Although the core of Mascot is the set of conventions for drawing design diagrams, the broader aspects of the Mascot method will be outlined first to set the scene. The overall philosophy is that hierarchical modular decomposition using a top-down approach is a good way to proceed and the best way to represent the complete design. The design itself is thought of as a network of concurrent processes which is represented by a type of data flow diagram.

In Mascot jargon, the word *template* is used instead of *module*, to emphasise re-usability. In most large software systems designs, many templates will be unique and used only once, but other templates will be of more general applicability and can be re-used in other parts of the same system or in other systems. Libraries of templates may be created also.

The Mascot method recommends six main stages of software development. In broad outline, these are as follows:

Stage 1   **External Requirements and Constraints** — a complete requirements analysis which may be subdivided into hardware and software system requirements, system test requirements, etc. Mascot does not prescribe the detailed method to be used here, but recommends any method compatible with the general principles of Mascot (e.g. CORE, JSD, SSADM).

Stage 2   **Design Proposal** — a top-level design proposal based on the software requirements identified in Stage 1.

Stage 3   **Network Decomposition** — a more detailed design of the software as a network of concurrent processes which interact with each other via data flow paths. The Mascot design diagram conventions are aimed primarily at this stage of software development, although they are very useful also in Stage 2 and again in Stage 4, and to a much lesser extent in the other stages.

Stage 4   **Element Decomposition** — the lowest level of design before programming, in which each sequential process is designed in more detail.

Stage 5   **Program Definition** — the programming of the templates (i.e. modules) specified in the previous stages. Any conventional program design technique may be used here (Mascot does not prescribe the method to be used for the detailed design of relatively small sequential sections of the program).

Stage 6   **Test System Definition** — the integration and testing of the complete software system.

Documentation is seen as a vital component throughout all six stages of software development, but no recommendations of particular techniques or standards for documentation are made. Any style of documentation is acceptable provided it is well structured and adequately comprehensive. The creation of the various volumes of documentation should proceed along with the corresponding stages of the software development.

10.2   Mascot Design Diagrams

Mascot design diagrams are essentially a design language in which to create and express the network designs of Stage 3. These design diagrams are relatively formal in the sense that the rules for drawing them are reasonably well defined and complete and the diagrams do not incorporate arbitrary natural language explanation (as is the case in many other diagramming conventions). Instead, all the important elements of Mascot diagrams are named and a full specification and explanatory description of the named elements is contained in the accompanying documentation which should be created along with the diagrams.

Mascot 3 also defines a textual representation of these diagrams which is intended primarily as a means of storing the diagrams in a machine readable database and communicating them in a machine independent form. It also contains somewhat more detailed information than can be included in the diagrams, in particular the names of interface routines and the types of their parameters. A variety of software tools are commercially available to support computer-aided software design using the Mascot conventions, and these mechanically translate the diagrams from graphical to textual representation and vice versa. The textual representation is of no particular interest, so we largely ignore it in the following description of Mascot design diagrams.

10.2.1   Basic Symbols

Mascot design diagrams are essentially a type of data flow diagram. There are two main outlines used: the *activity*, which is Mascot jargon for a process; and the *intercommunication data area* (IDA) which is, as the name suggests, any sort of shared memory area or buffer. The lines connecting these are known as *paths* and indicate data flow. Paths normally have arrowheads at one or both ends to indicate the direction of data flow. The activities and IDAs are the *components* of the diagram.

The Mascot convention, which is more-or-less consistent with other common data-flow diagramming conventions, is that active elements are denoted by rounded outlines (circles are often used, particularly in cases in which there is very little internal detail to show), while passive elements have rectangular outlines. The precise shape and size of the outlines is not prescribed, but we will draw them as shown in Fig. 10.1.

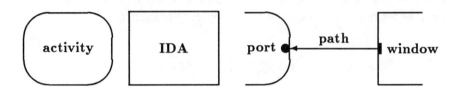

Figure 10.1: Basic symbols used in Mascot design diagrams.

The meaning of the terms *active* and *passive* in this context is rather subtle, but should become clearer shortly when we look at some examples. A path always connects a *port* and a *window*, as shown in Fig. 10.1. Ports (small circular blobs) and windows (narrow rectangular blobs) are always drawn just inside the boundaries of outlines such as those for activities and IDAs. The port denotes the active end of the path and the window the passive end of the path. Only one path may connect to a port, but any number of paths may connect to a window. In simple terms the window represents a set of one or more procedures, while the port represents the calling of these procedures.

Consider now the example shown in Fig. 10.2. This is our old friend the producer–consumer problem: the Mascot design diagram represents the overall structure of a simple bounded-buffer solution to this problem.

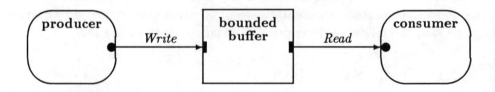

Figure 10.2: Mascot diagram for a producer–consumer system.

In this program, the producer and consumer are processes (i.e. activities) and are therefore represented by activity outlines in the Mascot design diagram. The bounded buffer, on the other hand, is not a process, but a purely passive object and hence shown as an IDA. The path from the producer activity to the bounded buffer IDA which is labelled *Write* can be interpreted as follows. It represents an interface between the two components linked by the path (in this case the producer and the bounded buffer), this interface usually being implemented by procedure calls. The port at the producer end of the path indicates that the producer calls a procedure (or possibly several procedures) which are implemented at the window end of the path, in this case as part of the bounded buffer module. The arrowhead on the path shows that data is passed from producer to bounded buffer.

Access Interfaces

The label on a path is the name of an *access interface*. This denotes the type of path. In the textual form of Mascot, an access interface defines a set of procedure names and the types of their parameters (somewhat like a definition module in Modula-2, but global variables are not allowed). It defines the form of the interface that the path represents, but says nothing about the meaning of the data that will flow down that path. The component containing the port end of the path may call the procedures specified in the access interface, while the component at the window end of the path must provide an implementation of them.

Mascot is more powerful than many programming languages in this respect. It is possible for several distinct paths to be labelled with the same access interface name if the form of communication along these paths is identical. Most programming languages do not allow several distinct instances of the same procedure to be created and then referred to by the same name because it would then be difficult to distinguish them, but in Mascot diagrams the paths are easily distinguished by their different positions in the diagram (see Fig. 10.3, for example).

Returning to our first example in Fig. 10.2, a possible implementation of this would be the Modula-2 program described in Section 8.3. It may help in understanding the Mascot diagram to look at the correspondence with this Modula-2 program (Figs. 8.2 and 8.3). The access interface *Write* consists of the single procedure *append*, which is called by the producer to pass a data record to the bounded buffer. The access interface *Read* consists of the single procedure *take*, which is called by the producer to obtain a data record from the buffer. The bounded buffer IDA is represented in the Modula-2 program by the monitor module *boundedbuffer*, which implements and exports the two procedures *append* and *take*. The definition module for *boundedbuffer* corresponds approximately to the union of the two access interfaces *Write* and *Read* in the Mascot design. In Modula-2, there is only one definition part and it specifies all the exports of the module (amongst other things), while in Mascot these have been split into two distinct access interfaces because they are used quite independently (the producer only calls *append*, while the consumer only calls *take*).

Thus Mascot allows the form of the interfaces between components to be specified rather more accurately and expressively than is possible in Modula-2 (or most other programming languages, for that matter). This does not prevent Modula-2 being used as a programming language for implementing designs expressed in Mascot, however. It simply means that the resulting program does not show all of the high-level structure that was present in the Mascot diagram (in much the same way that object code compiled from any high-level language program lacks much of the structure that was present in the original source program).

One of the main strengths of Mascot is that it uses the principle of information hiding rather more flexibly than it is used in Modula-2 or Ada. If two components are linked by a single path, they communicate only by means of the procedures defined in the access interface for that path. No communication whatsoever is permitted other than that explicitly denoted by paths. However, a single component may have any number of paths interfacing to it (via ports or windows).

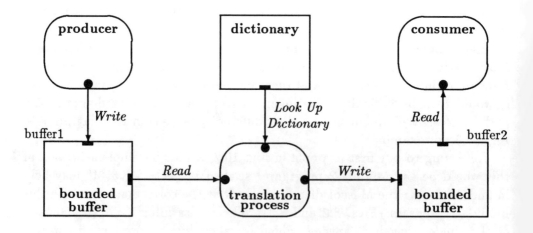

Figure 10.3: Mascot diagram for a system with an extra process between producer and consumer.

A slightly more complex example is shown in Fig. 10.3. Assume that we need to translate the data being passed from the producer to consumer. Suppose, for example, that the data passing from producer to consumer is mainly numerical but contains a sprinkling of English words (as headings or captions, say) which have to be translated into French on a simple transliteration basis. We insert an additional process between the producer and consumer to do the translation, and show the dictionary used for the translation as a distinct component (an IDA because it is passive).

Notice that none of the examples contain paths which directly link activity to activity or IDA to IDA. Mascot insists that an IDA must always be put on any path that would otherwise go directly between two activities, to force the designer to at least think about the mechanism for passing the data between activities and also about the form and structure of the data. In a very large system, different programmers, or even different teams of programmers, may implement different activities and the careful design of the interfaces is very important. Putting an IDA in the path between two activities means that an explicit component (i.e. the IDA) must be defined to handle communication between the activities. Mascot does not permit direct inter-process communication such as occurs with the rendezvous mechanism in Ada.

10.2.2 Hierarchical Design

More complex designs need to be hierarchically structured to avoid excessive complexity in individual diagrams. A special symbol is used in Mascot diagrams to denote a *sub-system*, as shown in Fig. 10.4. This is like the activity symbol, except that its outline is drawn with a double line (or a thick line). Mascot uses such double (or thick) lines elsewhere also to denote composite objects.

Figure 10.4: The sub-system symbol.

A sub-system may encompass any part of a Mascot diagram, except that the sub-system boundary may not cut through components (activities, IDAs and other sub-systems). A sub-system has ports and/or windows on its own boundary via which it communicates with other parts of the system. A complete system is also denoted by the same symbol. The only difference is that a complete system has no ports or windows for external interfacing.

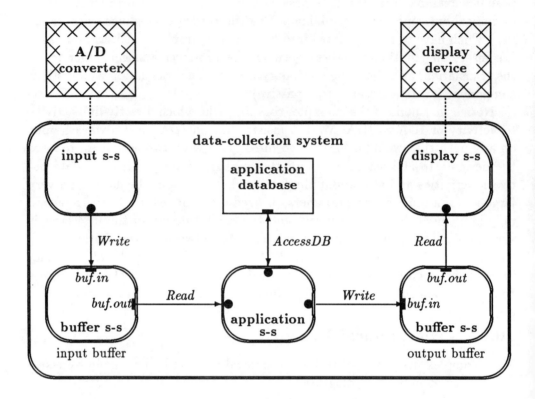

Figure 10.5: Network diagram for a complete data-collection system.

Consider the example shown in Fig. 10.5 which represents a fairly large complete system, as denoted by the large sub-system symbol which encloses everything except the two devices. The name of the complete system, 'data collection system' is written within the boundary of the symbol, as usual. The complete system has no ports or windows on its boundary but, of course, it must have some means of communicating with the outside world. This is shown by the broken lines to the hatched rectangles which represent hardware input/output devices. Alternatively, hardware devices may be denoted by schematic pictorial representations of the devices concerned.

This diagram represents a system which may be quite large in that it contains five sub-systems, which are themselves of as yet unknown complexity. The internal structure of these sub-systems would typically be shown in separate diagrams (as, for example, in Fig. 10.6). Two of these sub-systems are both labelled internally as 'buffer s-s', but labelled externally as 'input buffer' and 'output buffer'. The Mascot convention is that the internal label always denotes the type of object, while the external label denotes the particular instance of that object. Thus, the sub-systems 'input buffer' and 'output buffer' are both of type 'buffer s-s' and hence each provides identical interfaces to the outside world: i.e. the two windows labelled *buf.in* and *buf.out* which provide access interfaces of types *Write* and *Read*, respectively.

Each of the three other sub-systems in the diagram is of a unique type and so there is no need to distinguish the name of the type of object from the name of the particular instance. In this case, the Mascot rule is that the name of the object is shown as an internal label and the external label is omitted.

10.2.3 Sub-system Templates

In the initial stages of a top-down design, the complete system is designed in terms of components which are often sub-systems either because of their complexity, or simply because the designer does not yet want to decide upon their implementation. At a later time, the implementation of each of these sub-systems must be designed. These designs are shown in separate Mascot diagrams known as sub-system templates. Fig. 10.6 shows a template for the buffer sub-system. This template shows the internal structure of both the input buffer and the output buffer because each is of this type.

Notice that the window symbols are repeated where paths to windows (in internal components) pass through the outer boundary. This repetition of the window (or port) symbol enables different names to be used at different levels of the design where necessary or convenient. Normally, all the ports and windows in Mascot diagrams should be named, but it is sometimes not necessary to name everything. In the examples in this chapter, names are often omitted simply because we are not interested in the complete design details of every component used.

Templates for the input and display sub-systems are shown in Fig. 10.7. These contain a new Mascot component outline, which is called a *server* and represented by the D-shaped outline shown in the diagram (the orientation of the outline is arbitrary). Servers are the only components which may interface directly to hardware devices. This interface is not shown as a path, but is represented by a broken line from the rounded end of the server outline to the device outline.

The implementation of such a device interface may be by any of the usual means: ordinary programmed I/O, interrupt driven I/O, memory mapped, etc. In some respects the server looks like a passive component, while in other respects it may have properties that are normally regarded as active. For example, it may contain an interrupt handler which is properly regarded as a process in its own right, yet it is typically not known by the scheduler and

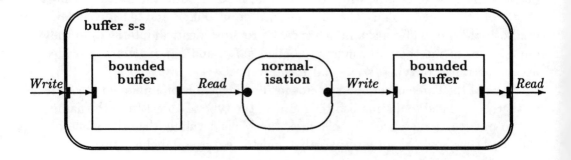

Figure 10.6: Template for the buffer sub-system.

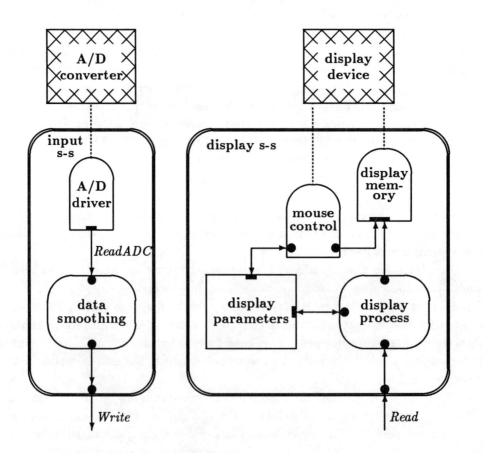

Figure 10.7: Templates for input and display sub-systems.

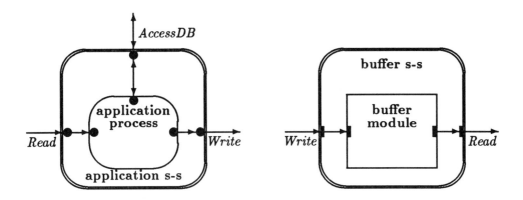

Figure 10.8: Template for application sub-system and alternative template for buffer sub-system.

hence not considered as a normal 'user' process. For this reason, the outline used has both rounded and rectangular corners to indicate the ambivalent active/passive nature of many servers. Servers may contain both ports and windows. Windows are always drawn on the straight side of the 'D' (opposite the curved side), while ports are drawn on either of the two parallel sides.

Two more sub-system templates are shown in Fig. 10.8, one for the application sub-system and the other for an alternative design for the buffer sub-system. Both of these are examples of sub-systems which consist of only a single component each (in one case an activity, in the other an IDA). Indeed, it is possible that a sub-system may be implemented without any components at all. In such degenerate cases it will contain only windows, ports and paths connecting these.

10.2.4 Other Mascot Symbols

Some Mascot implementations (i.e. implementations of software tools for computer aided software design in Mascot) provide further symbols beyond those described so far. The additional symbols include composite activities; composite paths, ports, windows and servers; and a few other special elements. These are not regarded as part of the basic set of Mascot design elements and are not necessary, although they may be convenient, particularly in the design of very large systems.

Composite paths are simply a graphical convention for coalescing a bundle of simple paths between the same two components into a single element in the design diagram (shown as a double line or thick line). Composite paths connect composite ports to composite windows. We do not examine any of

these in detail here; the interested reader is referred to the *Mascot Handbook*
(U.K. Ministry of Defence, 1987).

Composite activities are simply activities for which an internal decomposition is shown. A composite activity is still a single activity (i.e. process)
with a single sequential thread of execution; it is not possible to decompose
an activity into smaller activities. Instead, Mascot provides for decomposition
into modules which are known as *roots* and *sub-roots*. Each composite activity
has exactly one root (corresponding to a main program) and any number of
sub-roots which are connected by *links* (not paths). These links show the calling hierarchy. The root has links to sub-roots, which may have links to further
sub-roots, and so on. Thus the template for a composite activity does not show
data flow as in other parts of the Mascot diagrams, nor does it show control
flow as in conventional flow charts. Instead, it shows the calling hierarchy for
the procedures or modules that make up the activity (e.g. the main program
may call various procedures, which may themselves call other procedures, and
so on).

Earlier versions of Mascot distinguished two types of IDA: *channels* and
pools. A channel is an IDA that is used to pass a stream of data in one direction
only, the bounded buffer in Fig. 10.6 for example. A pool is a more general
form of IDA which may be accessed more-or-less as required; for example, the
dictionary in Fig. 10.3. Some Mascot implementations provide special symbols
for channels and pools which are minor variations of the usual IDA outline.

10.3   Implementation of Mascot Designs

Once a program design has been created in Mascot, it could be coded by hand
into any desired programming language. Computer based support for Mascot
is generally orientated to one or more particular languages only, Ada being a
common choice. Ada is suitable because it provides quite good facilities for the
very type of programming that Mascot is aimed at: real-time embedded systems. If a language without such facilities is used, the Mascot implementation
must provide suitable alternatives itself (concurrent processes, synchronisation
primitives, device drivers and/or the means to write them, etc.).

Most Mascot support systems provide a library of common templates. This
might include the specification and implementation of useful basic components
such as a bounded buffer IDA or a look-up table IDA (typically implemented as
a hash table). Other useful tools include aids to check that the program source
code conforms fully to the Mascot design, aids to testing and monitoring in
real-time environments, and aids to project management and documentation.

Chapter 11

Parallel Processing of Sets of Data

11.1 Introduction

The classical basic problems of concurrent programming such as the producer–consumer problem or the readers and writers problem have been distilled from the accumulated experience of several decades of programming real-time applications. In these problems, it is assumed that the programmer has already decided how to structure the program as several concurrent processes. The problem is then one of handling the synchronisation and communication between these processes. This is a realistic approach for real-time programs because the process structure is often suggested by the real-time constraints present in the problem definition.

For example, if it is required to drive a computer output device concurrently with other tasks, the obvious solution is to create a process which is synchronised to that device; i.e. it initiates the output of a record, then goes to sleep until the device has completed the output and is free to accept the next output record, whereupon the cycle is repeated.

In many parallel processing applications, however, there are no real-time constraints and nothing in the definition of the problem to suggest an obvious way to compose the program out of a number of concurrent processes. Parallel processors are used simply to gain better performance than can be achieved on uniprocessor machines. Any application for which processing speed is important can be a candidate for parallel implementation.

In this chapter, we look at some fundamental techniques for splitting up a processing task into many separate sub-tasks which can be run in parallel. Both multiprocessing (concurrent processes with shared memory) and distributed processing (concurrent processes with message passing) styles of

157

parallelism are considered. Both of these categories fall into what are often described as MIMD (multiple instruction, multiple data) architectures. The other common type of parallel architectures, the SIMD (single instruction, multiple data) architectures, are not considered at all because these machines will run only a single process at a time and achieve their parallelism in a completely different way (by performing exactly the same sequence of operations on several different sets of data simultaneously).

To complicate matters further, the division into multiprocessor and distributed processor architectures is only part of the story. Small details of the architecture of the particular parallel computer in use can have a large effect upon the choice of algorithm to solve a particular problem. All conventional uniprocessor computers are very similar in their organisation, following closely the von Neumann model of a computer. Hence an algorithm which works well on one machine will generally work equally well on other machines. Unfortunately, this is often not the case for parallel computers. Algorithms which work well on one parallel machine may be unsatisfactory on another type of parallel architecture even if it falls into the same general category.

These differences are largely glossed over in this chapter. We confine our discussion to algorithms which are very general and fundamental, and which can be adapted to run satisfactorily on a variety of different parallel architectures within the broad categories specified. They are often quite simple and even obvious (particularly with hindsight)!

Nevertheless, the most simple and obvious algorithms are often the most useful and important. Programming is almost invariably learnt using purely sequential techniques for uniprocessor machines and the great majority of today's programmers have little knowledge or experience of even the most basic parallel techniques. This chapter is an attempt to fill some of those gaps and provide a starting point for the study of more specialised parallel algorithms.

We will not attempt a detailed performance analysis of the algorithms discussed, because there are too many factors which can influence their performance. Meaningful performance analysis requires more specific details of the particular parallel architecture on which the algorithms are to be run, together with more details of how the algorithms are to be implemented on that architecture. Instead, the discussion is kept at a fairly general level that is applicable to a wide variety of parallel computers.

11.1.1 Sets of Independent Computations

The basic abstract problem we consider is that of doing a set of independent computations in parallel. This would appear at first sight to be completely trivial because, if the computations are independent, we can simply give different computations to different processors and let them run concurrently. It is not quite as simple as that, however, because we assume that the data is initially all in the one place (and hence we need to decide how to distribute it among the processors), and we require the results to be collected together in one place also.

We use the following program as the archetype of this basic problem:

```
FOR ALL i IN 1..n DO
    y[i] := f(x[i])
OD
```

where the construct

$$FOR\ ALL\ i\ IN\ 1..n\ DO\ .\ .\ .\ OD$$

is like a normal *FOR* loop except that the order in which the values of i are taken must be irrelevant (i.e. the implementation may use any order that it finds convenient).

The array x contains a set of data values, the function f defines the computation to be carried out on each, the set of results being put into the array y. The computation in this case is assumed to be a pure function without side-effects. In other words, the computation of $f(x[i])$ does not cause the state of the machine to be affected in any way; no variables are altered and no input or output occurs. Nor does the function f depend upon any data other than its argument (it must not access any variables other than its argument and local variables used as work space).

Thus the problem can be expressed in words as follows. Given n data items, from each compute a result which depends upon that data item alone. Clearly, in such a situation, all n computations can be performed independently and in parallel. In general, the function f may be as complicated as required and each data item, $x[i]$, and each result, $y[i]$, may be complex data structures of arbitrary size.

A simple example of a program which fits into this category is a payroll calculation in which the pay of a large number of different employees is computed independently for each. The value of i denotes the particular employee. The data item $x[i]$ denotes a record which contains components such as the employee's rate of pay, number of hours worked, tax rate, etc. The result $y[i]$ denotes another record containing the employee's computed total pay for the week, tax deducted, net pay, etc. The computation for each employee can be performed completely independently of the computations for all the other employees.

With Limited Side-Effects

A more general problem is one in which some limited side-effects are allowed. The term 'side-effects' means any action that causes a variable to be changed, in circumstances in which that variable does not appear explicitly on the left-hand side of an assignment statement. Simple examples of side-effects are incrementing a counter (to count the total number of data items, say) or printing a message for each data item processed. Side-effects are thus merely hidden assignment statements, including input and output (which are effectively assignments to the state of the peripheral device concerned; e.g. output to a printer changes the state of the paper: before printing it is blank, after printing it is filled with printed characters).

We take the following program as our archetype, in which the side-effects that we permit have been made explicit in the pure function *sideEffects* (both *f* and *sideEffects* are pure functions without side-effects of their own):

```
state := initialState;
FOR ALL i IN 1..n DO
    y[i] := f(x[i]);
    state := sideEffects(x[i],state)
OD
```

In practice, one procedure would probably be written for the function *f* together with its side-effects, which we have separated out here as the two pure functions, *f* and *sideEffects*. Note that the permissible side-effects depend only upon $x[i]$ and *state* (which denotes any set of global variables, but does not include x and y). Hence each separate computation (for one value of i) still depends upon only one data item, $x[i]$. We exclude situations in which each computation uses several data items, unless the programs can be rewritten into the form shown above.

The order in which *sideEffects(x[i])* is computed (for different values of i) is assumed not to matter. This does not necessarily mean that the final value of *state* will always be the same irrespective of the order in which the computations are performed. If it does differ, however, the differences do not matter. In our archetypal program, *sideEffects* is computed only once for each value of i and, in general, it will be important to preserve this property in any implementation.

A simple example of a problem falling into this category would be the payroll calculation described earlier, but extended so that the total amount paid to all employees for the week is also computed. This falls into the category of a permissible side-effect, i.e. one that can be expressed in the form shown in the archetype program above. Every time another employee's pay is computed, a variable representing the total pay is incremented by that amount. This operation is easily put into the required form: *state* is the variable in which the total pay is accumulated, and *sideEffects* simply computes the employee's pay from the data for that employee ($x[i]$) and adds it to the current value of the total pay (*state*).

Similarly, if a print-out is produced with an entry for each employee, this would also be classed as a side-effect. Even though it may be the main result required, we categorise it as a side-effect to the parts of the computation which can be done completely independently for each employee. This apparent perversity in terminology is simply because the parts of the computation which are totally independent for each employee are the parts that are easy to compute in parallel, and hence it is convenient to think about them first, as if they were the most important parts of the computation.

11.2   Multiprocessing Solutions

A multiprocessing algorithm consists of a number of processes which communicate via shared variables. In an ideal implementation of such an algorithm, each process would run on a different processor and the shared variables would be implemented in a shared memory unit. In practice, it is often necessary to have several processes sharing the same processor (those processes are time-shared on that processor in the usual way), simply because there are not enough processors to have only one process on each. The correct functioning of the algorithms described here is not affected by how they are distributed across the available processors, although clearly the performance will often be much better if processes do not have to share processors.

Consider the problem described in the previous section: that of carrying out a set of independent computations, which was subdivided into the two cases: (i) with limited side-effects and (ii) without side-effects. The specification tells us that the order in which the computations are done on the data items is unimportant. The results (i.e. the array y) must be required for some purpose, however, and that will involve reading elements of the array y whenever the results are required. As the value of $y[i]$ need not be computed until it is required (and, furthermore, if it is never required there is no need to compute it at all), we require the programmer wishing to use the result $y[i]$ to do so by using a specially written function $gety(i)$ which simply supplies the value of $y[i]$.

This function, $gety$, must be used whenever access to $y[i]$ is required. The advantage of using such a function is that we can implement it so that the first time it is called for a particular value of i, it computes the value of $y[i]$ from $x[i]$, while on subsequent calls it can simply read the value of $y[i]$ which was

gety(i)

```
BEGIN
    IF NOT  computed[i]
    THEN
        y[i] :=  f(x[i]);
        computed[i] := TRUE
    FI;
    RETURN  y[i]
END
```

Shared: *x : ARRAY [1..n] OF anytype1 (initially filled with the data)*
          y : ARRAY [1..n] OF anytype2 (initially undefined)
          computed : ARRAY [1..n] OF boolean (initially all FALSE)

Figure 11.1: First-come first-served algorithm for a set of independent computations without side-effects.

computed earlier. The multiprocessing algorithms which we now describe all follow this approach and hence each is expressed in the form of an algorithm for the function *gety*. This function may be called at any time by any processes that wish to use the results of our computation of the array *y*.

11.2.1   First-Come First-Served, Without Side-Effects

If there are no side-effects, it does not matter if we allow several different processes to perform the same computation simultaneously (i.e. they all simultaneously compute $f(x[i])$ with the same value of i). This may occur if several processes call $gety(i)$ with the same value of i, and at about the same time. An algorithm for *gety* which allows this is shown in Fig. 11.1. It uses a flag, *computed[i]*, to indicate whether or not the value of $y[i]$ has already been computed. The arrays *x*, *y* and *computed* must be located in shared memory, but the computation of $f(x[i])$ may be carried out entirely within the local memory of the processor concerned.

In this and subsequent algorithms, operations which must be indivisible (atomic) are shown in small thick-ruled boxes. The flag *computed[i]* is *TRUE* only when the value of $f(x[i])$ has been computed and saved in $y[i]$. If *computed[i]* is *FALSE* it indicates that the value of $y[i]$ cannot be relied upon, although its computation may be in progress (possibly on more than one processor). As every processor which computes $f(x[i])$ should get the same value, it does not matter if several of them each assign this value to $y[i]$. Even if $f(x[i])$ is indeterminate (i.e. it may give one of several possible values and we do not know, in advance, which one), this method may still be satisfactory, provided that it does not matter if different calls of $gety(i)$ can give different values.

If the function is indeterminate, so that different values of $y[i]$ could be assigned by different processes, all accesses to $y[i]$ must be performed as atomic operations (as shown in Fig. 11.1). This will also be necessary if a particular value of $y[i]$ can be represented internally in the computer in more than one way. If two processes simultaneously attempt to assign different bit patterns to $y[i]$ (either different representations of the same value, or different values because the function is indeterminate) and the accesses are not atomic, then the result could be an incorrect value for $y[i]$.

If the function is determinate (always gives the same value for the same argument) and the representation of every value is unique, then the requirement that the accesses to $y[i]$ be indivisible is no longer necessary.

11.2.2 First-Come First-Served, With Side-Effects

If side-effects are involved, it is necessary to ensure that each computation is done once only (for example, if a message is printed during the computation, or if a counter is incremented, then this must be done exactly once for each data item).

Our previous algorithm must be modified so that we do not allow a process to even start the computation once another process has started. For this purpose, another array of flags, called *start*, is used. This array is located in shared memory, along with x, y and *computed*. The algorithm is shown in Fig. 11.2. Note that an indivisible exchange instruction is used in the third line of this algorithm. It is not difficult to modify the algorithm to use test-and-set or other special indivisible instructions instead.

If the side-effects are such that it is essential that every value of the array y must be computed (e.g. to generate a print-out for the complete file) even if that element of y is not required anywhere else, then the programmer must ensure that $gety(i)$ is called for all values of i. If necessary, a process can be written which simply calls $gety(i)$ for each i in turn, and ignores the values returned. Of course, to improve performance, it may be better to write p processes (to run on different processors), each of which calls $gety(i)$ for a different set of n/p values of i (see the examples in Section 11.2.4).

gety(i)

```
BEGIN
     started := TRUE;
     started :=: start[i];                    {exchange}
     IF NOT started
     THEN
          y[i] := f(x[i]);
          state := sideEffects(x[i],state);
          computed[i] := TRUE
     ELSE
          WHILE NOT  computed[i]  DO OD
     FI;
     RETURN y[i]
END
```

Shared: *x : ARRAY [1..n] OF anytype1 (initially filled with the data)*
          y : ARRAY [1..n] OF anytype2 (initially undefined)
          computed : ARRAY [1..n] OF boolean (initially all FALSE)
          start : ARRAY [1..n] OF boolean (initially all FALSE)
          state : anytype3 (initialised as required)

Figure 11.2: First-come first-served algorithm for a set of independent computations with limited side-effects.

11.2.3   Partition by Location

In the first-come first-served algorithms (both with and without side-effects) the computation of a particular item may end up being done by any process. It depends solely upon which process gets to that item first. Now, in many circumstances, it may be much more efficient if the processes can be designed so that a particular data item will be computed by a particular process and no other. An example of such a situation is given later. For the moment, we simply assume that we wish to ensure that for each data item one particular process carries out the computation for that item. We assume that a function h is given such that $h(x[i])$ is the process number (an integer in the range $1..k$) of the process which must perform the computation on $x[i]$. The current process number is denoted by *processNumber* in the algorithm, as shown in Fig. 11.3.

In this case, there is no chance of two or more processes attempting the

gety(i)

```
BEGIN
     IF NOT  computed[i]
     THEN
          IF h(i,x[i]) = processNumber
          THEN
               y[i] := f(x[i]);
               state := sideEffects(x[i],state);
                computed[i] := TRUE
          ELSE
               WHILE NOT  computed[i]  DO OD
          FI
     FI;
     RETURN y[i]
END
```

Shared: *x : ARRAY [1..n] OF anytype1 (initially filled with data)*
         y : ARRAY [1..n] OF anytype2 (initially undefined)
         computed : ARRAY [1..n] OF boolean (initially all FALSE)
         state : anytype3 (initialise as required)

Figure 11.3: Partition by location algorithm for a set of independent computations with side-effects.

same computation simultaneously because we specify precisely which process will do each computation. Of course, this has the disadvantage that if a particular process requires the value of $y[i]$, and it has not yet been calculated, then that process must wait until the correct process computes it (in the first two algorithms given, it would simply go ahead and compute the value itself). Care must also be taken to ensure that each process that is responsible for the computation of $y[i]$ for a particular set of values of i does indeed compute all those values. If it omits any it may cause the permanent blocking of other processes which are waiting to use those values.

11.2.4 Examples

We consider now two simple problems involving the processing of English text, the solutions to which illustrate the multiprocessing techniques described earlier. The first problem is to sort the letters in an English word into alphabetical order and do this in parallel on a number of different words. The second problem is to find all the different words in a piece of English text and the number of times each occurs, the results being printed out in decreasing order of frequency.

These examples are illustrative of a very wide class of similar problems. In many problems requiring the processing of files of records, it is easy to identify at least part of the problem in which computations are carried out essentially independently on the different records. A certain amount of interdependence can be handled easily if the program can be structured in such a way that it falls within our definition of allowable 'side-effects'.

Example 1: Sorting Character Strings

The Problem — The shared memory contains an array of character strings, each being an English word or phrase. It is required to print these words in the order stored, each being followed by its characters sorted into alphabetical order (preserving duplicate characters), e.g. the, eht, passage, aaegpss, consists, cinossst, . . .

A computer with k processors which can all access a shared memory is available.

A Solution — There are no side-effects in computing the sorted character string for each word (ignoring, for the moment, the problem of printing the results), so any of the three methods described earlier would be suitable. The first method is simple and effective, but can be made even more efficient in many cases by organising things so that one process runs through computing all the records in order, printing the results as it goes, while a second process simultaneously runs through and computes records $n/k+1..2n/k$, a third process does records $2n/k+1..3n/k$, and so on, where n is the number of records (i.e. English words) and k is the number of processes (each intended to be run on a separate processor).

Then, assuming it takes about the same length of time to compute each record, each process will compute n/k records. The first process should find that all records have already been computed by the time it reaches record number n/k (which is where the second process started from). If the time to compute each record varies markedly, then the algorithm will still work correctly, but it may run a bit more slowly.

The algorithm is shown in Fig. 11.4. The array *word* contains the data words, while the sorted character strings are stored in the array *sortedWord*. The function *sort* sorts a character string into alphabetical order. This sorting is carried out within a single process, so conventional sorting methods may be used. Note that *getSortedWord* is not a process, but simply a function that is called by each of the p processes.

Process 1

```
FOR i := 1 TO n DO
    print(word[i]);
    print(getSortedWord(i))
OD
```

Process p, p=2..k

```
FOR i := (p-1)*n/k+1 TO p*n/k
DO getSortedWord(i) OD
```

getSortedWord(i:1..n)

```
BEGIN
    IF NOT  computed[i]
    THEN
            sortedWord[i] :=  sort(word[i]);

            computed[i] := TRUE
    FI;
    RETURN  sortedWord[i]
END
```

Shared: *word : ARRAY [1..n] OF string; (the words to be processed)*
              sortedWord : ARRAY [1..n] OF string; (initially undefined)
              computed : ARRAY [1..n] OF boolean; (initially all FALSE)

Figure 11.4: Algorithm for the parallel sorting of character strings on a multiprocessor.

Implementing the accesses to *sortedWord[i]* as indivisible operations may be non-trivial as *sortedWord[i]* is likely to be implemented as a character string of arbitrary length and hence not represented in a single word of memory. It will usually be necessary to use a mutual exclusion protocol to implement these accesses as critical sections.

This problem is not totally realistic because the processing time to sort the letters of a typical English word into order is very small. On many parallel computer systems the overheads involved in the parallel algorithm would outweigh the savings achieved. Nevertheless, it is easy to imagine a situation in which a great deal more processing is required on each separate data item and, in such cases, parallel implementation could lead to very significant savings in time.

Example 2: Counting Word Frequencies

The Problem — The shared memory contains an array of character strings, each being an English word. It is required to count the number of times each different word occurs, and print a table of words and the number of occurrences of each, in decreasing order of occurrence.

A computer with k independent processors accessing a shared memory is available.

A Solution — In this case the computation for each word is not independent as we need to identify words which are repeated and count how many times each occurs. The order of processing the words is not relevant, however, and we can create a side-effect to see if a word has occurred before and increment a counter for it. We keep a table of the different words found so far with the number of occurrences of each. This table is updated every time another word is processed. It is the *state* variable of our archetypal program.

We can split the processing of each word into two parts: (i) compute a hash value for the word and from this compute a processor number, (ii) update the table of different words and their occurrences. The table of different words and occurrences can then be partitioned across the processors (each part may be kept in local memory of the processor concerned). For this to work, the processor number must be a function of the word itself. Thus identical words will always be handled by the same processor (in fact, all words that give the same hash value will also be handled by the same processor). We use a hashing function of the word to obtain the processor number, and another hashing function can be used to create a hash table of different words and the number of occurrences of each, to be stored in the local memory of that processor.

We partition the hash table in this way because, on most multiprocessor systems, access to local memory is likely to be more efficient than access to shared memory (simply because frequent contention for shared memory is inefficient: if several processors simultaneously attempt access, some will be made to wait). A general aim for almost all multiprocessor algorithms is to keep the number of accesses to shared memory to a minimum (or to a sufficiently low figure that contention for shared memory is not significant).

When all the words have been processed, each processor can then sort its own part of the table of different words and occurrences, before writing the sorted list back into shared memory. Finally, one processor can merge the sorted lists and print the results. The algorithm is given in Fig. 11.5.

In this algorithm, the flag *computed[i]* is set to *TRUE* when both the hash

Process p, p=1..k

```
FOR i := 1 TO n DO
    IF NOT  computed[i]
    THEN
         hashvalue[i] := hash(word[i]);
         procno[i] := khash(word[i]);
          computed[i] := TRUE
    FI;
    IF procno[i] = p
    THEN
         IF word[i] is in hash table
         THEN add 1 to associated count
         ELSE enter word[i] into hash table with count of 1
         FI
    FI
OD;
sort hash table into required order;
write sorted table into shared memory;
IF p = 1
THEN
    WHILE other processes are still running DO OD;
    merge the sorted tables and print results
FI
```

Shared: *word : ARRAY [1..n] OF string; (the data words)*
hashvalue : ARRAY [1..n] OF integer; (initially undefined)
procno : ARRAY [1..n] OF integer; (initially undefined)
computed : ARRAY [1..n] OF boolean (initially all FALSE)
arrays for storing the sorted results

Local: *the hash table*

Figure 11.5: Parallel algorithm for counting word frequencies on a multiprocessor.

value has been computed and stored in *hashvalue[i]* and the processor number has been computed and stored in *procno[i]*. The functions *hash* and *khash* may be any suitable hashing functions. Each is assumed to always give the same representation of its result when called with the same argument value (otherwise the assignments to *hashvalue[i]* and *procno[i]* must be atomic).

The latter part of the algorithm has been described at very high level as it can be entirely conventional as each local hash table is entirely within one process and so requires no parallel processing techniques, and the merging and printing is carried out by Process 1 only, so again involves no parallel processing techniques.

The test to see if all other processes are finished is easy. Simply keep an array of boolean flags, one for each process, which are all initialised to TRUE. The last statement of each process sets its flag to FALSE. Then a logical OR of all the flags indicates whether or not any process is still running.

11.3   Distributed Processing Solutions

A distributed processing algorithm consists of a number of processes which communicate via a message-passing system. Typically each process would run on a different processor and the message-passing system would be a hardware communications network linking the processors.

In the multiprocessor algorithms given earlier in this chapter, the order of the data items is automatically preserved because they are stored in an array in the shared memory and never moved from their original positions. In distributed solutions this is not automatically achieved because the data is not retained centrally, but distributed to the separate processes and there is no automatic guarantee that it will be collected back together again in the same order. In fact, we assume that the order does not matter and the algorithms described in what follows make no attempt to preserve the ordering of data items.

For this reason, it is convenient to express the problem in a form that is slightly different from that used earlier. Assume, as before, that the data is supplied in an array $x[1..n]$. Now, however, we require the results as two arrays $xx[1..n]$ and $yy[1..n]$, where $xx[1..n]$ is any permutation of $x[1..n]$ and $yy[i]=f(xx[i])$.

11.3.1   Unbuffered Distribution, Without Side-Effects

In this solution, the computation of $f(x)$ is distributed over a number of parallel processes (which we name $COMPUTE[p]$, $p = 1..k$) which receive data from a single distribution process (called $DISTRIBUTE$), and which send the results

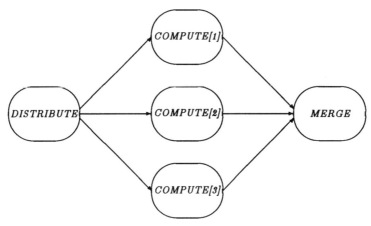

Figure 11.6: Data flow for unbuffered distribution.

Process DISTRIBUTE

```
FOR i := 1 TO n DO
    ACCEPT get(xval : OUT anytype1)
    DO
        xval := x[i]
    END get;
OD
```

Process MERGE

```
FOR i := 1 TO n DO
    ACCEPT put(xval : IN anytype1; yval : IN anytype2)
    DO
        xx[i] := xval;
        yy[i] := yval
    END put;
OD
```

Process COMPUTE[p], p=1..k

```
WHILE TRUE DO
    get(x);
    y := f(x);
    put(x,y)
OD
```

Figure 11.7: Distributed algorithm for a set of independent computations, without side-effects.

to a single collection process (called *MERGE*), as shown in the data flow diagram in Fig. 11.6 (for the case of $k = 3$).

The process *DISTRIBUTE* defines a procedure *get* which supplies the next item of data. Whenever a *COMPUTE* process is ready for a new item of data it calls *get* to obtain that data. When it finishes the computation on that data it calls a procedure *put* to pass on the results. The definition of *put* is in the process *MERGE*.

Note that the next item of data will always be given to the first *COMPUTE* process that requests it. Thus the *COMPUTE* processes will always be kept busy and never have to waste time waiting for further data (assuming, of course, that the time to get the data from *DISTRIBUTE* is not significant). This does mean, however, that we have no control over which process computes each item of data; hence this method is not suitable for situations in which we wish to partition the data items by value or by their original positions (as, for example, in the problem of counting word frequencies, described earlier).

The complete algorithm is shown in Fig. 11.7, using the Ada rendezvous mechanism for the message passing. It is assumed that messages can be passed directly between *DISTRIBUTE* and *COMPUTE[i]*, and between *COMPUTE[i]* and *MERGE* (for all *i*). In practice, a particular distributed computer system may not have direct links between all pairs of processors. In such cases, some effort may be required to map the algorithm efficiently onto the message-passing links available. We ignore such problems and simply assume that all the required links are available.

11.3.2   Buffered Distribution, With Side-Effects

We now describe an algorithm in which additional processes are incorporated to buffer the flow of data from the process *DISTRIBUTE* to the *COMPUTE* processes.

In this algorithm we specify which process will handle each item of data rather than simply sending it to the first process which becomes free. Thus *DISTRIBUTE* now uses a function, h, of the position index, i, and the data item itself, $x[i]$, to determine the process number to which that data should be sent. The buffer processes are needed to ensure that the *COMPUTE* processes are not kept waiting unduly. (*DISTRIBUTE* still passes out the data in the order that it is supplied and this typically will not be the order in which the *COMPUTE* processes become free.)

The data flow between processes is shown in Fig. 11.8, while the pseudocode for the processes themselves is given in Fig. 11.9 (*MERGE* is omitted as it is unchanged from the unbuffered case shown in Fig. 11.7). We have had to use arrays of entry names to distinguish between the buffer processes: *putbuffer[p]*

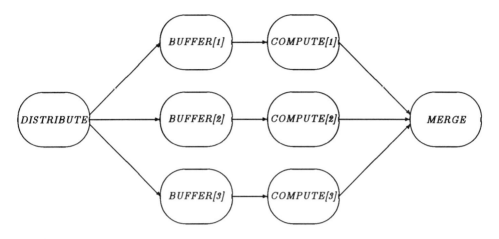

Figure 11.8: Data flow for buffered distribution.

is the entry name to put data into *BUFFER[p]*, and *get[p]* is the entry name to get data from *BUFFER[p]*.

In this algorithm, we allow limited side-effects to be included, but require that these can be partitioned in such a way that each *COMPUTE* process can handle its own side-effects independently of the other processes (we have no shared memory now, so a single *state* variable accessible to all processes is not possible, although more complex alternatives can be found: see Section 11.3.3). Instead, the variable *state* is local to each *COMPUTE* process, hence the state is effectively partitioned across the processes in the same way that the data records are partitioned. The algorithm given is incomplete in that the final value of the state is left partitioned across the processes whereas it would often be required to gather it together into the *MERGE* process, as has been done with the results vector *y*.

An example of a problem in which the side-effects can easily be partitioned in the way required is the problem of counting word frequencies, which we discussed in Section 11.2.4. In the multiprocessing solution to this problem, the *state* variable was partitioned across the local memories of the processors, and exactly the same form of partitioning can be used to obtain a distributed processing solution.

11.3.3 Emulating Shared Memory

Multiprocessor systems using a shared memory and distributed processor systems with message passing but no shared memory are not fundamentally different in what they can do. To exemplify this, we show how to emulate shared memory on a message-passing system. The message passing is expressed in

Process DISTRIBUTE

```
FOR i := 1 TO n DO
    procno := h(i,x[i]);
    putbuffer[procno](x[i])
OD
```

Process BUFFER[p], p=1..k

```
WHILE TRUE DO
    SELECT
        WHEN queue is not empty =>
            ACCEPT get[p](xval : OUT anytype1)
            DO
                xval := take next item from queue
            END get[p];
    OR
        WHEN queue is not full =>
            ACCEPT putbuffer[p](xval : IN anytype1)
            DO
                put xval into queue
            END putbuffer[p];
    END SELECT
OD
```

COMPUTE[p], p=1..k

```
state := initialstate[p];
WHILE TRUE DO
    get[p](x);
    y := f(x);
    state := sideEffects(x,state);
    put(x,y)
OD
```

Figure 11.9: Distributed algorithm for a set of independent computations, with side-effects.

terms of Ada rendezvous.

Shared Memory Process

```
WHILE TRUE DO
    SELECT
        ACCEPT fetch(i : IN address; x : OUT word)
        DO
            x := M[i]
        END fetch;
    OR
        ACCEPT store(i : IN address; x : IN word)
        DO
            M[i] := x
        END store;
    END SELECT
OD
```

Local: *M : ARRAY[0..(N – 1)] OF word*

Figure 11.10: Algorithm to emulate shared memory on a distributed system using the Ada rendezvous mechanism for message passing.

We create a process in which two entry names, *fetch* and *store*, are defined so that *fetch(i,x)* returns in *x* the contents of location *i* of the shared memory, and *store(i,x)* causes the value *x* to be stored at location *i* of the shared memory. An array, *M*, local to this process, is used to represent the shared memory itself.

Other processes wishing to access the shared memory call *fetch* and *store* to do so. The algorithm for the process which implements the shared memory is shown in Fig. 11.10.

11.4   Exercises

Exercise 11.1 Finding Anagrams Given a sequence of English words which are all different but in an unknown order, it is required to group the words into classes whose members are all anagrams of each other (anagrams are words with the same letters, but in a different order). For example, the sequence:

   eat, stare, rat, rates, tar, tears, art, tea

could give the result:

   (eat, tea) (rat, tar, art) (stare, rates, tears)

Suggest a suitable algorithm to perform this task on a multiprocessor system.

Exercise 11.2 Give a suitable algorithm for the anagrams problem of the previous exercise, but using a distributed processor system.

Exercise 11.3 In abstract terms, which of the algorithms you gave for the previous two exercises will give the better performance?

Chapter 12

Reliability

12.1 The Need for Reliability

Constructing highly reliable software is often both difficult and expensive. A great deal of existing software is quite unreliable, yet it is still widely used and tolerated, if somewhat grudgingly. There are several reasons for this state of affairs.

Foremost is that for many applications, high reliability, although desirable, is far from essential and users are not prepared to pay the additional cost. Even unreliable software can be very expensive and achieving a significant increase in reliability can multiply the cost by an unacceptably large factor. Certainly, as time goes by, users of software are becoming less tolerant of highly unreliable software and their expectations are rising more-or-less in line with our ability to produce greater reliability at an acceptable price. For historical reasons, however, software reliability has started from a fairly low base.

The very earliest computers were used primarily to support scientific research and development work. By its very nature, research and development is somewhat speculative and contains many uncertainties. The added uncertainty introduced by software unreliability is often quite easy to live with. If the program crashes, the researcher simply fixes or bypasses the bug and tries again. It is no worse that any other type of problem encountered in his research, of which there are generally many. The performance and functionality of the software were generally much higher on the researcher's list of priorities than was reliability.

Very early commercial software was not much different. Most computing was 'batch processing' and deadlines were measured in days. If a program failed, there was often time to patch it up before any really serious loss occurred (or even, in extreme cases, return to the manual system which the computer had replaced). Computers were slow and expensive, and performance was often the top priority.

Today the situation has changed radically. Computer hardware is very much cheaper and faster, and software now plays a crucial rôle in many applications with very demanding time constraints. For example, the latest generation of passenger aircraft are described as 'fly-by-wire'. The pilot's controls are inputs to a computer program which controls the actual flying surfaces of the aircraft. A bug in this software could cause the aircraft to very rapidly go out of control. In such situations, there is clearly no time to patch up the software and try again, nor is there a manual system to revert to. With some of the most advanced aerodynamic designs it may be effectively impossible to fly the aircraft manually, so there is little point in providing a manual backup system. Reliability is essential.

There are now many such computer applications in which the software is a critical link in a much larger system, often one on which people's lives depend or which is otherwise of very high value. High reliability is then worth paying for. The question is: how can we achieve it? The main approaches to making software more reliable will be introduced in this chapter.

12.2   Where to Start

Faults in software are faults in design. Although errors may occur in copying and running software, unless they are inherent in the software, they are caused by the hardware upon which the software is implemented. There are well established techniques for the detection and correction of such hardware errors. These techniques do not concern us here. Instead, we wish to address the problem of software design errors, commonly referred to as 'bugs'.

There are four broad lines of attack which can be mounted against software bugs:

- **During specification** — make sure that you have a reliable specification of the problem to start with.

- **Before the design begins** — try to reduce the probability of bugs being introduced in the first place.

- **During the implementation** — try to find and eliminate as many bugs as possible.

- **During software use** — try to live with the bugs by detecting and eliminating their effects (known as *fault tolerance*).

All three approaches are important in the battle for increased reliability. Each is described more fully below. Many of the techniques described in this chapter are really rather obvious, but the obvious is all too often overlooked.

If there is one single point that is the key to greater software reliability it is to be systematic and thorough. Bugs are due primarily to carelessness. While it is human nature to make careless mistakes, any techniques which make program design more systematic, more careful and more thorough are likely to increase the reliability of the final software.

12.3   During Specification

Quite obviously, if we do not have a statement of what the program is required to do (i.e. a specification), we cannot say whether or not it is correct. Nevertheless, many software 'errors' arise directly from ambiguities, omissions or errors in the specification. The best program development methodology in the world cannot produce a program that is more reliable than the specification which it has been designed to meet.

Programming problems discussed in textbooks (such as this book) are generally highly abstract and simplified situations that have brief and simple specifications (e.g. the mutual exclusion problem, the producer–consumer problem, the Dining Philosophers Problem). Problems in the 'real world' are typically much more complex with a large amount of fine detail. It is not unusual for commercial software projects to have requirements specifications running to hundreds of pages. In extreme cases they may even be longer than the programs which are later developed to meet them. The effort required to ensure an adequate level of reliability in such complex specifications may be relatively quite large, and must not be overlooked.

12.4   Before the Design

One of the most effective ways to improve reliability is to reduce the complexity of the design. There are several actions that can be taken in the early stages of a software development project to permit a greater simplicity of design to be achieved.

Use More Hardware Resources

Complex designs are often needed to obtain high software performance. Overall performance is a combination of software performance and hardware performance. A program can be made to run faster either by using a more efficient algorithm or by using a faster computer. If reliability is a high priority it may often be worth achieving the required performance by buying more hardware (a faster processor, more memory, etc.) and relaxing the demands on the software performance.

> Consider the Dining Philosophers Problem (see Section 1.2.6). Although this is a relatively simple resource allocation problem, the solution is non-trivial and many ordinary programmers might experience some trepidation in writing a program for this upon which their own lives would depend. The problem is made trivial by the simple expedient of buying five more forks so that each philosopher can have two forks of his own and no longer needs to share his forks with anyone else. He can now eat whenever he likes without interfering with the other philosophers.
>
> Of course, from an academic point of view this completely destroys any interest and challenge in the problem, but from a purely practical point of view it may well be the cheapest way to obtain a solution of extremely high reliability.

Use Better Software Engineers

There are many different ways to solve a programming problem. A good programmer will often find an algorithm which is both simpler and more efficient than that produced by a poor programmer. All aspects of the quality of the software produced, including its reliability, can be very highly dependent upon the skills of the software engineers who are writing the software.

> Looking once more at the Dining Philosophers Problem, whereas some programmers might be unsure of their ability to obtain a solution of extremely high reliability, those with a high level of competence at concurrent programming should be able to do so, without needing to simplify the problem by buying more forks.

Re-Use Tried and Tested Designs

Libraries of basic routines are used by most compilers, and more specialised software libraries are used in many application areas, particularly in numerical and statistical applications, graphics, data-base management, etc. Nevertheless, the re-use of software occurs on a very much smaller scale than is desirable, or, indeed, was predicted in the past. Part of the reason for this is that it has proved technically much more difficult than many people expected to write software that is widely and easily re-usable, yet acceptably concise and efficient. Recent advances in programming language design (data abstraction, object-oriented programming, etc.) should help in this respect. The other main factor is commercial pressures, which often work against the standardisation and re-use of software.

The need for improved reliability in safety-critical applications should be a spur to the development of more software libraries and to the development of effective quality control on the software in those libraries. Regrettably little is currently being done on any effective scale, however.

> Consider again the Dining Philosophers Problem. It is widely discussed in the literature, and any reasonably literate programmer should be able to implement a textbook solution rather than try to solve the problem himself. Unless this is done with a full understanding of the algorithm, however, its reliability is still somewhat dubious because printed matter often contains misprints or other errors. If a program to solve the problem can be obtained in machine readable form this is likely to be much more reliable, but even then its reliability is dependent upon its source, upon which a judgement needs to be made.

Keep it Simple

Much of the complexity of software is introduced to achieve greater efficiency in the use of resources. Often this is essential and the simplest imaginable programs are often totally unacceptable in practical applications. Nevertheless, programmers become so used to introducing complicated methods to improve performance that they easily get carried away and optimise programs when it is not really necessary.

Michael Jackson is often quoted for his advice on optimisation:

> Rule 1 — Don't do it.
> Rule 2 — Don't do it yet.

In other words, put simplicity first. A simple design will generally be much more reliable than a complex design, so complex designs should be used only if they are absolutely essential. It usually pays to put additional effort into the early stages of the work to find the simplest design which is acceptable, rather than go straight to a complex design on the assumption that it must be 'best'.

12.5   During Implementation

The approach at this stage is essentially one of finding (and then eliminating) the bugs that are introduced during design and coding. There are two main approaches, both of which play important rôles:

- Analysis and proof

- Testing

It is important to emphasise that these (and almost all the other methods for achieving increased reliability) are not alternatives. It would be perfectly feasible and sensible to use many different methods in the one project. No method can be guaranteed to eliminate all bugs, but the more approaches that are followed, the fewer the bugs that can be expected to escape detection.

Analysis and Proof

Analytical methods can be further subdivided into three categories:

- **Formal methods** — the verification (proof) of programs using rigorous mathematical techniques. This is essentially similar to proving theorems in mathematics. To formally and rigorously 'prove' a program, it is necessary to have a formal and rigorous statement of what that program is expected to do. Special formal specification languages exist and the whole area of formal specification and proof is an active field of research which is developing rapidly. These techniques are discussed further in the next chapter.

- **Semi-Formal Methods** — the partial analysis of programs using rigorous mathematical techniques. Rather than do a complete formal analysis which is extremely detailed and tedious, it is often possible to carry out a much more limited analysis to check some aspects of the program to see that it makes reasonable sense. Such partial analyses are generally computer assisted, although the interpretation of the results is generally left to the programmer.

  Examples of the type of thing that can be checked easily are:

  – Are any variables never used?

– Are any variables used before values are assigned to them?

– Are any sections of code unreachable?

Some good compilers automatically check these things, in other cases a special program must be run to perform the analysis. The types of things that can be checked for in this way are currently rather limited, but new tools are continually being developed in this field.

- **Review Techniques** — the subjective examination of the program by a team of experts, using inspections or structured walk-throughs. This approach is generally much less formal than the previous two methods, but, if done systematically and professionally, it can be surprisingly effective. It is an extremely adaptable technique and can be used to improve the quality of all aspects of software development, from the initial specifications, through all stages of design, the code itself, and all types of documentation associated with the project.

Testing

The basic idea of program testing is familiar to every programmer. Often testing is done in a rather haphazard way, and a very much more systematic approach is needed if a very high degree of reliability is to be achieved in the final program. Ideally, a program should be tested on every possible set of input data. For non-trivial programs this is usually totally impracticable because of the astronomical number of different sets of input data that would have to be used.

Testing methods differ primarily in the way in which the input data sets are chosen, the aim always being to choose a sufficient variety of different input values to detect all possible errors. Of course, this can never be achieved completely (without using all possible inputs).

The main types of testing are as follows (these should be regarded as complementary to each other rather than mutually exclusive):

- **Black Box Testing** — The test data is determined solely from the program specification without knowledge of the program design or implementation details. It is important to remember to include tests for cases which are implicitly as well as explicitly specified. For example, many specifications do not explicitly state all the cases in which error messages should be produced. It may still be sensible to test that the program gives useful error messages and does not fail catastrophically if supplied with invalid input data, even if the specification does not explicitly mention this case.

- **Glass Box Testing** (also called white box testing) — The test data is
  determined from a knowledge of the program design and implementation.
  It is then possible to ensure that all paths through the program are
  tested, extreme cases tested, etc.

- **Hierarchical Testing** — This is a special case of glass box testing in
  which the testing is structured in the same hierarchical modular way
  as the program design itself. Normally, testing is carried out on the
  modules as they are developed, but later tests on the completed system
  may also be structured in the same hierarchical way, and tests performed
  on individual modules at all levels in the system as well as on the system
  as a whole.

- **Statistical Testing** — Large-scale systematic testing using randomly
  generated test data sets to obtain a quantitative estimate of the reliability
  of the system. This tends to be a costly procedure because a large
  number of sets of test data must be used to obtain useful results. Even
  then, it is most suitable for very complex systems which would be very
  difficult to test thoroughly solely by the other techniques.

- **Simulation Testing** — With embedded real-time systems it may be
  necessary to construct quite large and complex simulators of the environment in which the computer is to be embedded in order to generate
  realistic test data (with realistic time behaviour) and also to evaluate the
  acceptability of the outputs (and the times at which they are supplied).
  Although it is best to test an embedded system in its real environment
  if possible, this is not always possible (e.g. the 'Star Wars' anti-ballistic
  missile system cannot be tested in its real environment, nor can a control
  system for a nuclear reactor), so simulation of the environment must be
  resorted to.

With all these types of testing one of the most difficult tasks is to assess the
thoroughness of the testing procedure itself. What is the probability of an error
remaining undetected after the tests are complete? There is no easy answer
to this question, but a useful technique in evaluating the testing procedure is
mutation analysis (also called *error seeding*). Deliberate errors are introduced
into the system which is then subjected to the test procedure to see if the
errors are detected. Do not be seduced into attributing too much weight to
this technique, however, as it is likely that many of the types of error which the
tester thinks of deliberately introducing are the very types which he thought
of writing the test procedures to look for. A totally unexpected error will often
escape both the original test procedure *and* the mutation analysis!

12.6 Fault Tolerance

There are many well established and widely used techniques for coping with hardware faults after the faults occur. Error detecting and correcting codes are highly effective in increasing the reliability of memory units, communication lines, etc. Nevertheless, these and similar techniques are designed to correct hardware failures in certain specified categories only. The likely modes of hardware failure are generally well known from experimental data, faults occurring in predictable patterns, with the same types of failure recurring many times.

Software faults, on the other hand, are all design faults. Once a design fault is recognised, it will normally be corrected as soon as possible and thereafter the same fault will never recur. Design faults rarely fall into predictable patterns. If faults are corrected as soon as they are found, then every failure will be different.

Design fault tolerance requires a more general form of redundancy than that commonly used for hardware fault tolerance. The requirement is for what is referred to as *design diversity* in the redundancy. The most general approach is known as *N-version software*. Here, N separate versions of the program are written, each ideally using a completely independent design from all the others. These N versions will be run concurrently on N separate computers whose output will to fed to an *adjudicator* unit to select the output which will be used. (Concurrent execution is not strictly necessary, the different versions could instead be run one after the other, then the adjudicator run finally to compare the results.)

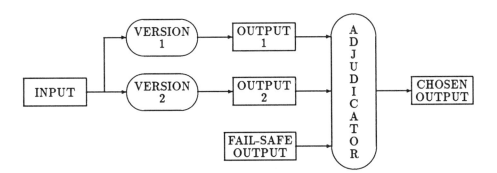

Figure 12.1: Dual-version software system.

The simplest case is dual-version software in which two independent versions of the software feed their output to the adjudicator unit as shown in Fig.

12.1. If the two outputs are identical, they are assumed to be correct, but if they differ one or other must be in error and the fail-safe output is selected instead. This system works well if a trivially simple fail-safe output can be generated (so that the reliability of the fail-safe output is very high) and it is acceptable to switch to a fail-safe output when an error is detected. For example, in the control of railway signals, the fail-safe output is to set all signals to red; or in the control of a nuclear reactor, the fail-safe output is to shut down the reactor.

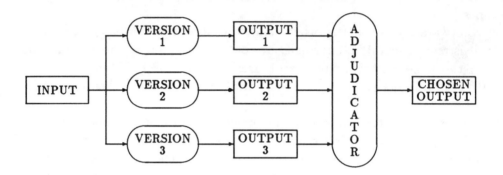

Figure 12.2: Triple-version software system.

In cases where a trivial fail-safe output cannot be found (e.g. in the control of the flying surfaces of an aircraft, there is no default setting which is 'safe'), or if the failure rate of the dual-version case is still too high, the next simplest alternative is to use triple-version software (see Fig. 12.2) with majority voting in the adjudicator. If any two of the three versions give the same output, they are assumed to be correct. Only if all three give different results is the adjudicator unable to choose an output, and this situation should be extremely rare if the three versions are properly independent and themselves reasonably reliable.

Clearly, *N*-version software does not compensate for design errors in the adjudicator or what follows it, nor in the mechanism for distributing the input. These parts of the system need to be sufficiently reliable on their own. Generally this can be achieved by ensuring that they are kept very simple. All of the more complex functionality (i.e. that most subject to design faults) must be handled within the *N* versions.

Both dual-version and triple-version software have been used in safety critical applications. Sometimes the different versions have been implemented on identical hardware and sometimes on different hardware. Some control software for fly-by-wire aircraft has used three versions implemented on three different types of microprocessor (computer systems in the NASA space shuttle use this approach also). This gives added benefits. Firstly, design faults in the computer hardware can also be detected and corrected. Secondly, design faults in the systems software (operating system, compiler, etc.) can also be detected and corrected. Thirdly, software designed for quite different machines is more likely to be truly independent: the design teams are less likely to borrow common routines or otherwise use common sources.

In fact, this highlights one of the most difficult problems with the N-version approach: ensuring that all versions are truly independent designs. Even if two design teams never communicate with each other, it is still possible for them to coincidentally choose to use the same textbook as the source of a standard algorithm or technique and reproduce an error from that common source.

Nevertheless, *N*-version software is a very widely applicable and highly effective way of increasing the reliability of software. So far, it has been used in relatively few applications, generally highly safety critical ones. There seems to be little reason why it should not be much more widely used. The increasing availability of suitable off-the-shelf hardware will make it much easier and cheaper to implement more modest systems using the *N*-version technique.

Chapter 13

Verification

13.1 The Philosophy of Program Verification

Program verification, often called program proving, is sometimes talked about as if it were the Holy Grail of programming: the long sought for and ultimate solution to bugs in software. Although the present state of the art permits only the smallest and simplest programs to be proved correct, considerable research activity in this field is steadily increasing our abilities in this direction. In the not too distant future it should be possible to verify much more substantial and realistic programs. Nevertheless, the subject of program verification and its aims continues to cause considerable confusion and misunderstanding. Program verification is a technique of fundamental importance, but it is not an 'ultimate solution' that will once and for all eliminate the possibility of bugs in software.

At first sight, it may appear obvious that a program that has been proved correct cannot possibly be incorrect. Unfortunately, it can. A program that has been verified (proved) is *not* immune from bugs, although the probability that it contains bugs is very much smaller than if it had not been verified. It is important to understand why this is so and to do this we need to look in some detail at the philosophy of proof.

The Meaning of 'Proof'

First of all, what is a proof? Rather surprisingly, this is not a trivial question and has indeed been the subject of some controversy among computer scientists in recent years (Fetzer, 1988). Yet mathematicians have been talking about proofs for centuries and usually appear to be satisfied that they understand what is meant. The meaning of the word 'proof' is generally not an issue among mathematicians.

This immediately suggests that computer scientists may be using the word 'proof' to mean something slightly different from what mathematicians use it for. [A similar fate befell the word 'variable', which is now used in programming languages with a distinctly different (although closely related) meaning from its original mathematical meaning.] In fact, the situation is even more complicated: computer scientists often use the word 'proof' rather casually, without defining precisely what they mean, and a variety of subtly different interpretations may be implied in different circumstances.

In mathematics, a proof is a systematic logical argument that shows that the required conclusion (the theorem being proved) can be logically derived from a set of axioms (which are assumed to be true). Proofs are rarely written in a completely precise and formal language; they are intended to be read by other mathematicians, not by a computer. Although highly symbolic and concise, the usual language of mathematical argument is only partially formal. Some ambiguity and incompleteness of language definition is tolerated provided that other experienced mathematicians can understand what is meant (in effect, they resolve the ambiguities and fill in the gaps by using their own experience of what is appropriate in the circumstances).

In computer science, at least three different meanings of the word 'proof' have been used, which we will refer to as proof-1, proof-2 and proof-3. They can be defined as follows:

Proof-1 A cast iron guarantee that the program will never fail to give results in accordance with its specification. In other words, a statement of belief that the program is 100% reliable, that there is no conceivable possibility of failure.

Proof-2 A systematic logical argument that the program meets its specification. This is essentially the same as the usual mathematical meaning.

Proof-3 A machine readable and checkable sequence of logical inferences that show that the program meets its specification. This is similar to the previous meaning, except that the logical argument must be expressed in a precisely specified language (rather like a programming language), and nothing may be omitted. It is similar to that which mathematicians call a 'proof from first principles'. Such a proof can be mechanically checked by a computer program to ensure that it is free from clerical and logical errors.

In all cases, the existence of a specification for the program is a prerequisite for program verification. The aim is then to verify that the program meets its specification; i.e. that it will always give results that conform to the specification. For the purposes of this discussion, we assume that the specification is correct and ignore the not insignificant problems of assessing the reliability of the specification.

Proof-1 is essentially a value judgement and a matter of opinion. There is no scientific way of confirming a claim that something is totally reliable (although if the thing fails, the claim is clearly disproved). While the reckless optimist may be quite happy to claim that a program is 100% reliable, more cautious people are very reluctant to make such claims.

Claims of total reliability are often said to be justified on the grounds that the software has been verified in the sense of proof-2 or proof-3. Consider first the case of proof-2, i.e. a proof in the usual mathematical sense. Writing a proof-2 is somewhat like writing a program, and is subject to error in the same ways that programs are subject to error. Most experienced mathematicians know of examples of mathematical proofs which have been published in reputable academic journals and have subsequently been found to contain errors. This occurs despite the fact that proofs in mathematics are generally relatively short (rarely more than a few pages) and studied in great detail and with great care. Proofs of programs are often longer than the programs themselves and are rarely studied with the same care and attention as proofs in mathematics. Consequently, it is reasonable to expect bugs to occur in these proofs just as much as in the programs themselves.

Proof-3, a machine checkable version of proof-2, would appear to solve this problem of bugs in the proof. Using a computer to check the logic of the proof should eliminate the possibility of errors in the proof, thus making it 100% reliable. Unfortunately, this argument holds only if the proof checker is itself 100% reliable. It is logically unsound to use the proof checker to check itself, and, even if we *could* guarantee its total reliability, there remains the possibility that a hardware fault in the computer may cause errors in the operation of the proof checker. Nevertheless, a machine checked proof-3 does give us a very high degree of confidence in the correctness of a program, even though it cannot guarantee total reliability; some chance of failure always remains, no matter how remote.

In fact, although a conventional proof-2 is subject to bugs itself, it still gives a substantial boost to our confidence in the reliability of a program. In this context it is worth remembering that typical software today is highly unreliable. A large program is almost certain to contains some bugs; in other words, its reliability is very close to zero (defining reliability in this instance as the probability that it is completely correct). The very act of constructing a proof-2 involves a careful analysis of the program and this usually uncovers many bugs which had previously lain undetected. It is the detailed analysis of the program which improves its reliability, the proof itself is of little value (unless the proof is subsequently checked further, either by machine or by hand, in which case the checking process may uncover bugs in the proof which may be traced back to yet more bugs in the program).

13.2   Verification Methodologies

Various methodologies are being developed for program verification. Few of these are in any state of maturity, and the next decade is likely to see significant advances in these techniques. An essential prerequisite for program verification is a precise specification: you cannot prove a program correct if you do not know precisely what it is supposed to do! Consequently, verification methodologies are often associated with methodologies for program specification. Two such methodologies which are easily accessible via readable textbooks are VDM (Jones, 1986) and Z (Spivey, 1989; Woodcock and Loomes, 1988). Unfortunately, these have so far been applied mainly to sequential programs and relatively little has been published on their use for concurrent programs. This situation may change in the next few years as there is increasing interest in applying such methodologies to concurrent programming.

Instead, at the present time, there are several methodologies aimed specifically at concurrent programming which concentrate on the concurrency problems and sometimes leave the sequential parts of the program to be analysed using other methods (see Barringer, 1985 for a survey of research in this area). We briefly introduce two such methodologies, Petri nets and CSP. The former is a graphically based way of modelling the synchronisation behaviour of a set of concurrent processes. It models only the synchronisation between the processes, and contains no facilities for describing what each process does.

CSP, on the other hand, looks more like a conventional programming language with primitives for inter-process communication and synchronisation. These primitives have simple and precise mathematical definitions which permit a rigorous mathematical analysis of programs written in CSP. Both Petri nets and CSP are intended as languages for writing programs which are to be subject to formal analysis rather than actual implementation.

As well as a brief look at Petri nets and CSP, we introduce the use of state diagrams as a general aid to the verification of basic concurrency algorithms written in any conventional programming language. In this situation, special methodologies like Petri nets and CSP are often inconvenient because they require the program to be modelled using their own specific synchronisation and communication primitives, which are not the same as the primitives used in many common programming languages.

13.3   Petri Nets

A Petri net graph is a diagrammatic representation of the synchronisation behaviour of a collection of concurrent processes. It models the relative ordering
of events in time. We do not attempt to give a complete description of Petri
nets, but the basic ideas are illustrated by means of several simple examples.

The main components in a Petri net graph are *places, transitions, tokens*
and *directed arcs*. The symbols used are:

Example 1: An Infinite Buffer

Consider now our old friend, the producer-consumer problem, with an infinite
buffer, as an example. A Petri net graph which models this situation is shown
in Fig. 13.1.

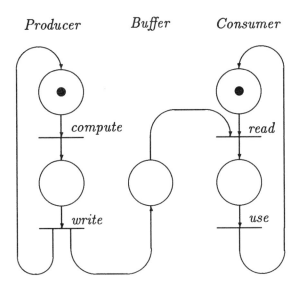

Figure 13.1: Petri net graph for an infinite buffer producer-consumer.

The rules for interpreting this Petri net are as follows. Each transition
in the Petri net represents an action that can take place in the execution
of the program. The four actions that we have chosen to represent are (i)
compute the data, (ii) *write* the data into the buffer, (iii) *read* the data from

the buffer, and (iv) *use* the data, and the four transitions in the diagram are labelled accordingly. A transition can *fire* (representing the execution of that part of the program) if and only if there is at least one token present in each of the input places of that transition. The input places of a transition are places (circles in the diagram) from which there are directed arcs leading *to* the transition. When a transition fires, one token is destroyed in each input place and one token is created in each output place (places to which there are directed arcs *from* the transition).

Hence the execution of this Petri net proceeds as follows. Initially there is only one transition that can fire, i.e. *compute* (*write* and *use* cannot fire because there are no tokens in their input places, *read* cannot fire because only one of its two input places contains a token). When the *compute* transition fires, the token disappears from the top left place and a new token appears in the bottom left place. At this stage the only transition which can fire is *write*. When this fires (representing the writing of data to the buffer by the producer process), the token in the bottom left place is destroyed, and two new tokens created, one in the top left place and the other in the middle place (in the *Buffer* part of the diagram).

Now there are two transitions which are able to fire: *compute* and *read*. This represents the behaviour of the program when there is an item of data in the buffer: the producer can compute the next item of data, but the consumer can also read an item of data from the buffer. Which of these two actions actually takes place is quite arbitrary, and so it is with the Petri net; we may arbitrarily choose which of the two transitions to fire next, or both may fire simultaneously.

Suppose the transition which fires is *compute*, followed by *write*. This will put a second token into the middle place (a place may contain any number of tokens). Tokens in this place represent items of data in the buffer (although tokens in other places do not, in general, represent data items). A little thought will convince you that this Petri net accurately models the behaviour of a producer-consumer program using an infinite buffer. The producer process is always able to run, putting data items into the buffer, but the consumer can execute the *read* transition only if it has finished using the last item of data (this state is represented by a token in the top right place) and there is something in the buffer (represented by one or more tokens in the middle place).

Example 2: A Bounded Buffer

The producer-consumer problem with a buffer which will hold at most N records can be modelled by the Petri net shown in Fig. 13.2.

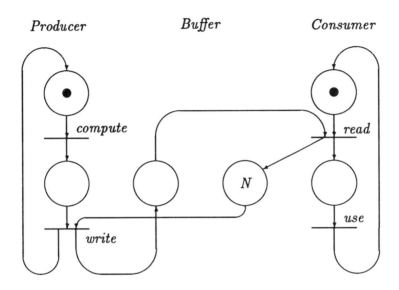

Figure 13.2: Petri net graph for a bounded buffer producer-consumer program.

The part of the diagram modelling the buffer now contains two places, the additional place initially contains N tokens (denoted by the symbol N inside the circle, as we clearly cannot literally draw N tokens). The tokens in this place represent vacant slots in the buffer, and when all these have been used up the *write* transition in the producer will be unable to fire thus preventing the producer from writing further data into a full buffer. The other place within the buffer part of the diagram is the same as in the infinite buffer case: the number of tokens in this place denotes the number of data items in the buffer.

Example 3: Mutual Exclusion

The Petri net shown in Fig. 13.3 models the behaviour of two processes with mutually exclusive critical sections. The middle place in this graph initially contains one token which means that only one of the transitions representing entry to a critical section can fire. Only after that process leaves its critical section (represented by the firing of the corresponding transition) can the other process enter its critical section. The middle place in this Petri net contains a token when neither process is in its critical section, and does not contain a token when one or other process is in its critical section.

This particular Petri net model of mutual exclusion is subject to starvation. A more complex Petri net is needed to model a mutual exclusion situation that

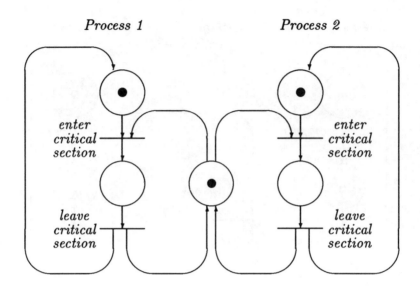

Figure 13.3: Petri net graph for mutual exclusion between critical sections in two processes.

is not subject to starvation.

Using Petri Nets

A considerable body of theoretical techniques have been built up for analysing Petri nets and verifying that their behaviour is as required by the program specification. The theory of Petri nets is mathematically well founded and so these analyses can be carried out with full mathematical rigour. There is currently considerable research interest in the theory and applications of Petri nets, and the importance of this technique is growing.

Petri nets provide a powerful mathematical and graphical technique for modelling the behaviour of complex concurrent systems. Nevertheless, they are more suited to modelling some situations than others. As we saw in the previous example, a simple Petri net can model mutual exclusion between critical sections in two processes if they are subject to starvation, but it is more complicated to model a starvation-free situation. Petri nets use a particular set of primitives for synchronisation, and concurrent systems which are defined in terms of a different set of primitives will usually be more difficult to model than those which are defined in terms of the same or a similar set of primitives.

13.4 CSP

CSP, an acronym for Communicating Sequential Processes (Hoare, 1978 and 1985), is an algebraic formalism for representing concurrent systems. It is aimed primarily at the precise modelling of concurrent systems for the purposes of specification, analysis and verification. In these respects its aims are similar to those of Petri net theory. Unlike Petri nets, it is not normally diagrammatic, but uses a concrete syntax which bears some similarities to programming languages (although in some other respects it is closer to conventional mathematics). Although CSP is close to being a programming language, it is not intended for implementation.

The discussion which follows attempts very briefly to give some of the flavour of CSP by highlighting a few key points, but omitting most of the less important detail. It is very far from complete and cuts corners for simplicity, but should give some idea of the ways in which CSP models concurrent systems.

Events and Synchronisation

A basic concept used in CSP is that of an *event* as an action which is instantaneous in time, but which may involve the participation of more than one process (hence it acts to synchronise the processes involved). A process in CSP is merely a collection of events and the relationships between them. A simple example of a process would be a sequence of events which follow one another in strict succession. CSP does not concern itself with the internal meaning of individual events, nor even with what causes each event. Instead, it provides a means of describing the time relationship of different events in a purely qualitative way (there is no quantitative measure of time, only the concepts of before and after). Processes synchronise with each other by having events in common.

Processes

A *process* is formally a pattern of behaviour of a collection of events (CSP talks about the *alphabet* of a process, being the names of all the events which may be referred to in the process definition). For example,

$$P = x \rightarrow y \rightarrow z$$

defines P to be the process which consists of x followed by y followed by z, where x, y and z are events. As another example,

$$Q = (x \rightarrow y \mid u \rightarrow v \rightarrow w)$$

defines Q to be the process which consists of either x followed by y, or u followed by v followed by w, where x, y, u, v and w are events. Sequencing (denoted by $\rightarrow$) and alternation (denoted by $|$) are the two main ways of relating events when defining processes.

Channels and Communication

Processes communicate by sending messages to each other through *channels*. The passing of a message through a channel is an event in which one process sends the message down the channel and another process receives the message from the channel. This is one event and so the sending and receiving of the message take place simultaneously (just like the rendezvous in Ada). Channels are named and the syntax used is illustrated by the example:

$$P = instream \ ? \ x \rightarrow outstream \ ! \ x$$

which defines P to be the process consisting of the event *instream ? x* followed by the event *outstream ! x*. The event *instream ? x* denotes the action of receiving a message from the channel called *instream*. The value of the message is denoted by x. The symbol *?* denotes input (receiving a message on a channel), while *!* denotes output (sending a message on a channel). Hence the complete process consists of exactly two events in sequence. The first is to receive a message on a channel called *instream* and the second is to send the same message (since x is used in both cases) on a channel called *outstream*.

Example: Producer–consumer with unbounded buffer

Consider now the producer–consumer problem with an unbounded buffer. In CSP it is necessary to use an extra process to do the buffering (just as it was in Ada, and for the same reasons: there is no shared memory available as a basic communication mechanism). The three processes (producer, consumer and buffer) can be modelled as follows:

$$PRODUCER = compute \rightarrow tobuffer \ ! \ x \rightarrow PRODUCER$$

$$CONSUMER = frombuffer \ ? \ x \rightarrow use \rightarrow CONSUMER$$

$$BUFFER = P_{<>}$$
$$P_{<>} = tobuffer \ ? \ x \rightarrow P_{<x>}$$
$$P_{<x> \wedge s} = (tobuffer \ ? \ y \rightarrow P_{<x> \wedge s \wedge <y>} \ | \ frombuffer \ ! \ x \rightarrow P_s)$$

Notice that these processes are defined recursively as infinite sequences of events. So, *PRODUCER* is defined to be the infinite sequence of events:

$$compute \rightarrow tobuffer \ ! \ x \rightarrow compute \rightarrow tobuffer \ ! \ x \rightarrow \ ...$$

Similarly, *CONSUME* is defined to be the infinite sequence of events:

$$frombuffer \ ? \ x \rightarrow use \rightarrow frombuffer \ ? \ x \rightarrow use \rightarrow \ ...$$

The definition of the buffer process makes use of some new syntactic constructs which require explanation. The angle brackets $<$ and $>$ are used to delimit a sequence. So, $< x, y, z >$ denotes the sequence containing x, y and z, in that order (x, y and z are any data items). This is a sequence in the usual mathematical sense, not to be confused with sequences of events through time, which are used in the definition of processes.

The operator $\wedge$ is used to concatenate two sequences, so, for example:

$$< x, y > \wedge < z >=< x, y, z >$$

The name P is used here to denote an infinite family of patterns of behaviour. Each individual member of this family is distinguished by a different subscript. The subscript used is a sequence of items, denoting the data items present in the buffer. So $P_{<>}$ denotes the pattern of events possible when the buffer is empty; while $P_{<x>}$ denotes the pattern of events possible when the buffer contains the single data item x; and $P_{<x> \wedge s \wedge <y>}$ denotes the pattern of events possible when the buffer contains x, s and y, where s is any sequence of data items, and x and y are any individual data items.

Thus the process called *BUFFER* is defined to behave as follows. Initially it is the event *tobuffer ? x* which receives the data x on the channel called *tobuffer*. Following that it is the pattern of events called $P_{<x>}$. The definition of $P_{<x>}$ can be deduced from the definition of $P_{<x> \wedge s}$ by taking s to be the empty sequence, i.e. $<>$. It is either (i) the event *tobuffer ? y* which receives the data y on the channel *tobuffer*, followed by the pattern of events denoted by $P_{<x> \wedge <y>}$, or (ii) the event *frombuffer ! x* which sends the data x on the channel *frombuffer*, followed by the pattern of events denoted by $P_{<>}$.

Specification and Verification in CSP

CSP contains facilities for expressing conditions which a particular concurrent system must satisfy; in other words, part or all of an algebraic specification of the system. CSP is essentially a well-founded mathematical formalism, and like other such formalisms, it obeys a number of basic mathematical laws.

These laws have been formalised into a collection of rules of inference which can be used as the basic building blocks of proofs (that a concurrent system formulated in CSP satisfies its specification, also formulated in CSP or in the basic formalisms of mathematical logic).

The full CSP language is quite large and it would take too long here to try to describe all the details necessary to write specifications and proofs. It uses many basic concepts from mathematical logic and set theory together with many other concepts relevant to programming in general and concurrent programming in particular. The interested reader should consult the Further Reading.

13.5   State Diagrams

How can we verify a concurrent program written in a conventional programming language (e.g. assembly code) which uses shared memory as its inter-process communication mechanism? Techniques such as Petri nets and CSP can be difficult to use in such situations because they are based on entirely different sets of communication and synchronisation primitives.

The proofs of well known algorithms as published in the research literature are generally much like proofs in conventional mathematics and demand a considerable degree of mathematical sophistication on the part of the reader. In other words, the author of the proof has found clever ways to short cut and abbreviate the large amounts of tedious detail usually required in proofs from first principles. These short cuts do not cause serious problems for those with adequate mathematical background, but they may be difficult for many programmers who are less mathematically inclined. Most programmers would have extreme difficulty in trying to construct such proofs for themselves.

What is needed is a method that can be used to analyse and verify concurrent programs without the need for a high level of mathematical exerience and insight. Of course, the price that must be paid is in handling a lot of tedious detail (after all, this tedious detail is exactly what the short cuts are intended to eliminate).

We assume that the analysis of the purely sequential parts of the program are not a problem and so concentrate solely on coping with the concurrency. The method selected to aid in the systematic analysis of the concurrency properties of the program is that of constructing a state diagram.

State diagrams have been used for decades as aids to the design of both computer hardware and software, and the general idea should already be familiar to the reader. They are easily applied to concurrent programs. To illustrate the method, consider the following examples.

Example 1

The mutual exclusion algorithm given in Fig. 3.5 is safe but subject to deadlock. Suppose we wish to verify these two properties by detailed analysis.

	Process 1		**Process 2**
	init1;		*init2;*
	WHILE TRUE DO		*WHILE TRUE DO*
1	*flag1 := 1;*	1	*flag2 := 1;*
2	*WHILE flag2=1 DO OD;*	2	*WHILE flag1=1 DO OD;*
	crit1;		*crit2;*
3	*flag1 := 0;*	3	*flag2 := 0;*
	rem1		*rem2*
	OD		*OD*

Shared: *flag1, flag2 : 0..1 (both initially 0)*

Figure 13.4: The mutual exclusion algorithm labelled as required.

Firstly, rewrite the algorithm in the form shown in Fig. 13.4, in which the statements involving access to shared variables have been numbered. There is no need to number the other statements as they cannot directly affect the synchronisation of the two processes. Numbering every statement does no harm, but it increases the number of states that have to be considered and adds to the amount of tedious detail that has to be handled. Some short cuts are necessary if the amount of detail is not to become quite prohibitive!

The state diagram for this algorithm is given in Fig. 13.5. Each circle denotes a different state, and the directed arcs linking the circles are state transitions allowed by the program. Each state is labelled with a four-digit number $abcd$, in which a denotes the abstract program counter of Process 1, b denotes the abstract program counter of Process 2, c denotes the shared variable *flag1* and d denotes *flag2*. The abstract program counter is defined to take on the values of the labels we put on the statements of the program as execution proceeds. If the abstract program counter of Process 1 is 3, this means that Process 1 has completed execution of the previous labelled statement (statement 2 in this case) but has not yet started execution of statement 3 (it could, however, be in the middle of executing its critical section, *crit1*, which is between statement 2 and statement 3).

For example, the state at the top left of the diagram, labelled 1100, is the initial state in which neither process has yet begun execution of their respective

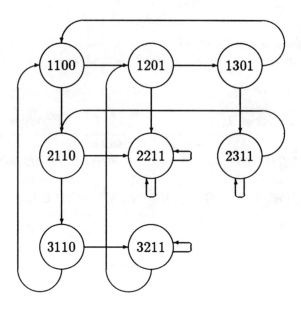

Figure 13.5: State diagram for the mutual exclusion algorithm of Fig. 13.4.

statements labelled 1, and $flag1 = flag2 = 0$. The graph has been drawn so
that arcs leaving a circle vertically downwards denote transitions produced by
the execution of statements in Process 1, while arcs leaving a circle horizontally
to the right denote transitions produced by Process 2. Each state has at least
two arcs leaving it because, at any time, either of the two processes may
execute its next statement. There are only two arcs leaving each state because
there are only two processes and all the statements in both processes lead to
unique state changes (the program contains no indeterminism). The diagram
is drawn by starting with the initial state and then adding all possible states
that can be reached by transitions produced by the execution of either of the
two processes. Only reachable states have been shown on the diagram. Other
states are generally not of interest.

It is easy to see that the algorithm is safe. If it were not, both processes
would be able to enter their critical sections simultaneously. This would be
denoted in the state diagram by a state of the form 33xx (where x denotes any
value). No such state is reachable from the initial state, 1100, so the algorithm
is safe.

It is equally easy to see that deadlock can occur. Look at state 2211 in the
middle of the graph. Both transitions from this state lead straight back to the
same state. Hence, once this state has been entered it is impossible to leave
it again. In general, deadlock manifests itself by the presence of a state from

which all paths lead back to itself without passing through the states which represent the doing of useful work by the algorithm. In this algorithm, 'useful work' means the statements *crit1, crit2, rem1* and *rem2*, not the statements which implement the mutual exclusion protocol.

Example 2: Peterson's Algorithm for Mutual Exclusion

As a slightly more complex example, consider Peterson's Algorithm for mutual exclusion, which we write with the statements labelled as shown in Fig. 13.6.

Process 1

```
   init1;
   WHILE TRUE DO
1      flag1 := 1;
2      turn := 1;
3      WHILE flag2 = 1 AND turn = 1 DO OD;
       crit1;
4      flag1 := 0;
       rem1
   OD
```

Process 2

```
   init2;
   WHILE TRUE DO
1      flag2 := 1;
2      turn := 2;
3      WHILE flag1 = 1 AND turn = 2 DO OD;
       crit2;
4      flag2 := 0;
       rem2
   OD
```

Figure 13.6: Peterson's Algorithm for mutual exclusion.

The state diagram for this program is shown in Fig. 13.7. Each state is denoted by a five-digit number *abcde*, in which *a* denotes the abstract program counter of Process 1, *b* denotes the abstract program counter of Process 2, *c, d* and *e* denote the shared variables *flag1, flag2* and *turn*, respectively. There are two possible initial states, 11001 and 11002 (the initial value of turn is unspecified). The graph has been drawn to include all states which are reachable from either of these.

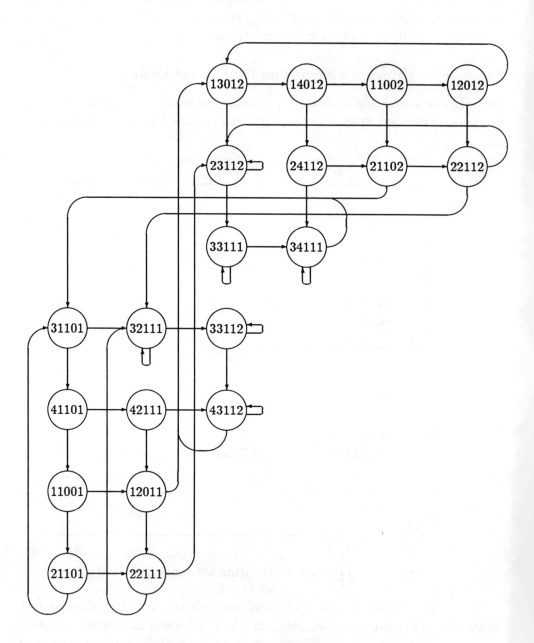

Figure 13.7: State diagram for Peterson's Algorithm for mutual exclusion.

The algorithm is easily seen to be safe because there is no reachable state of the form 44xxx, which would occur if both processes executed their critical sections simultaneously.

Showing that the algorithm is live requires more effort. Firstly, we can verify that it is not subject to starvation by showing that every closed path on the graph which includes at least one transition due to each process (i.e. at least one vertical and one horizontal arc) passes through states which denote the execution of all four of *crit1, crit2, rem1* and *rem2* (i.e. states of the form 4xxxx, x4xxx, 1xxxx and x1xxx respectively). This requires a detailed examination of the graph, but it is not difficult (just tedious). For example, consider the closed path through the states: 21102, 31101, 32111, 33112, 43112, 13012, 14012, 24112, 21102. This path clearly includes states of all four required forms.

Secondly, we need to verify that permanent blocking cannot occur if either process decides to remain in the non-critical part of the program (*rem1* or *rem2*) forever. The program is symmetrical between Process 1 and Process 2 (the graph is symmetric about a line drawn diagonally through the centre of the graph from top left to bottom right, although it has been drawn with the top-right half of the graph transposed slightly to the left to enable it to fit on the page more easily). Thus, we need only show that if Process 1 stays forever in *rem1*, Process 2 is not permanently blocked. If Process 1 stays in *rem1*, this means that the abstract program counter remains at 1, which is shown in the state diagram by replacing all vertical arcs leaving states of the form 1xxxx by arcs which loop back on themselves, as shown in Fig. 13.8.

Examination of this graph shows that all closed paths that include at least one vertical and one horizontal arc pass through at least one state of each of the following forms: x1xxx and x4xxx. This proves that Process 2 cannot become permanently blocked even if Process 1 stays in *rem1* forever.

13.6   Conclusions

This chapter has given a brief glimpse of some of the many formal methods currently being used or developed for program verification and analysis. These methods are continually being refined and improved, but the current state of the art in formal methods for program analysis is very immature, particularly for concurrent programs, and the next decade should see major advances in this field and the much more intensive and widespread use of such techniques.

It can be argued that the current high level of research interest in program verification has been accompanied by the relative neglect of other important aspects of program analysis (Stankovic, 1988). For real-time programs, not

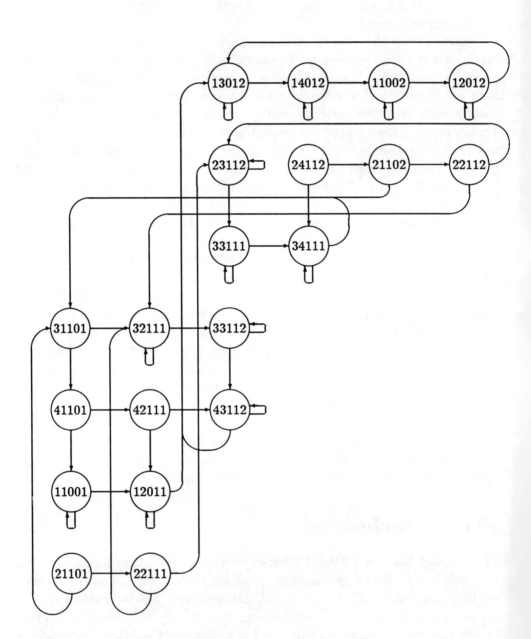

Figure 13.8: State diagram for Peterson's Algorithm modified to show Process 1 staying on statement 1 forever.

only is the correctness of the results important, but also the time at which those results are produced. A program which is required to monitor the temperature and pressure of a boiler and shut off the fuel supply if dangerous levels are reached is of no value if it correctly shuts off the fuel supply, but after the boiler has exploded! In Chapter 6 there was some discussion of timing analysis, but generally we have not been able to include as much analysis of execution times as the practical importance of the topic warrants. Considerably more research on this topic is needed.

Most programming languages that claim to support concurrent and real-time programming provide little, if any, help for the development of programs which must meet specified upper limits on response times. Ada, along with many other concurrent languages and systems, provides a delay statement to help with the control of timing, but this simply produces a delay with a guaranteed minimum value and no maximum value. What is often required just as much is more or less the converse: a statement to guarantee that part of a program will be executed within a specified *maximum* real time. Such a statement does not exist in any of the common real-time programming languages. This is an important problem which deserves much more attention than it has been receiving.

While the 1970s and 1980s have been the decades of structured programming (in the very broad sense — to include data abstraction, object-oriented programming and the program design methodologies such as JSP), the 1990s and beyond may well be the decades of concurrent programming with an upsurge of interest in both parallel and real-time systems.

Solutions to Exercises

1.1 Suppose that the stack is represented as an array, *a*, and an index, *i*, where $a[i]$ is the next free location in the array (therefore *i* is also the number of items on the stack). Typical code for *push* and *pop* is shown in Fig. A.1.

push(x)	**pop()**
$a[i] := x;$ $i := i + 1$	$i := i - 1;$ $return\ a[i]$

Shared: $a : ARRAY[0..n]\ OF\ anytype;$
  $i : 0..n$

Figure A.1: Typical routines for accessing a stack.

If we execute the first statement of *pop* followed by the first statement of *push*, followed by the second statement of *pop*, followed by the second of *push*, then the item originally on the top of the stack is overwritten and lost, which is clearly unacceptable.

1.2 The answer to this question can be either yes or no, depending upon the representation chosen for the queue and the routines to access the queue. If putting an item onto the tail of the queue is completely independent of taking an item off the head of the queue, then mutual exclusion is not necessary. This is the case if the queue is represented as an array, *a*, and two indices, *head* and *tail*, where $a[tail]$ is the next free location (i.e. the location at which the next item will be placed), and $a[head]$ is the location containing the next item to be removed from the queue. The indices are incremented modulo the size of the array, say *n*.

The routines to access the queue are shown in Fig. A.2. The slightly tricky part of these routines is the test for the queue being full, which is done when it contains only $n - 1$ items. The reason for this is that if we allowed the array to be completely filled (*n* items), then *head* and *tail*

put(x)   **take()**

```
IF (tail + 1 MOD n) = head          IF head = tail
    THEN error FI;                      THEN error FI;
a[tail] := x;                       x := a[head];
tail := tail + 1 MOD n              head := head + 1 MOD n;
                                    return x
```

Shared: $a : ARRAY[0..(n-1)]$ OF anytype;
               $head : 0..n$;
               $tail : 0..n$

Figure A.2: Typical routines to access a queue.

Entrance process

```
WHILE TRUE DO
    i := read number of vehicles entering tunnel;
    begin critical section;
    nvehicles := nvehicles + i;
    end critical section
OD
```

Exit process

```
WHILE TRUE DO
    i := read number of vehicles leaving tunnel;
    begin critical section;
    nvehicles := nvehicles - i;
    end critical section
OD
```

Traffic lights process

```
WHILE TRUE DO
    begin critical section;
    n := nvehicles;
    end critical section;
    IF n ≥ N THEN set lights to red
        ELSE set lights to green FI
OD
```

Figure A.3: Processes to control traffic flow in a road tunnel.

would be equal which is the same condition as we use to test if the queue is empty! The advantage of this approach, however, is that mutual exclusion is not necessary because the *put* routine writes to *a[tail]* and *tail*, while the *take* routine writes to *a[head]* and *head*. Provided the queue is not empty, these are four different variables and so there is no chance of their values being affected by the way the processes interleave. If the queue is empty, *a[head]* and *a[tail]* are the same, but *take* will fail if applied to an empty queue, so there is still no chance of corruption of the queue occurring.

On the other hand, we could use an additional variable, *size*, which is the number of items currently in the queue. This simplifies the tests for a full queue and permits us to use all *n* locations in the array, but mutual exclusion is now necessary because *put* will increment *size* and *take* will decrement it (it is easy to show that interleaving the incrementing and decrementing of *size* can lead to incorrect values of *size* being generated unless atomic instructions are used for the incrementing and decrementing).

1.3 We use a shared variable, *nvehicles*, to denote the number of vehicles currently in the tunnel. The three processes are shown in Fig. A.3. In the traffic lights process, the critical section is needed only for the read access to the shared variable, *nvehicles*. If *nvehicles* is a single memory word and its access is indivisible, then the critical section in the traffic lights process is not needed.

2.1 Typically, string instructions are interruptible, but only at specific points in their execution. An alternative, and convenient, way of looking at it is to redefine a string instruction as not one instruction but many, purely with regard to its execution. Under this new definition, when a string instruction is executed, only one element of the string is processed. If this is the last element of the string then the complete string operation has been completed and the program counter is incremented in the usual way so that the instruction following the string instruction will be executed next.

On the other hand, suppose the element just processed is not the last element of the string (this is always known by testing the value of a count which is kept in one of the normal registers and decremented by one as each element is processed: when it reaches zero the end of the string has been reached). In this case the program counter is *not* incremented in the usual way, but remains the same. Thus, the same string instruction will be repeated on each element of the string. What we previously thought of as the execution of one instruction is now seen as the repeated execution of the same instruction, once for each element of the string. Control moves to the next instruction only when the string counter hits zero.

With this new definition of what constitutes an 'instruction execution', we can maintain our general rule that no instruction is interruptible in the middle of its execution, even string instructions. Of course, what is really important in deciding when an interrupt may occur is that the state of the machine, which is preserved when an interrupt occurs, must contain sufficient information to enable the process to be resumed later without corruption. This is clearly satisfied in this case, assuming the state of the machine is defined in the usual way. Both the Intel 8086 and the DEC VAX, as well as many other architectures, operate in this way.

2.2 This would largely defeat the object of a multiprocessor machine which is to provide a number of processors which can run in parallel to increase the overall speed of the computer. When conventional interrupt mechanisms are provided on multiprocessors, the disabling of interrupts usually affects one processor alone. Other processors run as usual. Hence the disabling of interrupts can no longer be regarded as a simple means of locking out all other processes: it now applies only to processes running on the same processor.

2.3 The updating of a variable which is packed with other objects into a memory word takes place in the following three stages:

1. Read the contents of the memory word into a register.
2. Update that part of the register that corresponds to the variable.
3. Write the register contents back into the memory word.

If two processes perform such an update concurrently so that the separate stages of these operations are interleaved, only one of the updates will be effective, the other being overwritten and hence completely lost.

Equally, if two *different* variables are packed into the *same* word of memory, concurrent updating of these variables can suffer the same fate also (i.e. only one of the updates is effective, the other being lost).

3.1 The shared temperature and pressure variables each require more than one memory access, so the indivisibility of memory accesses is insufficient to ensure the safe reading and writing of these variables.

Instead, we must treat as critical sections the code which accesses these variables (a different class of critical sections for each). The simplest way to implement the mutual exclusion for these critical sections of code is to disable interrupts during the critical sections. If this is not possible or not desirable, most of the other methods described in Chapter 3 would also be suitable in appropriate circumstances.

3.2 (i) The algorithm is safe. The proof is as follows.

Suppose two processes are in their critical sections simultaneously. The process that executed *bolt* := *1* first we call Process A. The other process we call Process B. Now when A finishes executing *bolt* := *1*, B must have completed the wait loop (if it hasn't, it will remain in it because now *bolt* = *1*). But that is impossible, because it is not possible to switch from B to A after B finishes its wait loop and before it completes *bolt* := *1* (because interrupts are disabled). Hence our assumption must be wrong, i.e. the two processes cannot be in their critical sections simultaneously.

(ii) The algorithm is not live. It is deadlock free, but subject to starvation. The proof that it is deadlock free is as follows.

Suppose the two processes are in deadlock. The only place that each can be is in its wait loop. Thus *bolt* = *1* (if not, each process will immediately exit from the wait loop). This is not possible, however, because whichever process last executed its critical section will have executed *bolt* := *0* afterwards, and the only other assignment to *bolt* is immediately after the wait loop, so there is no way it can have been executed between executing *bolt* := *0* and getting into deadlock.

The proof that it is subject to starvation is as follows.

Suppose that, by chance, Process 1 gets interrupted only while it is in its critical section (interrupts are enabled during that time). Process 2 will then run and will always find that *bolt* = *1*, thus preventing it from entering its own critical section. This situation could recur indefinitely, resulting in starvation of Process 2.

3.3 Suppose that Process 1 is interrupted in its first execution of its critical section with *bolt* = *1*. Process 2 then proceeds and enters its wait loop with $x2 = 1$ and *bolt* = *1*. It is then interrupted and Process 1 continues, exiting from its critical section, setting *bolt* = *0*, returning to the start of its main loop and proceeding to enter its critical section, at which point it is interrupted again and Process 2 proceeds. Process 2 remains stuck in its wait loop (because Process 1 set *bolt* = *1* again before re-entering its critical section). This situation can recur indefinitely, resulting in starvation of Process 2.

3.4 The proof in this case is similar to that given in the previous answer. In fact, *any* algorithm which does not disable interrupts (or otherwise inhibit process switching) during the critical section and which relies on a single shared boolean variable to indicate when a process is in its critical section, must be subject to starvation in the same way. Notice that Peterson's algorithm, which is starvation free, uses three shared boolean variables, so it is always known which process last executed its critical section and also whether the other process is currently waiting to enter its critical section.

L[i]

```
WHILE TRUE DO
    receive(message);
    IF message = token THEN
        IF NOT tokenexpected THEN send(dummy) FI;
        IF waiting THEN critical := TRUE FI;
        WHILE critical DO OD;
        send(token);
        tokenexpected := FALSE
    ELSE {message = dummy}
        IF tokenexpected THEN send(token) FI;
        send(dummy);
        tokenexpected := TRUE
    FI
OD
```

Figure A.4: Message-passing process for a circulating token algorithm with dummy token for resilience.

3.5 The first part of the algorithm (the user process, $P[i]$) is identical to that for the simple circulating token case (Fig. 3.9). The message passing process, $L[i]$, is as shown in Fig. A.4.

The real token (the one that is used for mutual exclusion) we call the *token*, and the second token we call the *dummy*. An extra local variable *tokenexpected* is set to false when the token is received, and to true when the dummy is received. If the dummy is received when the token is expected, then the token must have been lost and is regenerated and sent on ahead of the dummy. If the token is received when the dummy is expected, then the dummy must have been lost and is regenerated and sent on ahead of the token. The regenerated message must be sent ahead of the other, otherwise the next processor on the ring will also think it is lost and it will be regenerated again.

4.1 When *sleep* is called, it causes the state of the Current Process to be saved in the system data segment, and the Current Process to be entered into a queue of processes sleeping on the specified event. Now, whether or not interrupts are disabled is simply part of the state of the process.

A/D device driver

> (entered on system call requesting A/D read)
> *initial housekeeping and checks;*
> *start A/D conversion;*
> *disable interrupts;*
> *timeout(wakeup,ADevent,ADdelay);*
> *sleep(ADevent);*
> *enable interrupts;*
> *read value from A/D converter;*
> *final housekeeping;*
> *return to user process*

Figure A.5: Device driver for analogue to digital converter.

and will be saved along with the rest of the process state. The scheduler will decide which process to run next and restore its state from its system data segment (including whether or not it had disabled interrupts). That process will then be run.

4.2 An interrupt handler is a process in its own right, but it is *not* a user process. Thus it has no system data segment and the scheduler knows nothing about it (it thinks the interrupted user process is still running). The procedure *sleep* may only be called by user processes. If *sleep* was called by an interrupt handler, the user process which had been interrupted (i.e. the Current Process) would be put to sleep instead, but with its state set to that of the interrupt handler. This would cause considerable havoc when that process was woken up again!

On the other hand, *timeout* does not affect the calling process in any way, so it is safe to call from an interrupt handler or anywhere else. All it does is make an entry in a table which is examined on every clock interrupt.

4.3 The function given as an argument to *timeout* is run when it is called by the clock interrupt handler, which is not a user process. Therefore, this function may not call *sleep*, for the reasons given in the solution to the previous exercise.

4.4 A possible solution is as follows. A new device driver would be incorporated into the kernel. The code for this device driver would be entered on a system call from a user program requesting input from the A/D converter, and would have the form shown in Fig. A.5.

Modem driver

(entered on a system call requesting a phone call to be made)
initial housekeeping and checks;
phoneflag := TRUE;
disable interrupts;
initiate telephone call;
timeout(abortphone,0,ringdelay);
sleep(phonevent);
enable interrupts;
phonesuccess := phoneflag;
phoneflag := FALSE;
final housekeeping;
return(phonesuccess) to user process

abortphone(x)

IF phoneflag THEN
    phoneflag := FALSE;
    wakeup(phonevent)
FI

Modem interrupt handler

(entered upon an interrupt from the modem)
read modem status (answered or engaged);
IF engaged THEN phoneflag := FALSE FI;
wakeup(phonevent);
return to interrupted process

Global: *phoneflag : boolean*
 Local: *phonesuccess : boolean*

Figure A.6: Kernel routines for an autodial modem.

ADevent is an integer constant (different from all other event numbers used in the kernel — conventionally the address of the start of the device driver routine is taken as a convenient value), *ADdelay* is 1 (the time delay in sixtieths of a second).

Interrupts are disabled between the calls of *timeout* and *sleep* to ensure that no process switching occurs during this time. Therefore the timeout cannot expire and cause *wakeup* to be called before the process goes to sleep (otherwise there is a risk that the process will sleep forever).

Problems can arise if another process starts to read the A/D converter before the first process is finished. The initial checks in the A/D device driver must prevent this happening.

4.5 A possible solution is shown in Fig. A.6.

In this algorithm, *phonevent* is an integer constant (e.g. the address of the start of the modem driver routine to ensure uniqueness). Interrupts are disabled between initiating the phone call and going to sleep. This is to prevent any process switching occurring during this period so that neither the timeout can expire nor the modem interrupt occur before the process goes to sleep.

Problems can arise if two processes try to make phone calls nearly simultaneously, so checks against this must be included in the initial checks of the modem driver routine.

This solution is not totally satisfactory because the timeout continues to run even after a phone call has been completed. Thus, if a new phone call is started before the timeout expires, that new call will get aborted well before its 15 seconds are up. One way to overcome this difficulty is to use another global variable to record the serial number of the phone call (an integer which is incremented every time a new call is begun). This serial number can be supplied as the parameter of *abortphone* and the code of *abortphone* modified so that if its parameter is not the same as the current serial number it does nothing. A more direct method would be to cancel the timeout when the call is completed, but there is no easy way of doing this without knowing the implementation of *timeout* and then writing a routine specially for the purpose.

4.6 A suitable algorithm is shown in Fig. A.7. The variable *currentblockno* is global, along with the arrays *block, transfer* and *transferaddr*, as specified in the question. Interrupts are assumed to be disabled throughout the disc interrupt handler.

5.1 Boolean semaphores have only two possible values, 0 and 1, so they can be implemented as follows. Instead of allocating space to store the value of each semaphore, we make use of the knowledge that the majority of

writedisc(blockno,discaddr)

```
transfer[blockno] := WAITWRITE;
disable interrupts;
IF disc is not busy THEN
    initiate disc write to disc address discaddr
    (data taken from block[blockno]);
    currentblockno := blockno
FI;
sleep(blockno);
transfer[blockno] := NOTWAITING;
enable interrupts
```

readdisc(blockno,discaddr)

```
(similar to writedisc)
```

disc interrupt handler

```
(entered on EOT interrupt from disc)
wakeup(currentblockno);
currentblockno := nextdisctransfer();
IF transfer[currentblockno] = WAITREAD THEN
    initiate disc read from transferaddr[currentblockno]
    (data put into block[currentblockno])
FI;
IF transfer[currentblockno] = WAITWRITE THEN
    initiate disc write to transferaddr[currentblockno]
    (data from block[currentblockno])
FI
```

Figure A.7: Algorithm for a disc driver.

boolean semaphores are 1 for much longer periods than they are zero in typical applications. So we keep a set, called *zerosemaphores*, of all those semaphores which are zero. All others (not in this set) are 1. Each semaphore is identified by an integer value (just as events for *sleep* and *wakeup* in UNIX are identified by integer values). The pseudocode for P and V (*init* does nothing) is shown in Fig. A.8. The set, *zerosemaphores*, could be represented in many different ways, but a simple array of values with sequential search is likely to be acceptably efficient if the number of semaphores which are simultaneously zero is usually small.

Integer semaphores are more complicated to implement. Various methods are possible depending upon the efficiency required and the circumstances of use that are expected.

5.2 We assume integer semaphores. For each semaphore, s, we keep three global variables in the kernel: *s.value* is the value of the semaphore (a non-negative integer), *s.first* points to the first process in the queue of processes waiting for the semaphore (i.e. the one to proceed next), and *s.last* points to the last process in the same queue. In addition, *active.first* and *active.last* are global variables which point to the first and last processes in the chain of active processes. Suitable algorithms for P and V are given in Fig. A.9.

The routine *transferto(s)* moves the current process (i.e. the first process in the active queue) out of the active queue and into the queue for semaphore s, while *transferfrom(s)* moves one process from the queue for semaphore s and puts it into the active queue. The implementation of these routines involves purely pointer manipulation and has no special real-time features, so we omit the details.

The difference between strong and weak semaphores lies in the way in which *transferto* and *transferfrom* are implemented. For strong semaphores, processes should be put into and removed from the semaphore queues in FIFO order to ensure that starvation cannot occur. Any order is acceptable for weak semaphores.

5.3 A possible solution is shown in Fig. A.10.

The value of the integer semaphore *freeslots* denotes the number of free character positions in the print queue (total number of character positions is N). It is assumed that the operation of putting a character into the print queue does not need to be implemented as a critical section. If it does, then changes to the algorithm are needed to ensure mutual exclusion. Of course, taking a character off the print queue is automatically indivisible because it is within the interrupt handler, during the execution of which interrupts are disabled.

P(s)

```
disable interrupts;
IF s∈zerosemaphores THEN sleep(s) FI;
enable interrupts
```

V(s)

```
disable interrupts;
IF s∈zerosemaphores THEN
        delete s from zerosemaphores;
        wakeup(s)
FI;
enable interrupts
```

Figure A.8: Implementation of semaphores in terms of *sleep* and *wakeup*.

P(s)

```
disable interrupts;
IF s.value = 0 THEN
    transferto(s)
ELSE
    s.value := s.value − 1;
FI;
enable interrupts
```

V(s)

```
disable interrupts;
IF s.first ≠ NULL THEN
    transferfrom(s)
ELSE
    s.value := s.value + 1
FI;
enable interrupts
```

Figure A.9: Implementation of semaphores by transferring processes between queues.

Printer driver

> (entered on a system call from the user process, where
> $a[1..n]$ is the character string to be printed)
> *FOR i := 1 TO n DO*
>   *IF printer is not busy THEN*
>   *print a[i]*
>   *ELSE*
>   *P(freeslots);*
>   *put a[i] into print queue*
>   *FI*
> *OD*

Printer interrupt handler

> (entered on an interrupt from the printer)
> *IF print queue is not empty THEN*
>   *print next character from queue;*
>   *V(freeslots)*
> *FI;*
> *return to interrupted process*

Shared: *freeslots : integer semaphore (initially N)*
         print buffer

Figure A.10: Implementation of a printer driver with semaphores.

sleep(event, priority)

```
P(access);
IF event is in table already THEN
    nprocs[event] := nprocs[event] + 1;
ELSE
    nprocs[event] := 1;
    sem[event] := any free semaphore;
FI;
V(access);
P(sem[event])
```

wakeup(event)

```
P(access);
FOR i := 1 TO nprocs[event] DO V(sem[event]) OD;
nprocs[event] := 0; (i.e. remove event from table of sleeping events)
return sem[event] to list of free semaphores;
V(access)
```

Figure A.11: Implementation of *sleep* and *wakeup* using semaphores.

Philosopher i

```
WHILE TRUE DO
    think and sleep;
    P(fork[i]);
    pick up left fork;
    P(fork[i + 1 MOD 5]);
    pick up right fork;
    eat;
    put down left fork;
    V(fork[i]);
    put down right fork;
    V(fork[i + 1 MOD 5])
OD
```

Shared: *fork : ARRAY[0..4] OF semaphore (initially all 1)*

Figure A.12: A simple solution to the Dining Philosophers Problem, which is subject to deadlock.

This solution is not very efficient because it calls P and V for every character put into the print queue. A more efficient solution may be desirable in many circumstances.

5.4 A possible solution is given in Fig. A.11, using a boolean semaphore, *access*, and a number of integer semaphores (initially kept in a list of free semaphores). The method keeps a set of sleeping events (i.e. events on which one or more processes are sleeping). Two fields are kept for each sleeping event: the number of processes sleeping on that event, *nprocs[event]*, and the semaphore currently being used by those sleeping processes, *sem[event]*. These are represented as two arrays indexed on *event*. In practice, the range of possible values for *event* would probably be too large to do this, and instead we could use a sequential table of events or a hash table if speed was important and the number of events being slept upon at any one time was expected to be large. This table (and the number of integer semaphores initially in the list of free semaphores) should be large enough for the maximum number of events being simultaneously slept upon. Entries are made in the table only for events upon which processes are sleeping.

5.5 A simple solution, but one subject to deadlock, is shown in Fig. A.12. Philosopher i uses *fork[i]* (on his left) and *fork[i + 1 MOD 5]* (on his right), where $i = 0, \ldots, 4$. A semaphore is associated with each fork,

Philosopher i

```
WHILE TRUE DO
    think and sleep;
    P(total);
    P(fork[i]);
    pick up left fork;
    P(fork[i + 1 MOD 5]);
    pick up right fork;
    eat;
    put down left fork;
    V(fork[i]);
    put down right fork;
    V(fork[i + 1 MOD 5]);
    V(total)
OD
```

Shared: fork : ARRAY[0..4] OF semaphore (initially all 1)
          total : integer semaphore (initially 4)

Figure A.13: A deadlock-free solution to the Dining Philosophers Problem.

Process X1

```
WHILE TRUE DO
    P(s1);
    P(mutex);
    V(either);
    delay;
    P(either);
    V(mutex);
    V(s1)
OD
```

Process X2

```
WHILE TRUE DO
    P(s2);
    P(mutex);
    V(either);
    delay;
    P(either);
    V(mutex);
    V(s2)
OD
```

Shared: s1, s2 : boolean semaphore
          mutex : boolean semaphore (initially 1)
          either : boolean semaphore (initially 0)

Figure A.14: An algorithm to permit waiting on either of two semaphores.

being one when the fork is free and zero when it is in a philosopher's hand.

5.6 There are exactly five forks, so if only four philosophers are wanting to eat simultaneously, at least one must be able to pick up two forks (because every fork can be reached by at least one of these four philosophers, no matter which four are chosen). Similar arguments can be used if only two or three philosophers are hungry at the same time. Hence deadlock cannot occur if no more than four philosophers attempt to eat simultaneously.

An algorithm based on this property is given in Fig. A.13. This is similar to the previous algorithm, but uses an additional semaphore, *total*, which becomes zero when four philosophers are attempting to eat simultaneously and is used to prevent the fifth from attempting to pick up either of his forks if he becomes hungry also. The algorithm is subject to starvation if weak semaphores are used.

5.7 Create two new processes, X1 and X2, which wait for the two semaphores, *s1* and *s2*, respectively. The original processes use the operation *P(either)* instead of the hypothetical *P(s1 OR s2)*, followed by *V(either)* when it is required to release the semaphore (whichever of *s1* or *s2* was selected by *P(either)*). Two additional boolean semaphores, *either* and *mutex*, are required. The algorithm is shown in Fig. A.14.

The algorithm is not particularly efficient unless the *delay* is long, but it is simple and easily generalised to permit waiting on one of **n** semaphores by creating additional processes X1,...,Xn corresponding to the semaphores *s1*,...,*sn*.

6.1 A solution is to use three boolean semaphores: *free* indicates when the buffer is free, *Afilled* indicates when the buffer contains data from process A, and *Cfilled* indicates when the buffer contains data from process C. The algorithm is shown in Fig. A.15.

6.2 Our solution uses the array *buff[0..1][0..255]* for the two line buffers, boolean semaphores *full[0..1]* to indicate when each is full, and boolean semaphores *empty[0..1]* to indicate when each is empty. The local variable *i* indexes the buffer currently being filled and the local variable *j* indexes the buffer currently being printed. The local variable *posn* indexes the next free character position in the buffer currently being filled. The interrupt handler process must be a normal user process known to the scheduler so that *P* and *V* operators work correctly. It must also be linked to the printer interrupt. The algorithm is shown in Fig. A.16.

6.3 A minor difficulty with this problem is finding a convenient way to express the solution. It is no longer convenient to use the same name *data* for the

Process A
WHILE TRUE DO
compute data;
P(free);
put data into buffer;
V(Afilled)
OD

Process B
WHILE TRUE DO
P(Afilled);
get data from buffer;
V(free);
use data
OD

Process C
WHILE TRUE DO
compute data;
P(free);
put data into buffer;
V(Cfilled)
OD

Process D
WHILE TRUE DO
P(Cfilled);
get data from buffer;
V(free);
use data
OD

Shared: *free : boolean semaphore (initially 1);*
                 Afilled, Cfilled : boolean semaphore (initially both 0)

Figure A.15: Two producer–consumer pairs sharing a single buffer.

local variables in the producer and consumer because one of these must be shared. One of the producer and consumer must contain a statement to copy the contents of the variable *data* in one to the variable *data* in the other. A suitable algorithm is given in Fig. A.17.

Notice that *pdata* need only be readable by the consumer process. An equally valid alternative is to put the statement

$$cdata := pdata$$

in the producer instead, in which case *cdata* becomes the shared variable, writable by the producer, and *pdata* is only local.

6.4 A solution is given in Fig. A.18.

7.1 No, it cannot. The producer is not simply a writer. It must read the queue pointers to find out where to put the next record and also to check that the buffer is not full. Similarly, the consumer is not just a reader. It must update the queue pointers to show that it has removed a record from the buffer (otherwise the same record could be read a second time).

7.2 Suppose that Reader 1 is about to execute the statement

$$reading := reading - 1$$

putchar(c)

```
IF c = EOF THEN
    pad out buff[i] with nulls;
    V(full[i])
ELSE
    IF posn = 256 THEN
        V(full[i]);
        i := i + 1 MOD 2;
        P(empty[i]);
        posn := 0
    FI;
    buff[i][posn] := c;
    posn := posn + 1;
FI;
return
```

interrupt handler process

```
(entered on a printer interrupt)
V(empty[j]);
j := j + 1 MOD 2;
P(full[j]);
initiate printing of buff[j];
return to interrupted process
```

Shared: *full : ARRAY[0..1] OF boolean semaphore*
(initially both 0)
empty : ARRAY[0..1] OF boolean semaphore
(initially both 1)

Local: *i,j : 0..1 (initially both 0)*
posn : 0..256 (initially 0)

Figure A.16: Double buffering lines of output.

and no other reader is into its critical section (so the value of *reading* is 1). If, after Reader 1 computes the value of *reading* – 1 as zero, it is interrupted and Reader 2 proceeds into its critical section, updating *reading* to 2 on the way, and then (while Reader 2 is still in its critical section) Reader 1 continues, setting *reading* to zero, we are then in an unsafe situation: *reading* is zero, yet Reader 2 is still reading the data. If the Writer attempts to access the data it will be able to do so, which is exactly the situation we are trying to prevent.

This algorithm is unsafe if the statement

$$reading := reading - 1$$

is a divisible operation. Not only is it unsafe if the value of *reading* becomes zero when it should not be, but also the writer could become permanently locked out if the value of *reading* becomes larger than it should be and never returns to zero even though no readers are accessing

Producer

```
WHILE TRUE DO
    compute(pdata);
    V(readytowrite);
    P(finished);
OD
```

Consumer

```
WHILE TRUE DO
    P(readytowrite);
    cdata := pdata;
    V(finished);
    use(cdata)
OD
```

Shared: *readytowrite, finished : semaphore (initially both 0)*
          pdata : anytype
Local: *cdata : anytype*

Figure A.17: Producer-consumer with no buffer.

Build case

```
WHILE TRUE DO
    get raw materials;
    build case;
    P(casehold);
    put case into holding area;
    V(case)
OD
```

Build circuit

```
WHILE TRUE DO
    get raw materials;
    build circuit;
    P(circuithold);
    put circuit into holding area;
    V(circuit)
OD
```

Final assembly

```
WHILE TRUE DO
    P(case);
    get case from holding area;
    V(casehold);
    P(circuit);
    get circuit from holding area;
    V(circuithold);
    assemble product;
    deliver finished product
OD
```

Shared: *casehold : integer semaphore (initially 10)*
          circuithold : integer semaphore (initially 25)
          case, circuit : integer semaphore (initially both 0)

Figure A.18: Processes simulating factory production lines.

the data. All these problems could be solved if both the incrementing and decrementing of *reading* could be implemented as indivisible operations. On a uniprocessor, implementing them as single instructions would be a simple cure.

Writer	Reader i (for i=1..n)

WHILE TRUE DO
    compute(data);
    preprotocol(write);
    WHILE reading ≠ 0 DO
OD;
    writing := 1;
    postprotocol(write);
    buffer := data;
    writing := 0
OD
	WHILE TRUE DO
	    preprotocol(write);
	    WHILE writing ≠ 0 DO
	OD;
	    preprotocol(read);
	    reading := reading + 1;
	    postprotocol(read);
	    postprotocol(write);
	    data := buffer;
	    preprotocol(read);
	    reading := reading − 1;
	    postprotocol(read);
	    use(data)
	OD

Figure A.19: Readers and writer algorithm modified to avoid deadlock.

7.3 This algorithm is very similar to that of the previous exercise; the only difference being that the statement which decrements *reading* has been made into a critical section by enclosing it within a mutual exclusion pre- and post-protocol pair. This certainly cures the faults present in the previous algorithm, but this method of ensuring that *reading* is updated in a critical section is unfortunately subject to deadlock.

Suppose that Reader 1 is accessing the data and the value of *reading* is 1, when the Writer attempts to access the data. It will be caught in the WHILE loop inside the critical section implemented by the pre- and post-protocol pair and will stay there until *reading* becomes zero. The reader cannot make *reading* zero, however, because it cannot pass the pre-protocol statement (which precedes the decrementing of *reading*) until the Writer exits its critical section, thus we have a deadlock situation where each is held up waiting for the other.

A solution to this difficulty would be to use two classes of critical sections, enclosing the statements which increment and decrement *reading*

```
MODULE mutex[1];
    EXPORT pre, post;
    IMPORT SIGNAL, SEND, WAIT, Init;
    VAR
        event : ARRAY[1..N] OF integer;
        complete : ARRAY[1..N] OF SIGNAL;
PROCEDURE pre(s:integer);
BEGIN
    IF s is in the array of events (at position i)
    THEN WAIT(complete[i])
    ELSE put s into the array of events (error if full)
    FI
END pre;
PROCEDURE post(s:integer)
BEGIN
    IF s is in the array of events (at position i)
    THEN
        SEND(complete[i]);
        remove s from array of events
    FI
END post;
BEGIN
    Initialise global arrays
END mutex.
```

Figure A.20: Modula-2 pseudocode to implement routines *pre* and *post* for mutual exclusion.

in a different pre- and post-protocol pair to those used already, as shown in Fig. A.19.

7.4 It is advantageous if the minimum *compute* time is less than the maximum *read* time. The algorithm is exactly the same as in Fig. 7.6, except that the third line of the Writer is changed to:

$$bn := latestbuf + 1 \ MOD \ b$$

8.1 Use a monitor module to define the procedures *pre* and *post*, with the class of critical sections being represented by an integer value (like the event argument in UNIX *sleep* and *wakeup*). The global variables in the monitor are an array of N events for the processes which are currently inside critical sections, and an array of N signals used to indicate when those processes

```
MODULE MessageSystem[1];
    EXPORT send,take;
    IMPORT anytype, SIGNAL, SEND, WAIT, Init;
    CONST N = {required number of buffers};
    TYPE      Buffer =
                  RECORD
                  src : integer; {source process}
                  dst : integer; {destination process}
                  body : anytype; {the message}
                  END;
    VAR
        buffer : ARRAY [0..N] OF Buffer;
        freebuffers : 0..N; {number of free buffers}
        nonfull : SIGNAL;
PROCEDURE send(source : integer, dest : integer, message : anytype);
    IF freebuffers = 0 THEN WAIT(nonfull) FI;
    i := 1;
    WHILE buffer[i].src = -1 DO i := i + 1 OD;
    freebuffers := freebuffers - 1;
    buffer[i].src := source;
    buffer[i].dst := dest;
    buffer[i].body := message
END send;
PROCEDURE take(VAR source : integer, dest : integer,
                                VAR message : anytype);
    i := 1;
    WHILE i ≤ N AND buffer[i].dst ≠ dest DO i := i + 1 OD;
    IF buffer[i].dst = dest THEN
        source := buffer[i].src;
        buffer[i].src := -1;
        message := buffer[i].body;
        freebuffers := freebuffers + 1;
        SEND(nonfull)
    ELSE source := -1 FI
END take;
BEGIN {Initialisation}
    freebuffers := N;
    Init(nonfull)
END MessageSystem.
```

Figure A.21: Modula-2 pseudocode for the monitor *MessageSystem*.

leave their critical sections. The pseudocode for the monitor is shown in Fig. A.20.

8.2 Our solution uses N buffers with fields in each for source, destination and message. Empty buffers are denoted by the value -1 in the source field. We assume that process identifiers are integers. The two procedures are implemented within a monitor module called *MessageSystem* as shown in Fig. A.21.

8.3 We use a monitor for the procedures *delay* and *tick*. Its global data is a table of N locations, each with three fields: *inuse* indicates whether or not that location in the table is being used, *event* is a signal used to wake up the process when its delay has expired, and *wakeuptime* denotes the time at which it should be woken up. The pseudocode for the monitor is shown in Fig. A.22.

9.1 Create a new process (a task in Ada) which defines the entrynames *pre* and *post* as shown in Fig. A.23.

Different classes of critical sections may be handled by creating a separate process for each class, each process being similar to the one shown above. Of course, they must have distinct entrynames, and that can be achieved in several ways. The Ada language allows arrays of tasks and entrynames to be declared in such a way that a single piece of code similar to that shown above can be used to define an array of N distinct instantiations of the task containing *pre* and *post*. The particular class of critical section to be implemented is specified by selecting a particular instance of the entrynames *pre* and *post* from the array. An integer index is used to specify which instance, in just the same way as an integer index is used to select an element from any other type of array.

9.2 We create a new process with the entrynames *startread, startwrite, stopread* and *stopwrite*. Two local variables are used: *readers* is the number of readers currently accessing the shared data, and *writers* is the number of writers currently accessing the shared data. The code for this process is shown in Fig. A.24.

The liveness properties of this solution depend upon the liveness properties of the rendezvous mechanism used. In the definition of the Ada language, although tasks waiting for the same entryname are queued and achieve their rendezvous strictly in first-come first-served order, there is no such requirement for tasks waiting for *different* entrynames within the same *SELECT* statement. Hence, writers cannot cause starvation of each other, but writers can cause reader starvation (of all the readers), and readers can cause writer starvation (of all the writers). It is unlikely that a uniprocessor implementation of Ada would allow this to happen, but

Delays monitor

```
MODULE Delays[1];
    EXPORT delay, tick;
    IMPORT time, timenow, SIGNAL, SEND, WAIT, Init;
    VAR
        inuse : ARRAY[1..N] OF boolean;
        event : ARRAY[1..N] OF SIGNAL;
        wakeuptime : ARRAY[1..N] OF time;
PROCEDURE delay(t : time)
BEGIN
    find a free location (say i) in the table (error if full);
    inuse[i] := TRUE;
    WAIT(event[i]);
    inuse[i] := FALSE;
END delay;
PROCEDURE tick()
BEGIN
    FOR i := 1 TO N DO
        IF inuse[i] AND wakeuptime[i] ≥ timenow
            THEN SIGNAL(event[i]) FI
    OD
END tick;
BEGIN
    Initialise global arrays
END Delays.
```

Figure A.22: Modula-2 pseudocode for a monitor to implement real-time delays.

```
unlock : boolean;

unlock := TRUE;
WHILE TRUE DO
    SELECT
        WHEN unlock =>
            ACCEPT pre() DO unlock := FALSE END pre;
        OR
            ACCEPT post() DO unlock := TRUE END post;
    END SELECT
OD
```

Figure A.23: Ada pseudocode for a process to implement routines *pre* and *post* for mutual exclusion.

```
readers : 0..numberofreaders;
writers : 0..1;

readers := 0;
writers := 0;
WHILE TRUE DO
    SELECT
        WHEN writers = 0 =>
            ACCEPT startread()
            DO readers := readers + 1 END startread;
    OR
        WHEN readers = 0 AND writers = 0 =>
            ACCEPT startwrite()
            writers := 1 END startwrite;
    OR
            ACCEPT stopread()
            DO readers := readers - 1 END stopread;
    OR
            ACCEPT stopwrite()
            DO writers := 0 END stopwrite;
    END SELECT
OD
```

Figure A.24: Ada pseudocode for a process to implement a readers and writers protocol.

```
inuse : ARRAY [1..N] OF boolean;
i : 1..N;
totalused : 0..N;

totalused := 0;
FOR i := 1 TO N DO inuse[i] := FALSE OD;
WHILE TRUE DO
    SELECT
        WHEN totalused < N =>
            ACCEPT claim(OUT d : 1..N) DO
                d := {any i for which inuse[i] = FALSE}
                inuse[d] := TRUE;
                totalused := totalused + 1
            END claim;
        OR
            ACCEPT release(IN d : 1..N) DO
            IF inuse[d]
            THEN
                inuse[d] := FALSE;
                totalused := totalused - 1
            FI
        END release
    END SELECT
OD
```

Figure A.25: Ada pseudocode for a process to control the use of N tape units.

Philosopher 1 process

```
WHILE TRUE DO
     think and sleep;
     getforks1();
     eat;
     returnforks1()
OD
```

table process

```
fork1, fork2, fork3, fork4, fork5 : boolean;

fork1 := fork2 := fork3 := fork4 := fork5 := TRUE;
WHILE TRUE DO
   SELECT
       WHEN fork5 AND fork1 =>
           ACCEPT getforks1() DO fork5 := fork1 := FALSE END;
       OR WHEN fork1 AND fork 2 =>
           ACCEPT getforks2() DO fork1 := fork2 := FALSE END;
       OR WHEN fork2 AND fork3 =>
           ACCEPT getforks3() DO fork2 := fork3 := FALSE END;
       OR WHEN fork3 AND fork4 =>
           ACCEPT getforks4() DO fork3 := fork4 := FALSE END;
       OR WHEN fork4 AND fork5 =>
           ACCEPT getforks5() DO fork4 := fork5 := FALSE END;
       OR ACCEPT returnforks1() DO fork5 := fork1 := TRUE END;
       OR ACCEPT returnforks2() DO fork1 := fork2 := TRUE END;
       OR ACCEPT returnforks3() DO fork2 := fork3 := TRUE END;
       OR ACCEPT returnforks4() DO fork3 := fork4 := TRUE END;
       OR ACCEPT returnforks5() DO fork4 := fork5 := TRUE END;
   END SELECT
OD
```

Figure A.26: Ada pseudocode for processes to implement a protocol for the Dining Philosophers Problem.

Process p, p=1..P

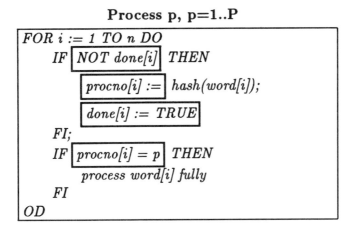

```
FOR i := 1 TO n DO
    IF  NOT done[i]  THEN
            procno[i] :=  hash(word[i]);
            done[i] := TRUE
    FI;
    IF  procno[i] = p  THEN
        process word[i] fully
    FI
OD
```

Figure A.27: Multiprocessor algorithm for finding anagram classes.

the language definition does not rule it out.

9.3 Let the device codes of the installed tape drives be *1,2,...,N*. Create a process (Fig. A.25) in which *inuse[i]* indicates whether or not the *i*-th tape drive is currently in use, and *totalused* denotes the total number of tape drives currently in use.

9.4 A simple, if rather crude, solution is shown in Fig. A.26. Each philosopher is represented by a separate process (only the first is shown), and a sixth process (called **table**) implements the protocol. The first philosopher calls *getforks1()* when he wishes to eat, and *returnforks1()* when he finishes eating; the second calls *getforks2()* and *returnforks2()*; and so on. Local variables (*fork1, fork2*, etc.) in **table** are used to indicate whether or not each fork is free.

This solution is deadlock free because a rendezvous cannot occur unless *both* forks required by a philosopher are free. Only *after* the rendezvous has occurred are the forks marked as in use. Thus there is no way that all philosophers can claim a fork each and then wait indefinitely for each other to release a fork. The Ada rendezvous mechanism is powerful enough to ensure this without needing to restrict the number of philosophers simultaneously trying to eat to four or less.

Starvation is possible with this solution if the rendezvous mechanism allows it. In Ada, starvation may occur because the philosopher processes call several different entrynames and Ada guarantees fair servicing of rendezvous only if all the processes call the same entryname.

11.1 An outline solution is as follows.

Firstly, find a hashing function which is independent of the order of letters in the word (this shouldn't be too difficult, but if a standard hashing function is preferred, simply sort the letters of the word into order first). The value obtained must be in the range 1 to P (where P is the number of processors) and will be used to determine which processor handles the word. All words which are anagrams of each other will thus be handled by the same processor.

We assume that the input sequence is already stored in shared memory. With each word ($word[i]$) is stored a flag ($done[i]$) indicating whether or not it has already been hashed, together with the hash value ($procno[i]$), which is to be used as a processor number. All P processors work concurrently on the input sequence.

The program for the p-th processor is shown in Fig. A.27. n is the number of words in the input sequence, all the $done[i]$ must initially be *FALSE*, and the statement '*process word[i] fully*' denotes the processing of the word by a normal sequential algorithm (e.g. sorting the letters into alphabetical order and then using this as the key to insert the word into a hash table or other data structure in which the anagram classes are built up). On completion, the complete set of anagram classes is simply the union of the separate sets of anagram classes found by each of the P processes. For many purposes, the anagram classes can remain partitioned as they are, no further processing being necessary.

11.2 The method is essentially similar in principle to that used in the previous exercise. A hash function which is independent of the order of letters in the word can be used to decide which processor will handle each word, thus ensuring that all words which are anagrams of each other go to the same processor.

One processor is used to compute the hash function for each word and then send that word to the appropriate processor for further processing. Assuming a buffered distribution algorithm, the configuration of processes is as shown in Fig. 11.8 (with as many branches as there are processors available, assuming the process configuration can be mapped efficiently onto the processor configuration).

The algorithm for the distribution process is simply:

```
FOR i := 1 TO n DO
    procno := hash(word[i]);
    send word[i] to buffer[procno]
OD
```

The buffer processes are perfectly standard, and the p-th computation process simply reads a sequence of words from the p-th buffer and processes them sequentially as if they were the complete sequence of words. On completion, the complete set of anagram classes is partitioned over the computation processes (in the same way as in the previous exercise).

11.3 The two methods are, in principle, the same. The complete set of input words is partitioned in the same way in both cases, and each part is processed sequentially by a single processor. The bulk of the processing is this sequential processing of the separate parts of the input sequence, but with all processes running concurrently. This is identical for the two methods. The only differences are in the way in which each computation process receives its part of the input sequence. In the multiprocessing case, each process examines all words but ignores those which will be handled by the other processes. In the distributed processing case, an extra distribution process scans the input sequence once only and passes each word to the appropriate computation process (via a buffer process).

Only if the number of processors becomes very large is the distribution likely to dominate the overall processing time. In this case, contention for the shared memory (in the multiprocessing case), or the time delays in passing messages through the network (in the distributed processing case) may become significant and start to have a major effect on the overall speed of the program.

Further Reading

I have attempted here to select some good advanced textbooks and other publications which will provide a relatively easy path by which the interested reader may expand and deepen his knowledge of the topics introduced in this book. Most of these references can be used as stepping stones into the research literature: many of them contain extensive lists of further references.

Algorithms

Raynal, M. (1986). *Algorithms for Mutual Exclusion*, North Oxford Academic.

A comprehensive and well-presented collection of algorithms for mutual exclusion in both centralised and distributed systems. Also contains algorithms for the producer-consumer and the readers and writers problems. The best reference for fundamental synchronisation algorithms. It also contains a good bibliography.

Raynal, M. (1988). *Distributed Algorithms and Protocols*, Wiley.

Another useful collection of algorithms, this time exclusively for distributed processing systems, i.e. algorithms in which the interprocess communication is solely by message passing. The problems for which algorithms are given include: mutual exclusion, election of a single leading process out of many equivalent processes, detection and resolution of deadlock, detection of termination, message transmission protocols, management of distributed data, and gaining consensus in the presence of uncertainties. A variety of different topologies are considered for the message-passing network. Comprehensive lists of references are included.

Kronsjö, L. (1985). *Computational Complexity of Sequential and Parallel Algorithms*, Wiley.

About half this book is devoted to detailed description and analysis of parallel algorithms, including algorithms for: sorting, finding zeros of functions, matrix multiplication, fast Fourier transform, graph searching, graph traversal, and general iterative algorithms.

Gibbons, A. and Rytter, W. (1988). *Efficient Parallel Algorithms*, Cambridge University Press.

A collection of fast parallel algorithms based largely on tree structured methods. It includes algorithms for graphical problems, expression evaluation, parsing of context-free languages, sorting and string matching.

Language Mechanisms

Perrott, R.H. (1987). *Parallel Programming*, Addison-Wesley.

A good introduction to the range of programming languages available for parallel processing. It includes a chapter each on Modula-2, Pascal Plus, Ada, Occam, Cray-1 Fortran, CDC Cyber Fortran, Illiac IV Fortran and ICL DAP Fortran. Several other languages are covered in less detail. Little on algorithms except by way of examples of use of the programming languages.

Wirth, N. (1985). *Programming in Modula-2* (3rd Edn.), Springer-Verlag.

The definitive text on Modula-2 by the designer of the language. Many other good texts are also available.

International Standard ISO 8652 (1987). *Reference Manual for the Ada Programming Language*, published (as ANSI/MIL-STD-1815A-1983) by the American National Standards Institute, 1430 Broadway, New York, New York 10018, U.S.A.

The official definition of Ada. Many good textbooks on Ada are also available, and it is much easier to learn the language from one of these, although the official definition is an essential reference for the serious student of Ada.

Watt, D.A., Wichmann, B.A. and Findlay, W. (1987). *Ada Language and Methodology,* Prentice-Hall.

A good textbook on Ada that includes discussion of the more advanced features such as those for concurrent and real-time programming.

U.K. Ministry of Defence (1987). *The Official Handbook of Mascot, Version 3.1*, Defence Research Information Centre, Kentigern House, 65 Brown Street, Glasgow G2 8EX, U.K.

The official definition of Mascot. At present very few other references on Mascot are available.

The UNIX Kernel

Thompson, K. (1978). 'UNIX Implementation', *Bell System Technical Journal*, **57**(6), 1931–46.

This paper is part of a complete issue (Volume **57**, Number 6) of the *Bell System Technical Journal* which was devoted to various aspects of the UNIX operating system. The paper by K. Thompson, one of the original authors of UNIX, describes the functions and structure of the kernel.

Bach, M.J. (1986). *The Design of the UNIX Operating System*, Prentice-Hall.

A comprehensive account of the design of the UNIX kernel and other central features of the UNIX operating system. This is the 'official' text on the internals of UNIX, sponsored by Bell Telephone Laboratories.

Reliability and Formal Methods

Quirk, W.J. (ed.) (1985). *Verification and Validation of Real-Time Software*, Springer-Verlag.

A brief compendium of the main techniques for improving the reliability of real-time software, the emphasis being on semi-formal techniques (systematic testing, statistical testing and simulation), although both formal and informal methods are covered briefly also.

Peterson, J.L. (1981). *Petri Net Theory and the Modeling of Systems*, Prentice-Hall.

The standard text on Petri nets. Although primarily mathematical in its approach, this is a fairly readable text. It also contains a number of examples of the application of Petri nets to both software and hardware concurrency.

Hoare, C.A.R. (1985). *Communicating Sequential Processes*, Prentice-Hall.

A comprehensive description of Hoare's CSP formalism and its applications in modelling concurrent systems. Written as a textbook for programmers, it introduces CSP from scratch, together with the basic ideas of mathematical logic needed for a thorough understanding of CSP. Although all the mathematical symbolisms used are explained carefully when they are introduced, this is likely to be a difficult book for those with no experience of discrete mathematics.

References

Barringer, H. (1985). *A Survey of Verification Techniques for Parallel Programs (Lecture Notes in Computer Science,* Vol.191*)*, Springer-Verlag.

Ben-Ari, M. (1982). *Principles of Concurrent Programming*, Prentice-Hall.

Deitel, H.M. (1984). *An Introduction to Operating Systems*, Addison-Wesley.

Dijkstra, E.W. (1965). 'Cooperating Sequential Processes', in *Programming Languages* (Ed. F. Genuys), Academic Press.

Fetzer, J.H. (1988). 'Program Verification: The Very Idea', *Communications of the ACM*, **31** (9), 1048–1063. [This paper provoked a great deal of correspondence, e.g. *Communications of the ACM*, **32** (3), 287–289 and 374–381. Sadly, this debate sometimes reads more like the propaganda of religious fanatics than rational scientific argument.]

Hoare, C.A.R. (1978). 'Communicating Sequential Processes', *Communications of the ACM*, **21** (8), 666–677.

Hoare, C.A.R. (1985). *Communicating Sequential Processes*, Prentice-Hall.

Inmos Ltd. (1988a). *Occam 2 Reference Manual*, Prentice-Hall.

Inmos Ltd. (1988b). *Transputer Reference Manual*, Prentice-Hall.

ISO 8652. (1987) *Reference Manual for the Ada Programming Language, ANSI/MIL-STD-1815A-1983*, American National Standards Institute.

Jones, C.B. (1986) *Systematic Software Development Using VDM*, Prentice-Hall.

Maekawa, M., Oldehoeft, A.E., and Oldehoeft, R.R. (1987). *Operating Systems: Advanced Concepts*, Benjamin/Cummings.

Morris, J.M. (1979). 'A Starvation Free Solution to the Mutual Exclusion Problem', *Information Processing Letters*, **8** (2), 76–80.

Peterson, G.L. (1981). 'Myths About the Mutual Exclusion Problem', *Information Processing Letters*, **12** (3), 115–116.

Peterson, G.L. (1983). 'Concurrent Reading While Writing', *ACM Transactions on Programming Languages and Systems*, **5** (1), 46–55.

Peterson, J.L. and Silberschatz, A. (1983). *Operating System Concepts*, Addison-Wesley.

Raynal, M. (1986). *Algorithms for Mutual Exclusion*, North Oxford Academic.

Spivey, J.M. (1989). *The Z Notation: A Reference Manual*, Prentice-Hall.

Stankovic, J.A. (1988). 'Misconceptions About Real-Time Computing: A Serious Problem for Next-Generation Systems', *Computer* **21** (10), 10–19.

U.K. Ministry of Defence (1987). *The Official Handbook of Mascot, Version 3.1*, Defence Research Information Centre, Kentigern House, 65 Brown Street, Glasgow G2 8EX, U.K.

Wirth, N. (1985). *Programming in Modula-2 (3rd Edn.)*, Springer-Verlag.

Woodcock, J. and Loomes, M. (1988). *Software Engineering Mathematics: Formal Methods Demystified*, Pitman.

Index